# Marketing

For Bright Flower

# Marketing

## A critical introduction

# Chris Hackley

Los Angeles • London • New Delhi • Singapore • Washington DC

First published 2009

SAGE Publications Ltd
1 Oliver's Yard
55 City Road
London EC1Y 1SP

SAGE Publications Inc.
2455 Teller Road
Thousand Oaks, California 91320

SAGE Publications India Pvt Ltd
B 1/I 1 Mohan Cooperative Industrial Area
Mathura Road, Post Bag 7
New Delhi 110 044

SAGE Publications Asia-Pacific Pte Ltd
33 Pekin Street #02-01
Far East Square
Singapore 048763


**Library of Congress Control Number 2008935545**

**British Library Cataloguing in Publication data**

A catalogue record for this book is available from the British Library

ISBN 978-1-4129-1148-1
ISBN 978-1-4129-1149-8 (pbk)



Typeset by C&M Digitals (P) Ltd, Chennai, India
Printed in Great Britain by CPI Antony Rowe, Chippenham, Wiltshire
Printed on paper from sustainable resources

# CONTENTS

# CHAPTER 1

# MARKETING STUDIES: THE CRITICAL STANDPOINT

---

## CHAPTER OUTLINE

Chapter 1 introduces the rationale and approach of the book. The chapter outlines some penetrating criticisms which have been levelled at Marketing practice and Marketing studies. The chapter goes on to examine the critical standpoint in Marketing studies and offers a simplifying typology of critique with examples of how this typology might play out in terms of some of the general and specific criticisms of the managerial Marketing approach. This typology is revisited throughout the book.

---

## Introduction

As a critical introduction to Marketing studies, this book assumes that readers already have a working knowledge of the applied management principles, the 'tools and concepts', of Marketing. Taking these as a starting point, it develops lines of argument which critique those tools and concepts and the various assumptions which underpin them. The intention is to set the typical Marketing studies topics within a more rounded intellectual, historical and institutional context than is found in mainstream books and courses. The book is written for students, academics, researchers and practitioners to offer a resource for a deeper sense of intellectual engagement with Marketing, which includes but also goes beyond the applied, managerial perspective.

The critical tone of this book will jar with many students of Marketing more used to the very upbeat, positive and affirmative tone of typical textbooks on the subject. Professor Philip Kotler's (still) original *Marketing Management: Analysis, Planning, Implementation and Control* (1967) epitomizes the normative managerial Marketing approach with which so many thousands of students are familiar. The reach of Kotler's Marketing management approach (and its many imitators) has been such that many students of the subject already possess a working knowledge of its conceptual vocabulary of consumer orientation, segmentation, positioning and targeting even before they begin their formal studies.

Marketing studies have become so closely identified with a technical enterprise of managerial problem solving that criticism can hardly penetrate the glossy veneer covering its mass-market textbooks. Wealth and value creation are the espoused values of managerial Marketing. What can there be to criticize about a set of techniques designed to make organizations work more effectively for managers, shareholders, customers and society? The Marketing concept of customer orientation, its techniques of market research and product development and its persuasive targeting, branding, retailing and advertising approaches are typically deployed in an uncritical managerial agenda which promotes organizational effectiveness above all else. But the vacuum of critique in the discipline has serious personal, educational, civil and environmental implications. There is a striking need, therefore, for a thoroughgoing critical stance as an intellectual and moral counterpoint to the managerial problem-solving style of Marketing studies and the values which sustain it. Indeed, there is a need for an organic Marketing studies to balance the heavily processed, chemically constituted managerial Marketing brand.

The idea of critique can mean very different things in different contexts. Marketing studies is typically conceived as an applied management field in which critique does not normally extend beyond functional evaluation of its problem-solving techniques. Marketing, many popular textbooks claim, is a 'critical' organizational function. By this, they do not mean that it is intellectually rigorous, but merely that it is important. It is hard to deny that Marketing is important, to wealth distribution, economic growth, employment and industrial competitiveness. It is a collection of activities, processes and practices with wide-ranging organizational, economic and social implications. But a critical focus which falls narrowly on the technical efficiency of Marketing is hardly adequate because it does not examine the ways in which ideas are constructed and sustained and the forms of social and economic organization they support. This book, then, takes Marketing studies, as it is typically understood as a managerial discipline, as a relatively critique-free zone which would benefit from a radical reappraisal.

Criticisms of Marketing are, by implication, criticisms of the role of Marketing studies in management education and training. There are resonant calls for Marketing practice to serve the world better, for example, by developing more environmentally friendly products and services; by using resources more effectively and efficiently; by working for sustainable and socially positive forms of consumption; and by generally incorporating a stronger sense of ethics and social responsibility within the theories, the practice and the educational programmes of Marketing. Within the Marketing field, there is a crisis of confidence as regards the power of its ideas to influence markets and fulfil the strategic objectives of organizations, while Marketing academics wonder whether their theories and research really engage in the right way with any of the key audiences for Marketing studies: practitioners, students, employers, citizens and society in general. So, even the most vocationally inclined student of Marketing, lacking even a shred of intellectual curiosity, will benefit from an appreciation of critical perspectives in the subject, if only so that he or she can engage with the kinds of criticism inevitably faced by professional Marketers with suitably adroit sophistry. For those with a more detached curiosity about the world, an engagement with critical Marketing studies can be a surprising and fascinating adventure.

## Criticizing Marketing: Where to Begin?

The tone of many Marketing textbooks (Brown, 1995a; Hackley, 2003a) implicitly signals to students that criticism is outside the boundaries of Marketing studies. The style of writing in many such books casts Marketing as an ideology to be accepted, or rejected, uncritically. So criticizing aspects of the subject will seem unsettling for some students used only to the conventional style of Marketing text. But the edifice of Marketing studies does not collapse if it is subject to criticism. Instead, possibilities for a new Marketing studies emerge. So, disorientating as it may be for students of managerial Marketing, it is probably best to dive straight in at the deep end. A frank encounter with some of the main criticisms of managerial Marketing studies might feel like a cold shower of disillusionment to some, given that framed Marketing degree certificates take pride of place on so many living room walls. But it isn't the subject itself which is being criticized, nor is it the ability or sincerity of its students or teachers. Rather, it is the values which have come to frame the way Marketing studies is popularly conceived which attract such vehement criticism.

### General Criticisms of Marketing Studies

Given the level of acceptance Marketing concepts and Marketing studies have achieved globally, it may come as a surprise to many students of the subject that, for many of its critics, it simply has no features which redeem its fatal ethical, practical and intellectual shortcomings. The ways the subject is typically conceived, practised and taught have been roundly criticized for, among many other things: (see Alvesson, 1994; Brownlie et al., 1999; Burton, 2001, 2005; Crane, 2000; Cova, 2005; Jack, 2008; Klein, 2000; Tadajewski, 2006a; Witkowski, 2005; and Dholakia et al., 1980, in Tadajewski and Brownlie, 2008; Firat and Venkatesh, 1995; Gronroos, 1994; Gummesson, 2002a; Hastings and Haywood, 1994; Sheth and Sisodia, 2005).

- a perceived lack of real intellectual engagement with other disciplines
- a lack of response to criticisms of practising managers that Marketing does not deliver
- an over-emphasis on narrow managerial priorities and consumer self-interest
- complicity in environmental issues such as waste and destruction of resources
- a lack of theory development as a result of a misguided model of practice
- a tendency to cling uncritically to outdated concepts of limited value
- an overriding focus on transactions and profit rather than relation-ships and value
- intellectual shallowness, emphasizing naive instrumentalism over critical reflexivity
- a lack of moderation and a tendency to universalize North American neo-liberal values
- an over-emphasis on quantitative modelling in a positive-empiricist social science

Arguments over the declining role of critical thinking and the dumbing-down influence of positivistic learning objectives go on in all university sub-jects. No teaching subjects are immune to the commercial and ideological forces facing universities, and all entertain deep intellectual divisions and impassioned debates. In many subjects, these debates are largely invisi-ble to students on mainstream courses. Criticisms such as those above reflect sincere debates within the field. They are not dissimilar to the kinds of argument which go on in other fields of management, social and human studies, and they should be taken seriously if we are to understand why they arise, what they mean and what response is appropriate.

Criticisms of Marketing do not end with nice intellectual distinctions about the most appropriate sources of theory or research methods. There are widespread perceptions that the business function of Marketing sim-ply does not deliver on its claims. Sheth and Sisodia (2005) write in the academics' top Marketing journal, the *Journal of Marketing* (*JM*), that:

Marketing effectiveness is down. Marketing is intrusive. Productivity is down. People resent Marketing. Marketing has no seat at the table at board level and top management. Academics aren't relevant. And we have an ethical and moral crisis. Other than that, we're in good shape. (p. 10)

A thoroughgoing critical Marketing studies must, then, acknowledge not only the ethical and intellectual criticisms levelled at the subject and also the charge that it is guilty, at best, of political naivety, but must also take on board the admission of the field's top research journal that Marketing falls considerably short of its claims as a management technique.

Depressingly, Marketing and business management academics get little credit for acknowledging the weaknesses in their discipline and are seen by the unsympathetic as no more than corporate ideologists. In fact, some Marketing academics are quite indifferent to such a label and see no need for critique at all. This indifference, though, invites serious criticism from outside the discipline. For many critics, Marketing studies is a field of science which can demonstrate no progress, a field of social science which does not engage with social issues, and a field of human study which, reduced to technical problem solving, is thoroughly dehumanized. A critical appreciation of Marketing studies needs to engage with these criticisms to understand why they arise and to evaluate their fairness.

Scott (2007) (herself an internationally eminent Marketing academic) expresses the widely held view that Marketing is a part of a relatively 'homogenous and uncritical' management and business enterprise which attracts the undisguised contempt of academicians outside business and management because of its 'ostrich-like' intellectual blindness which renders it incapable of meeting 'the challenges of either practice or ethics' because 'it so totally lacks critical perspective'. Scott (2007) goes on to say that 'regardless of the level of scientific rigour that may be flaunted, the determination of business schools to be the unquestioning handmaids of industry make them a laughing stock at the campus level of most universities' (p. 7).

Such severe criticism might seem unfair, even perverse. It is, at least, a serious charge given the resources devoted to Marketing education, the importance of management education to the economy and to wider society and the amount of time and money invested in Marketing courses by thousands of individuals. Many Marketing academics feel that criticisms such as these are indeed unfair. They argue that its scholarship enjoys a rich and varied connection with the statistical and social sciences and the humanities, even if this breadth of influence is seldom evident in typical taught courses or textbooks. Most Marketing and management academics feel that they are academics first, and management academics second. They feel that intellectual values guide their teaching and research. Clearly, management subjects have an applied character too. But management academics feel that a direct connection with worlds of practice can be intellectually enabling.

If they have failed in communicating or preserving these values, there is a case to answer.

## Specific Criticisms of Marketing Studies

So much for general criticisms of Marketing studies. These are comprehensive enough, and will be elaborated upon throughout the book, but will seem very abstract to many students of Marketing management. An outline of some more specific criticisms of managerial Marketing's concepts might provide a more concrete point of departure for a critical Marketing studies. Once the more direct criticisms of Marketing's functionality as a management technique have been outlined, it is possible to ask deeper questions about why, if these criticisms have any grounds, the discipline has not evolved new theories to challenge or replace the old ones.

## Does the Marketing Concept Work?

Whether the Marketing concept deserves to be taken seriously as a management maxim is a big question which deserves a lengthier treatment than it is given here. Suffice to say that the way the concept is generalized into a one-size-fits-all panacea for organizational problems in popular textbooks is regarded with no little scepticism in some quarters (Brown, 1995a; Wensley, 1988; 2007). According to Ted Levitt's influential article, 'Marketing myopia' (1960), organizations flourish by finding out what customers want and then giving it to them. This is the essence of the Marketing concept, which holds that Marketing is not merely an organizational function concerned with sales and customer service but is no less than a philosophy of business (Drucker, 1954) which, in the Marketing oriented organization, should permeate every department. Organizations which focus on production, cost efficiency or sales will, ultimately, fail, according to Levitt's (1960) vision of Marketing orientation. The customer-focused and market-oriented organization will succeed. Kotler (1967) averred that this managerial concept can be put into action through a sequence of market analysis, strategic planning, implementation and control. Market success can, on this model, be directed by skilled Marketing managers armed with the right market information, primed with the right strategy and operationalized with the right Marketing techniques.

All of which will sound very familiar to people even superficially acquainted with managerial Marketing. The Marketing concept of organizational success through customer focus and market orientation is rather too general to prove or to refute. And this is one criticism levelled at it. It simply doesn't amount to anything more than folklore, at least according to its detractors. But, to take it seriously as a heuristic or 'rule of thumb' for management action, it seems to imply a rather static business model. Conventional Marketing's most persistent credibility problem lies in the evidence that significant numbers of business success stories seem to owe little or nothing to Marketing's key precepts. On the face of it, some highly successful organizations which claim to be customer-focused treat customers badly on occasions and don't necessarily base their activities on detailed market analysis. Instead, their success seems to be founded on a customer value proposition which people find attractive. The organization then exploits all the market power it can to push that offer into the market.

The point that the classic Marketing concept does not seem to fit many organizational successes has been made forcefully by many commentators. Brown, for example, (2001a, 2003, 2005b, 2006a, 2007) has argued that teasing, rather than satisfying, customers has been the key for some global Marketing successes, including the Harry Potter phenomenon and Ryanair, and also for unconventional Marketing geniuses like P. T. Barnum and 'Colonel' Tom Parker. Some of the typical examples of Marketing success cited in mainstream textbooks (McDonald's, Avis, Reader's Digest, Microsoft, Ford, etc.) are open to the charge that Marketing textbooks depend on them more than their success depended on Marketing textbooks. Entrepreneurial flair, imagination, drive and leadership might explain those iconic brands rather better than the Marketing concept. Counter examples might include Microsoft, the now-ancient history lesson in innovation leadership of the Sony Walkman, and more recent developments in internet business models. YouTube.com, for example, built up huge volumes of customer traffic by giving away its service free. Subsequently, Google paid a vast sum for its advertising potential. In effect, Google was buying a customer base from a provider that didn't sell any products. That is a business model which would seem highly improbable, were it not for the fact that YouTube was sold for some $1.65 billion in 2006.

It could be argued that these examples of business successes did not, on the face of it, seem to owe anything to the classic Marketing concept. More specific criticisms have been made of the managerial efficacy, and also the evidence base and logical coherence, of other well-established Marketing concepts such as the Product Life Cycle or PLC (Hooley, 1994); segmentation (see, for example, Saunders, 1993; Wensley, 1995), and the Four Ps of the Marketing Mix (Brownlie and Saren, 1992), to mention just a few examples. Other scholars have argued that the classic Marketing concept has an outdated focus on transactions, products and tangible resources, and that there needs to be a turn in the post-industrial economic era to services which utilize intangible resources to try to build customer relationships (Vargo and Lusch, 2004; for a critique of the service-dominant logic in marketing, see Brown, 2007).

It is axiomatic in Marketing texts that the Marketing function is strategic in the broad sense that it is sometimes the result of planned activity drawing on significant resources and designed to further the goals of the entire organization. It should be noted though, that the typical emphasis of managerial Marketing studies and texts on large consumer goods manufacturers has been criticized by those who feel that

Marketing studies ought to reflect more closely the fact that the vast majority of business enterprises are small ones (Carson, 1993; Carson et al., 1995). Nevertheless, Marketing and the heavy hitting management discipline of strategy are often thought to fit together hand in glove (e.g. Hooley et al., 2008) even though they are sometimes located in different organizational departments, and often in different academic departments. Every textbook on Marketing principles or Marketing management has a chapter (or several) devoted to strategic Marketing planning. Yet the strategic planning element of many commercial successes is as difficult to see as the presence of the Marketing concept.

The commercial insight of visionary entrepreneurs such as Ray Croc, Akio Morita, Bill Gates, Richard Branson and Henry Ford, to take a few examples,[1] apparently owed little to formal, textbook models of strategic Marketing planning. Of course, there is a danger here of conflating different things. Marketing, for many, is a word that evinces creativity, innovation and intuition, even if its managerial prescriptions fail comprehensively to explain radical innovations and creative leaps forward in commerce and administration (Cova and Svanfeldt, 1992). Yet the strategic planning approach within which Marketing is usually located is associated with rationality and bureaucracy. Planning formulation and planning implementation, though, can be seen as two distinct processes (Mintzberg, 1994) that are not necessarily connected. There are many tales of organizational life in which elaborately and expensively devised strategic planning documents are created at great cost in time and expense, then put in desk drawers, never to be read again, as people go back to operating in their usual interactional, intuitive and political way.[2]

Peters and Waterman (1982) created a case-based deconstruction of pretensions of strategic planning, but the notion that market success can be formalized in written documents and executed with a high degree of control persists. This does not, of course, mean that there is no value in pursuing such ideas in management and Marketing education and research. The important point to make here is that typical Marketing texts and courses seldom acknowledge or engage with criticisms of the functionality, evidence base or logical coherence of the main concepts of the subject. In particular, the Marketing concept seems to treat the organization as a blank canvas for the execution of Marketing ideas. Organizations are profoundly complex, human institutions (Watson, 2001a, 2001b), and managerial Marketing texts and courses completely ignore the institutional dynamics which have to be negotiated in order for the Marketing concept to be enacted.

It is already clear, then, that the charge that Marketing precepts don't work in practice is more complex than it appears. If they do not, why is that? Is it because they were not based on sound evidence? Is it because they lack intellectual robustness? And, in any case, by what standards can organizational effectiveness in Marketing be judged? Are there not many other possible explanations for organizational failure? Does the fault for the failure of new products, lack of innovation, falling demand, loss of market share or other organizational ills have to lie with Marketing management ideas? Or can it be blamed on the human error of the managers, deficiencies of staff training, quality management or resourcing, or simply the infinite uncontrollable variables in the marketplace? Looking beyond practice at Marketing studies and management education, is it fair or appropriate to judge Marketing ideas by social scientific standards? And if not, why not? If they should be, then do Marketing theories stand up to critical social scientific examination? And what, for that matter, is a theory?

So, not only is criticism of Marketing difficult to categorize and balance; each criticism implies deeper ones. Ultimately, a critical Marketing studies has to move beyond naive and ultimately insoluble considerations of organizational relevance and effectiveness to engage with issues of ethics, values, intellectual standards and the sociologies of knowledge and practice.

## Consumer Behaviour Models

Continuing this brief outline of points which criticize managerial Marketing studies on its own terms, on grounds of effectiveness, relevance and practicality, the model of the consumer upon which Marketing activity is predicated has come under close and continuing scrutiny. It seems clear that the anthropology, psychology and sociology of consumption are central to Marketing studies. Above all else, Marketing's claims are based on a privileged understanding of consumers, their wants, needs and inner drives and aspirations. The market is the consumer, and knowledge of the market drives Marketing management. It has been argued that the 'black box' models of consumer behaviour derived from Howard and Sheth (1968) offer only a partial representation of the consumer, and one which, in its emphasis on consumer rationality, flies in the face of anthropological accounts of consumer motivations (Levy, 1959). Even if the consumer can be understood by Marketing managers, can consumers really be managed (Gabriel and Lang, 2006) or is the entire edifice of Marketing management based on managerial vanity and pretension? Is managerial Marketing studies based on an overblown claim about the power of managers to control the idiosyncratic, accidental and paradoxical world of consumer Marketing? Indeed, is power the elephant in the Marketing room? Is it the key issue underpinning organizational life and market processes? And if so, in what ways can managerial Marketing studies engage with this issue?

Perhaps the Marketing texts imply a degree of control over the destiny of their brands which is simply not available to Marketing managers. Holt (2004) has suggested that the Marketing managers behind iconic brands are riding a cultural wave which they can neither control nor predict. In other words, customers and situations can be exploited, perhaps even anticipated with luck, but not controlled. That there is planning, strategy, segmentation, targeting and a sense of what consumers want behind organizational Marketing practice can hardly be denied. But exactly what these activities mean, how they play out in different organizational settings and precisely what their role is in Marketing processes may not necessarily be captured by the typical models and concepts of the managerial Marketing studies curriculum.

To be sure, Marketing is but one element of organizational success among many non-Marketing components. They include effective supply chain management, ownership of intellectual property rights or of raw materials, competitive scale and efficient manufacturing processes, creative and astute design and technology, among others. All these impinge on the Marketing offer while practical Marketing management usually focuses on issues closer to consumers like customer service delivery, pricing, promotion, distribution, product development and merchandising. So perhaps it is a little vague to say that Marketing 'doesn't work'. Nonetheless, Marketing is the discipline that has set itself up as the defining feature of organizational success, so it cannot be said to be behind all success yet at the same time not responsible for all failure.

The preceding paragraphs have opened up some questions about the functionality of Marketing concepts. These will be returned to in the book but serve, for the present, to introduce a few criticisms of Marketing studies which students familiar with the managerial style of the subject might be able to relate to. It is important to recognize, though, that criticisms of managerial Marketing's functionality are only one aspect of critique in the field. A thoroughgoing critical Marketing studies has to engage not only with criticisms of its claims as a technique of management problem solving but also with deeper issues of its implied positions on ethical, intellectual and political questions.

## How Can Marketing Studies Respond to Criticisms?

There are competing visions of critical Marketing studies, many of which will be discussed later in the book. What tends to confuse students is what, exactly, they are being asked to do when asked to take a critical perspective of their studies. There is vehement debate on the nature, scope and methods of Marketing studies so, naturally, ideas of what critique in the subject ought to look like differ as well. There is a colloquial aspect to critical scholarship and practice, which we outline here, while more theoretically based notions of critique in social study are introduced as the book progresses.

This book, then, offers a discussion around the notion of critique in Marketing. It is designed to bring disparate areas of thought in the field together in a form which can be accessed by students of the subject as a starting point for their own critical thinking, however that might be conceived. 'Critical' thinking is, simply, good thinking. But this does not mean that a critical approach to Marketing studies lacks a distinctive and different character to mainstream studies. A critical intellectual position questions assumptions about facts, relationships and values and offers new ways of understanding these and their relationships with each other. Critical thinkers look at things in new, different and creative ways. Critical thinking, in any subject, carries political, ethical and intellectual values, but the absence of critical thinking does not mean that political, ethical and intellectual values are irrelevant or not present. Marketing, broadly conceived as the activities, processes and practices of markets, influences lives and values in immediate ways. Marketing matters, since it has serious and far-reaching organizational, economic, cultural, environmental, ethical and educational implications. It is too important not to be critical, and too important not to be subject to critique.

## Critical Scholarship

The typical use of the word 'critical' in the context of academic studies is as a symbol of higher intellectual achievement. Few students have not been implored to write essays which 'critically evaluate' a topic, 'critique' a way of thinking about something or write a 'critical' analysis of a theory or body of work. But in spite of its importance as a foundational concept to academics, there is no agreed definition of what critical thinking or writing really entails. For many students, the instruction to be 'critical' in their essay probably means 'better', 'more' or just 'I don't exactly know but I'll award marks for it'. But even if it is difficult to define explicitly, most educators sincerely feel that critical thinking is a tangible scholarly virtue which we recognize when we see it. Academics look for critical thinking in students' work because they regard it as a mark of excellence, more difficult and creative than mere 'descriptive' work. Critical thinking is demanded in any field of scholarship and involves going beyond merely repeating and applying received ideas, even if they are repeated accurately and applied correctly. It involves taking ideas and demonstrating a thorough understanding of them by comparing, evaluating and interrogating their standards of logic and evidence. So, in this sense, critical thinking is just a term to denote the higher levels of intellectual achievement, in Marketing studies or any other subject. Academics use a similar distinction when discussing students' work between 'analytical' and 'descriptive'. Critical thinking is analytical in the sense that it does not merely describe ideas but analyses them.

# A Typology of Critique in Marketing

So much for the colloquial uses of 'critical', and the powerful but rather mystical meanings academics project onto the term. How might critical thinking, however it is designated, be applied in Marketing? Criticisms of Marketing studies persist, then, in spite of seemingly unceasing demand for its ideas in the form of management education, books and courses. But it is precisely this popularity which adds urgency to calls for Marketing studies to open up to more critical approaches. This book explores a number of lines of critical engagement in response to several persistent critical positions. Broadly, these fall into four overlapping categories, outlined here and developed throughout the book. These are labelled as functional, intellectual, ethical and, finally, political critique. This typology is used here not as a theory but simply as a literary and pedagogic device to help organize forms of critique in Marketing into more manageable subdivisions.

Put simply, functional critique asks the question: 'Do Marketing techniques work as management problem-solving devices?' Intellectual critique poses the question: 'Does this idea/theory/concept make sense in terms of its internal coherence and its relation to the world it describes?' Ethical critique asks what impact Marketing ideas and practices have on the world in terms of sustainability, social responsibility, individual freedom and other human and environmental values. Political critique asks: 'In whose interests is it to express Marketing ideas this way as opposed to a different way?'

It is worth saying a little more about these categories of critique here.

## Functional Critique

The first category, examples of which have been outlined above, concerns criticisms which accept the discipline's key assumptions as a technical, managerial problem-solving enterprise but challenge the validity and efficacy of particular ideas within this approach. In other words, we can ask the question: 'Do Marketing techniques work?' So Marketing studies is seen as an applied management field, and the academic role is to try to research and develop Marketing techniques to improve management training, education and practice. This inward-looking Marketing studies has two main dimensions. On the one hand, Marketing tools and concepts are evaluated in the light of evidence of how, and if, they get results in application. On the other hand, and equally importantly, they are evaluated in terms of their internal coherence and evidence base. Many criticisms in this vein imply both an evaluation of outcomes, however they might be measured, and a critical appraisal of the intellectual coherence of Marketing management prescriptions (Thomas, 1994, 1996).

For example, few Marketing textbooks do not draw on the 'AIDA' linear model of persuasive advertising adapted from the work of Strong (1925). This 85-year-old communication theory, based on personal selling, conceptualizes Marketing communication in terms of a sequence of internal states through which the receiver of the communication progresses. In order to be effective, a Marketing communication is said to have to get the *Attention* of the targeted receiver, then to generate *Interest*, promote *Desire* and finally persuade the receiver into *Action*, that is, purchase. This model has been criticized on many grounds. It is neat and simple, but some argue that it is simply wrong (Heath and Feldwick, 2008) from a practice point of view, others that it fails to capture the social character of Marketing communication (Ritson and Elliott, 1999), while still others have argued that it is such a gross simplification that it fails to teach students anything useful (Buttle, 1995). In this way, functional criticisms of Marketing management ideas overlap into evaluations of their internal coherence and evidence base.

Criticism of Marketing's practical effectiveness, its functionality, then, entails an evaluation of its key managerial principles, tools and concepts. In particular, it focuses on the challenges which unpredictable, quirky and creative human beings, and the complex social dynamics of markets and organizations, pose to the simplistic formulae of the managerial Marketing concept.

### Ethical Critique

So much for the question of whether particular Marketing ideas work in practice. One thing seems clear, which is that Marketing does indeed 'work', even if it may not be in the ways described in the standard textbooks. Marketing is held up as a social force for good and, often, for ill. Environmental destruction, waste of resources, over-pricing, labour exploitation, spreading values of greed and acquisitiveness – these are just a few of the crimes laid at Marketing's door. Marketing practice is subject to many criticisms of its ethics and standards of social responsibility (Hastings and Haywood, 1994; Smith, 1995), and especially the effects of Marketing activities on the vulnerable, particularly children (Nicholls and Cullen, 2006). Marketing studies has been criticized for not incorporating an ethical stance more deeply into its teaching and theorizing. Some argue that Marketing discourse and logic have spread far beyond markets and reach deeply into the everyday lives of citizens and individuals, commodifying even human relationships (Reuter and Zitziwitz, 2006). The managerial Marketing approach tends to look at organizational problems as technical difficulties of Marketing efficiency, with consumers seen as the means to achieve organizational ends. So ethical critique focuses on the moral and social values implied in the activities of organizations and the implications these might have for the world and for individuals. This suggests an examination of the ethical and social values which surround Marketing practice and which are embedded in Marketing education, research and theory, as well as an examination of the regulations and laws which delimit Marketing activity (Hackley et al., 2008). This would include a challenge to the managerial problem-solving approach as the rationale for Marketing studies, to take account of its broader societal role. It has been argued, as Chapter 2 describes, that Marketing studies has taken a wrong turn and that, because it has forgotten its history, it has left behind the concern with the wider effects of Marketing on society which were once central to the way the Marketing discipline was conceived (Witkowski, 2005).

### Intellectual Critique

Marketing studies, and management and organization studies in general, are typically thought of as fields of application rather than of pure intellectual endeavour. Yet Marketing, even if it is seen simply as a managerial problem-solving discipline, has to draw on many other disciplines for insights and conceptual frameworks. The mainstream Marketing management approach to research and theory has been criticized for being highly selective in the way it draws on and uses theories from other fields of human and social science (Brown, 1995; Firat and Venkatesh, 1995; O'Shaughnessy, 1997). What is more, it has to justify its place intellectually in university curricula all over the world. So intellectual critique focuses on the internal coherence, elegance and depth of Marketing theories and ideas. In part, this category of critique draws attention to criticisms of the intellectual standards of Marketing studies and challenges the intellectual basis which sustains the managerial Marketing agenda. It calls for Marketing studies and research to draw on a broader intellectual heritage to engage fully with other fields of social and cultural study and take account of historical and institutional forces which shape Marketing studies and practice. These calls have come from within the Marketing studies field as well as from other intellectual disciplines. The criticisms in this category entail an examination not only of the coherence of Marketing's managerial concepts but also of its intellectual scope and ambition as a discipline. Marketing studies can be seen as a simply managerial discipline, or more broadly as a field of social and human study based around the activities and processes of markets, consumption and the various implications of these activities for individual humans and the wider world. Marketing's theories, its assumptions, its intellectual values and its very modes of representation, the way it is written about and described in different media, are, then, subject to an examination which asks why things make sense in this way, when they could also make sense understood in a different way.

To make this more tangible, many Marketing scholars explore the outer reaches of the scope of the discipline from social scientific and humanistic perspectives. Marketing studies have not only been concerned with the scientific analysis of markets, need satisfaction and competitive success but have also explored topics as diverse as the psychoanalysis of klepto-mania (Fullerton, 2007), Nestlé's Marketing strategies in the Ottoman Empire (Köse, 2007), the inversion of the male gaze in advertising (e.g. Patterson and Elliott, 2002) and the tragic life and death of jazz legend Chet Baker (Bradshaw and Holbrook, 2007), not to mention the symbolic, hedonistic, existential and sexual motivations behind consumer behaviour (Elliott, 1997; Gould, 1991; Hirschman and Holbrook, 1982; Levy, 1959) and the postcolonial undertones of the Irish pub industry (Patterson and Brown, 2007). These topics, studied from many theoretical approaches which could hardly be further removed intellectually from the typical topics of Marketing management, hint at the scope of Marketing studies which occur outside of the Managerial mainstream.

## Political Critique

An examination of the values of a discipline includes looking at how ideas have evolved and what institutional forces formed them and sustain them. This, in turn, implies an examination of who stands to gain and why, by making Marketing studies into one thing rather than a different thing. Marketing studies is a vast, diverse and plural field of social scientific and human study. In its 100-year history in universities, it has been character-ized by perpetual tension and contest over its values, methods and scope (Marion, 2006; Wilkie and Moore, 2003). Not only is the field subject to internal tensions and political contexts over which theories and approaches are accepted as legitimate and which are not, Marketing also has a wider political dimension in the sense that it is intimately implicated in the play of power in social life. It has been argued that Marketing is essentially an ideology (Marion, 2006; Whittington and Whipp, 1992) and this implies that it confers power on those who control the way it is under-stood. In organizations, Marketing discourse justifies the power of man-agers who have control over what is seen as 'customer orientation' or appropriate levels of service. Marketing discourse, the use of Marketing ideas in everyday interaction, is used to justify many kinds of change, both organizational and social (Willmott, 1999). Since Kotler and Levy (1969) called for the Marketing management concept to be broadened to be applied in non-profit, public sector, professional service and charitable sectors as well as commercial manufacturing sectors (see also Kotler and Zaltman, 1971; Kotler and Roberts, 1989), Marketing ideas have spread to become a force for the marketization of all walks of life (Reuter and Zitziwitz, 2006). To this extent, Marketing studies and Marketing practice can be seen as having a political dimension because they are concerned with the power which plays through the use of certain ideas. Typical Marketing management texts and courses tend to ignore this aspect of Marketing, treating it as a neutral, technical exercise with no social, per-sonal or political implications.

Political critique overlaps with intellectual critique in the sense that any serious examination of ideas should involve a historical and institutional perspective. Yet, in Marketing studies, there is a good deal of intellectually sophisticated research which fails entirely to engage with the politics of the discipline. Marketing studies is big business, and of course so is Marketing. If Marketing is, crudely, about making money, Marketing studies isn't far behind in money-making ability. The Marketing education and research business recruits hundreds of thousands of paying students and thousands of paid academics. It sustains an industry of textbooks, courses and management-consulting operations. Intellectualizing about Marketing can be an empty exercise unless ideas are evaluated not only in their own terms but in terms of how they arose and what institutional forces combined so that particular ideas became accepted and others ignored. This means that a critical Marketing studies requires a historical perspective and a political focus on Marketing studies as a discourse, including a critical deconstruction of its writing, its voice and its styles of representation. Marketing is said not to merely describe but to construct consumers (Elliott, 1997; Elliott and Wattanasuwan, 1998) and workers (Brownlie and Saren, 1997; Willmott, 1999) as well as citizens. So a politically informed critique of Marketing studies would entail the use of critical theories to analyse the social and political dynamics embedded in the deep assumptions behind typical managerial Marketing approaches to the subject (Bradshaw and Firat, 2007; Hetrick and Lozada, 1994).

These categories are the points around which the book turns. They intersect each other and many of the issues discussed henceforth could be grouped under more than one of the categories. Nevertheless, the aim of the book is to offer a tentative organizing scheme for critique in Marketing, which might assist in bringing some of the wide-ranging and disparate yet vital and passionate debates in the field within the scope of more of the thousands of students and managers who have an interest in the area.

## Marketing Studies and Critique

Finally, we return to the question of why critique might be considered a virtue in Marketing studies. Marketing knowledge is itself a marketed commodity (Holbrook, 1995). But what Marketing studies is, is not widely agreed upon. What goes into a university syllabus or management training course is political and contested. Typical Marketing courses and texts mobilize the ideological influences at work in the Marketing discipline at the time (Marion, 2006), and reduce the scale and complexity of the subject into a package which fits curricula needs and bends to commercial forces. Historical and critical perspectives on the subject can be neglected or lost under the weight of political and commercial influence. It is important for students of Marketing to appreciate that the content of curricula is not the result of an outbreak of agreement and consensus, but a tentative, changeable and highly selective compromise which masks diverging views and detailed debates. Marketing is far from unique in this, though it does have a pressing need for critical perspectives to be more visible to the average student.

All this may sound disconcerting to students who are used to Marketing knowledge being packaged and delivered in tidy bullet points with glossy colour pictures. If the academics can't agree, what hope do the students have? But in this, Marketing is no different to any other field of thought. The educational point, if we need to state it, is to encourage and enable critical thinking, so that students learn to assimilate and evaluate competing viewpoints in order to better understand the thing itself. Marketing is not merely a chaos of competing views any more than Philosophy, Psychology, Theology or History. There may be majority points of view on particular issues, and there are also significant numbers of dissenters. In particular, 'critical' thought, by implication, takes a position against the popular or received view. In its everyday usage, 'criticism' can mean simply criticizing. On the other hand, critique can also refer to the application of new viewpoints to a topic, not so much in a spirit of antagonism but rather in a spirit of intellectual vitality where taken-for-granted assumptions and truths are continually questioned and new strains of thought introduced to refresh old ideas. There might sometimes be dialogue and perhaps cross-fertilization between the competing ideas. Of course, there can also be resistance, argument, and political influence over ideas. Such is the nature of every academic subject. After all, knowledge is never neutral, it is invariably invested with power for those who define it (Foucault, 1977, 2000).

This book, then, is an introduction to some of the many critical viewpoints which can be found in Marketing. Readers inclined towards critical thinking might already be asking themselves 'Is this little book really an innocent inquiry into the intellectual standards and practical felicity of Marketing? Or does it carry implicit assumptions which reflect the values, interests and priorities not of readers, students, consumers or managers, but of the author?' The answers to these questions are, naturally, 'yes' and 'yes'. The book's main point is that the questions should always be asked.

This book is intended not to prescribe an agenda for critical Marketing studies but to enrich the Marketing curriculum for students by showing ways in which spaces for dialogue, intellectual perspective and critique might be opened up on Marketing's typical subject areas. To this end, it is intended as an aid to critical thinking in Marketing with the end of assisting deeper student engagement with Marketing studies. It is aimed also at Marketing researchers and practitioners who are curious about the kinds of debate over topics, methods and priorities which occupy Marketing academics. It explores questions about why particular topics are usually conceived in this particular way and not in alternative ways. Finally, it is intended as a basis for further scholarship in Marketing to the extent that it brings together strands of debate and intellectual influences which are, for reasons which are explored in the book, excluded from typical Marketing texts and courses.

So many students, practitioners and academics find Marketing an exciting subject to study because of its many-faceted engagement with the social world, its openness to different kinds of intellectual treatment, and its connection to our personal experiences as consumers, managers, workers and citizens. It is a subject of study which is both enabled and restricted through its basis in a field of professional practice. This book is an attempt to convey something of the excitement of Marketing and consumer research and study, to pay tribute to the depth and breadth of scholarship in the field and to open up critical spaces with which students and practitioners might engage, as well as academics.

The book will explore more arguments as it progresses. For now, it might be useful to look more closely at what Marketing studies has become by examining where it came from. One, frequent criticism of typical Marketing textbooks in the managerial tradition is that they offer little in the way of historical perspective. The subject is presented as if it is timeless. The absence of historical perspective in typical Marketing books and courses makes the subject easier to teach, but produces a critical vacuum around its key concepts and silences debate around which of its 100-year history of theories should be retained and which should be abandoned. Some sense of historical perspective then should be a starting point for a critical Marketing studies.

## CHAPTER SUMMARY

Chapter 1 opened up some criticisms which have been levelled at Marketing studies and Marketing practice and contrasted these with the lack of critique in the popular managerial problem-solving approach with which the subject has become identified. It outlined a typology of critique consisting of functional, intellectual, ethical and political categories of critique which will be revisited throughout the book. To further develop the context for critique in Marketing studies, Chapter 2 will explore the origins and institutional dynamics of Marketing studies.

## CHAPTER REVIEW QUESTIONS

1. The typology of critique outlined in Chapter 1 divides critical approaches to Marketing into functional, ethical, intellectual and political categories. Look at the criticisms of Marketing listed earlier in the chapter and discuss which categories each particular criticism might fall into.

2. Critically evaluate the argument that Marketing studies needs a critical dimension.
3. Take three debates in Marketing discussed in Chapter 1 and evaluate the role of critique in terms of each. What questions have been asked in each debate and what assumptions have driven those questions? What end might be achieved by these debates?
4. Consider three Marketing encounters you have recently had. They might be products (a new car or watch), services (a meal in a restaurant, a course of education) and/or experiences (a day at a theme park or a date through a dating agency). Discuss to what extent you feel your encounter conformed to classic Marketing principles. That is, were your needs as a consumer anticipated and satisfied? Or were the dynamics of the encounter more complex than that, and if so in what way?

---

## CHAPTER CASE

### Coke Zero and the Limits of Marketing Research

Coca Cola, the world's number I brand,[3] has found that the classic Marketing planning model sometimes runs up against unpredictable events. New products are typically pre-tested before launch using research techniques of survey research, experiments and consumer taste tests. After launch, the sales are carefully monitored. The UK *Sunday Times*[4] reported data from market research company AC Nielson suggesting that Coca Cola's most important new product in the UK for two decades was suffering a sales decline. Coke Zero, the sugar-free brand targeted at young men, was reported to have lost roughly 30 per cent of its take-home sales in under a month. This report evinced memories of the company's attempt to enter the UK bottled water market in 2004 with its Dasani brand. A press story revealed that the Dasani production facility was piped into the UK mains water supply. So Coke were selling bottled tap water. Coke claimed at the time that their production processes refined the water making it more pure than normal tap water, but the PR damage was done and the brand withdrawn from the UK after a reputed £7 million marketing launch. Dasani remains a popular brand elsewhere. Coca Cola is reputed to research its market with great care before launching new products, and stories such as these suggest that there is more to Marketing success than detailed pre-launch market research. It should be noted, though, that Dasani is a successful brand in the USA and Canada and, at the time of writing, the marketing press is speculating that Coke might re-launch it (possibly under a different name) in the UK in the future. Bottled water is projected to exceed carbonated drinks sales globally so the market is important for Coke.

......................................................................................................................................................

## Case Questions

1.  Do these examples of Coke Zero and Dasani imply that there is a flaw in Coke's Marketing logic, or might there be other reasons behind the reported failures?
2.  Is it ethical to sell bottled water? What are the long-term implications of this business for the environment?
3.  How might the role of Marketing research in these two new product launches be evaluated in the light of each of the four categories of critique described in Chapter 1?

**Notes**

1  Ray Croc created the MacDonald's empire from a small hamburger store, while Akio Morita, CEO of Sony, invented and marketed the original Walkman in spite, according to legend, of negative market research results. Consumers simply couldn't grasp the concept, but Morita was convinced they wanted the Walkman, even if they didn't know they wanted it. Bill Gates, Richard Branson and Henry Ford are, of course, widely known through their entrepreneurial achievements. Like most legendary entrepreneurs, they had no formal management education.
2  'Why Strategic Planning Doesn't Work (and how to create plans that do)' by Bryan Feller (www.marketing.org/ArticleDetails.asp?AId=674 – Business Marketing Association website accessed 2 September 2006).
3  Source: Business Week Online website – bwnt.businessweek.com/brand/ 2005/ – 'The Top 100 Global Brands Scoreboard', data provided by Interbrand (accessed 20 July 2006).
4  Coke Zero sales fall to deflate sugar-free fizz', by Mark Kleinman, *The Sunday Times*, 27 August 2006, p. 3, Business section.

# CHAPTER 2

# THE ORIGINS AND INSTITUTIONS OF MARKETING STUDIES

---

### CHAPTER OUTLINE

Chapter 1 introduced the idea of a critical discipline of Marketing studies which takes account of, among other things, the historical and institutional forces which shape a field of knowledge. Chapter 2 explores these origins and outlines the key institutions of the discipline. In particular, it is important to trace the subject back beyond the popularization of management studies in the 1950s and 1960s to its founding academics at the turn of the century, in order to place its subsequent development in a broader context. The chapter goes on to examine the impact that key professional institutions, especially the American Marketing Academy, have had on the way in which the Marketing subject is understood. Some views on the ways in which this historical and institutional infrastructure may have influenced Marketing studies are then examined.

---

## Introduction: Marketing's Development as a Subject of Academic Study

Marketing is a discipline with a history, scale and intellectual scope that few students have the opportunity to grasp in typical one- or two-semester courses or airport lounge 'How to do Marketing' paperbacks. In over 100 years as a subject of higher study, research and scholarship, the field has developed strands of thought which reach further, wider and deeper than many people might suspect. Some of these strands of thought will be opened up as the book progresses, but for now it is important to outline some of the historical work which locates the field in a context of development. Today, there is a widespread view that Marketing studies have two pre-eminent characteristics. One is a focus on managerialism, the implicit assumption that the legitimate scope of Marketing studies is delimited by the interests, values and instrumental priorities of organizational managers. The other is that the subject is typically conceived as a pseudo-scientific technical discipline which has no need of historical perspective.

The question of whether Marketing studies has lived up to the aspirations and values of early thinkers is a persistent source of debate in the Marketing literature. It has been suggested that modern Marketing has neglected the historical perspective essential to a critical understanding (Tadajewski and Brownlie, 2008b) and therefore condemned itself to endless repetitions and reassertions of previously voiced ideas (Fullerton, 1987). One way of underpinning such arguments is to study Marketing history but, while Marketing history is a contested and vibrant area of scholarship in the field, it is one which has virtually no presence in the typical curricula of mainstream Marketing management courses. Importantly, the dominant technical problem-solving arm of Marketing studies tends to be ahistorical in its approach. So, it is important to ask where Marketing studies came from in order to understand what it has become.

## Marketing Studies Origins in the USA

It is usually claimed that the popular genre of normative or 'how-to-do' Marketing texts dates from the 1950s but the first college courses called 'Marketing' were recorded at the turn of the twentieth century in the USA (Halbert, 1965). Marketing developed initially as a branch of applied microeconomics concerned with the distribution of goods and the buying behaviour underlying market clearing processes in conditions of surplus production (Wilkie and Moore, 2003). It grew, partially, out of a sense of the inadequacy of economics for explaining, and offering policy prescriptions for resolving, market inefficiencies.

Marketing did not become formally established as a field of written ideas until the period between 1900 and 1920, in the USA. Marketing studies has a long presence in university education in the USA and a distinguished history as a multidisciplinary tradition of thought, research and writing (Bartels, 1951). The managerial (Sheth et al., 1988) model of Marketing studies which dominates the world of management education emanates from the USA but was not taken up in the rest of the world until the 1960s and 1970s. As Witkowski (2005) notes (citing Fox et al., 2005), it is telling that the first Marketing text published in Soviet Russia in 1980 was Philip Kotler's classic *Marketing Management (1967)*. This is a measure of the way the managerial vision of Marketing as a technical discipline which transcended cultural and political barriers became widely acceptable. According to some Marketing scholars, though, the subject was not originally conceived in that way.

Jones and Monieson (1990) argue that early Marketing education was driven by the desire to place Marketing management activity on a basis of firmly secured knowledge. They suggest that early Marketing educators at the University of Wisconsin were influenced by the German Historicist School of social science and interpreted this in terms of inductive fact-gathering (about consumption and distribution patterns) supported by descriptive statistics. The aspiration of Marketing education from the beginning of the century was to create a positivistic Marketing management science which would inform the activities of Marketing 'middlemen'. This was reiterated by Paul Converse (1945) 40 years later in a well-known paper which is often taken as the starting point for Marketing science. Yet Jones and Monieson (1990) show that the managerial orientation and scientific aspirations of Marketing research and education were present from the very beginning of the discipline's history. What was evident then, which is less so today, was a concern with Marketing as a societal function (Witkowski, 2005). The overall goal of Marketing studies was to improve Marketing effectiveness in order to improve the economic welfare of all.

## Marketing Management and the Harvard Case Method

While Marketing studies at Wisconsin were focused on the scholarly study of the systemic properties of markets, later at Harvard Business School, the emphasis was more closely on the normative or how-to-do Marketing aspect of the discipline. Harvard's engagement with management practice evolved into the famed Harvard Business School Case Method.[1] Management education at Harvard entailed a close analysis of a real business situation, preferably through direct experience with visits to the company and discussions with company officers (Contardo and Wensley, 2004), followed by intense class debate about possible solutions. The idea was for managers to experience cases, much as clinical education is based on practice case work as well as theory. Incidentally, the Harvard approach must have created a bear-pit which sharpened the rhetorical skills of the protagonists, not unlike the Oxford Union. And throughout classical education rhetoric, the art of being able to persuade others with the force of reasoned argument was considered the ultimate transferable skill.

Marketing studies consisted of two main aspects. One was the analysis of market trends, activities and processes. This was conceived as a social scientific exercise in the broadest sense, based on a historical case method. Descriptive statistics were used to gain insights into the structure and dynamics of particular markets, set in their cultural and historical context. The second main aspect was managerial in the sense that this market information was designed to improve managerial decision making at the policy level.

At Harvard, the education of managers was developed by a different approach to case analysis, which relied less on a market-level analysis and focused more on an organizational problem-level analysis from the managerial perspective. To put this another way, it could be seen as a shift from a more academically disinterested, social scientific and historical account of market dynamics towards a more problem-focused and vocational style of management education. Importantly, the Harvard approach was based on live case studies. Participants were encouraged to go into the companies they were discussing to understand more thoroughly the context of the problem. The term 'case' tends to be used in Marketing education today to refer to any kind of managerial problem-focused activity, most typically based on a narrative written up and published specifically for the purpose. This second-hand case material, often carefully crafted to spin a particular story, clearly lacks the experiential and ethnographic aspect of case analysis which entails a first-hand exploration of a real organization. So the idea of 'case study' most commonly understood today is quite a different thing to the traditional Harvard case idea. Case-based management education, which entails first-hand research in the form of discussions with managers in the organizational context, mimics ethnographic social scientific study. The use of written-up case studies for hypothetical decision analysis lacks this aspect and, if the exercise is conducted as a written one, also lacks the element of public argument and debate so important to the development of analytical and rhetorical skills. Nevertheless, the written case study has become a staple of Marketing management education and no self-respecting Marketing textbook (including this one) can afford not to have them.

## The Adoption of Marketing Studies in the USA and UK

The rest of the world lagged many years behind, not in the practice of Marketing but in accepting that Marketing studies has a place in the university curriculum. In the UK, for example, Marketing was, for a long time, regarded largely as a vocational subject suitable only for sub-degree education. The first professorial university Chairs in Marketing were instituted in the UK in the early 1960s, at the universities of Strathclyde and Lancaster. Many leading UK universities have been even slower to establish business and Marketing programmes as a central part of their provision. The Said Business School at Oxford University was established in 1996 (amidst some considerable controversy and opposition). The Judge Management School at Cambridge University was established in 1995, though at both institutions, management studies was taught for some years before. Royal Holloway, University of London established its School of Management in 1992 and its first Chair in Marketing in 2004.[2] In contrast, the School of Business at the University of Wisconsin-Madison was established in 1900, and Harvard Business School in 1908. The collegiate School of Business at Wharton, University of Pennsylvania, was established in 1881 and was offering its first courses in product Marketing by 1904.[3] Wharton were relative laggards in Marketing education though, since E. D. Jones of the University of Wisconsin is credited with teaching the first university course in Marketing (Jones and Monieson, 1990, citing Bartels, 1951, and Maynard, 1941) although Jones and Monieson (1990) concede that there may have been earlier university courses in Marketing distribution in Germany.

Early Marketing thinking, then, focused mainly on issues of market clearance. There was apparent waste in distribution processes resulting from poor coordination of demand and supply. The engagement with practice was considered enabling, in contrast to traditions of academic studies in which abstraction and theorization carried greater intellectual kudos. The Harvard case method has been highly influential in promoting a practice-driven ethos of Marketing (Bartels, 1951, in Jones and Monieson, 1990), as well as inspiring the MBA educational approach. The case method of management education pioneered at Harvard largely eschewed theoretical principles in favour of an applied problem-solving approach grounded in case-based facts and, where possible, generalized rules-of-thumb (Contardo and Wensley, 2004). Marketing studies, in short, were founded in the USA with the dual aim of generating Marketing facts and discovering management principles and communicating them to practising or aspiring managers, for the general betterment of organizational effectiveness, consumer welfare and society as a whole (Wilkie and Moore, 2006).

To sum up, early theorists saw Marketing studies as central to the enterprise of management and business studies education. They brought back a view from German universities that Marketing should be understood through inductive, case-based research methods allied with descriptive statistics and oriented to the practical education of managers. Jones and Monieson (1990) suggest that Marketing's claims as a knowledge-based subject originally rested on a statistical methodological approach which was mediated by a keen sense of history and of the specific behavioural and social contexts of markets. This approach was adapted into a case-specific approach to management education, though the case study based on a purposively written text is quite a different educational experience to the live case study based on personal first-hand organizational research.

As the presence of Marketing studies became established in American universities, its infrastructure of academic and practitioner journals and societies began to grow.

# Marketing Studies Institutions: Academic Journals and Professional Societies

## Marketing Journals

Today, academic research in Marketing[4] is booming on the back of robust student recruitment and a powerful infrastructure of professional and scholarly institutions such as the US American Marketing Association, the Marketing Science Institute, the Academy of Marketing Science, the British Chartered Institute of Marketing, the European Marketing Academy, the UK Academy of Marketing, not to mention the Association for Consumer Research, the American Advertising Federation, the American Academy of Advertising, the Australia and New Zealand Academy of Marketing, the UK Institute for Practitioners in Advertising and numerous others of which Marketing forms a significant sub-category. The existence of so many bodies points to the success of the field as a highly professionalized area of research and writing, as well as practice.

Something of the reach of Marketing studies can be understood from the selection of journals listed in Box 2.1, which publish scholarly articles on Marketing topics. The academic publishing of research in Marketing has become a huge business. The variety of titles hints at the way Marketing has fragmented around an increasing number of themes related to the scope, values, methods or key audiences for research in Marketing. However, the top US-based Marketing journals tend to share a managerial focus and statistical bias.

---

## BOX 2.1

### SELECTED ACADEMIC JOURNALS PUBLISHING RESEARCH IN MARKETING AND THEIR ORIENTATION[5]

Marketing as a superordinate management function:
*Journal of Marketing; Journal of Marketing Management; Journal of Strategic Marketing; European Journal of Marketing; Marketing Management Journal*

Marketing as a statistical or social science:
*Marketing Science; International Journal of Research in Marketing; Psychology and Marketing; Journal of the Academy of Marketing Science; Academy of Marketing Science Review; Journal of Consumer Psychology; Journal of Empirical Generalizations in Marketing Science*

Marketing as human and cultural studies:
*Journal of Historical Research in Marketing; Consumption; Markets and Culture; Journal of Material Culture*

---

Marketing as an interdisciplinary theoretical subject:
*Journal of Consumer Research; Marketing Theory; Journal of Marketing Theory and Practice*

Marketing as a generic set of management tools for application in any field:
*Journal of Non-Profit and Voluntary Sector Marketing; Journal of Travel and Tourism Marketing; Journal of Financial Services Marketing; International Journal of Bank Marketing; Journal of Political Marketing; Journal of Marketing for Higher Education; Journal of Business and Industrial Marketing; Journal of Fashion Marketing and Management; Journal of Services Marketing; Journal of Retailing; Journal of Business-to-Business Marketing; International Journal of Sports Marketing and Sponsorship; Journal of Research in Marketing and Entrepreneurship; International Journal of Medical Marketing; International Journal of Mobile Marketing; Journal of Direct Marketing; Journal of Health Care Marketing*

Marketing as an intelligence-based management function:
*Journal of Marketing Research; Journal of Database Marketing and Customer Strategy Management; Marketing Intelligence and Planning; Journal of Advertising Research; Qualitative Market Research – An International Journal; International Journal of Market Research*

Marketing as scholarship and pedagogy:
*Journal of Marketing Education; Marketing Education Review; Management Learning*

Marketing as an area of social concern:
*Journal of Public Policy and Marketing; Social Marketing Quarterly; Journal of Business Ethics; Business Ethics – A European Review; Journal of Consumer Affairs; Journal of Consumer Policy; Journal of Macromarketing*

Marketing as a management function with specialized sub-functions:
*Journal of Targeting; Measurement and Analysis for Marketing; Journal of Interactive Marketing; Journal of Relationship Marketing; Journal of Consumer Marketing; Journal of Brand Management; Journal of Customer Behaviour; Journal of Product and Brand Management; Journal of Personal Selling and Sales Management; Journal of Marketing Communication; International Marketing Review; Journal of Advertising; International Journal of Advertising; Journal of Consumer Satisfaction; Dissatisfaction and Complaining Behaviour; Corporate Communication*

The journals widely regarded as the top eight in rank – the *Journal of Marketing, Journal of Marketing Research, Journal of Consumer Research, Journal of Retailing, Journal of Advertising, Journal of Advertising Research, Industrial Marketing Management* – and *Marketing Science* are each over 30 years old and are all US-based (Sividas and

Johnson, 2005).[6] Many of the journals in Box 2.1 are less, reflecting the rapid rise in recent decades of the number of research academics working in the Marketing teaching departments of university business and management schools. Many of the journals could have been placed in more than one of these fairly arbitrary categories – the *Journal of Macromarketing*, for example, could have been in three as it deals with theoretical as well as social concerns and carries social scientific articles as well as historical essays and anthropological analyses. The *European Journal of Marketing*, similarly, carries non-mainstream research as well as the more conventional managerial problem-solving research. But, necessary overlaps and oversimplifications aside, the list suggests that the field does have a certain vitality, provided you know where to look.

Many Marketing journals are sponsored by professional bodies. The top-ranked journal and one of the most cited social science journals in the world (Lusch, 1999), the *Journal of Marketing (JM)*, is produced through the most prominent professional association, the American Marketing Association (AMA), which in turn sponsors a series of major academic and practitioner conferences. The AMA enjoys a powerfully influential position with a 'relative hegemony' over US Marketing journals (Wensley, 1998, p. 80). The *Journal of Marketing* reports a circulation of over 10,000 per issue (Stewart, 1999). Other examples include the *International Journal of Research in Marketing* which is published by the European Academy of Marketing (EMAC), the *Journal of Consumer Research* by the Association for Consumer Research (ACR), and the *Journal of Marketing Management* by the UK Academy of Marketing.

As Brown (1995) has pointed out, the written style of research papers in the top Marketing journals has changed markedly over the last 50 years. In the 1950s and 1960s, the key management journals, *Harvard Business Review* and the *Journal of Marketing,* had a far more practitioner-oriented readership. Articles now regarded as classic expositions of marketing theory such as those by Levitt (1960) and Kotler (1972) featured some relatively anecdotal analysis followed by decisive recommendations for management, supported by a few citations to other work. Nowadays, most articles published in these journals are profoundly technical with scores of citations and, often, detailed statistical calculations. A few journals carry critical, qualitative and conceptual papers, but generally speaking, the pre-eminent mode of paper published in the top ten Marketing journals is in the managerial problem-solving vein with arguments supported by statistical evidence.

Wensley (1988) suggested that the UK has a less well-defined academic and professional institutionalization than the USA, although it does have a pre-eminent association, the UK Academy of Marketing (formerly Marketing Education Group), which sponsors a major conference and a range of journals, the highest ranking being the *Journal of*

*Marketing Management*. The European Marketing Academy (EMAC), itself sponsored by the European Institute for Advanced Studies in Management (EIASM),[7] is a major European academic Marketing society with around 1000 members which (as noted above) published a highly rated journal and organizes major academic conferences around Europe. In the UK, there is a major trade association for professional Marketing practice which runs its own set of qualifications. The Chartered Institute of Marketing (CIM)[8] is a self-contained institution entirely separate from the Academy of Marketing. In the USA, the AMA acts as the principal association for both Marketing practitioners and academics.

The domination of the USA in business education is also reflected in the relative prestige and influence of USA-based Marketing academic journals. With no less than 136 academic Marketing research journals listed by the American Marketing Association and by the British organization the Association of Business Schools,[9] at the time of writing, the field is varied and comprehensive but also fragmented and divided. Many of the journals carry tacit preferences for particular topics or methods. For example, the EMAC-sponsored *International Journal of Research in Marketing* ranks highly and is modelled on the US journal style with a preference for statistical argument and a managerial problem-solving orientation. However, in a study of its own 1000-strong membership, EMAC found that while the journal was regarded as high quality, there was a perception that, because of its preference for econometric modelling, it was not relevant to managers, did not offer insights into Marketing practice and did not reflect the diversity of academic European Marketing research.[10]

The field-leading *Journal of Marketing (JM)* lays itself open to similar criticisms. Its website[11] states that its remit is to 'demonstrate new techniques for solutions to marketing problems and review those trends and developments by reporting research'. However, it also seeks to 'contribute generalizable, validated findings'. In keeping with the Ford and Carnegie reports into business education (Kniffin, 1966), this means that it is a very particular research approach based on a model of natural science which is heavily positivistic and statistical. Consequently, many of the research studies which appear in *JM* are highly technical validations of parts of larger models, accessible only to those with profound technical and statistical knowledge.

The evidence that top journals in Marketing are the central source of knowledge, which then disseminates to the lower ranked journals is confused (Wilkie and Moore, 2003). Academics can build careers focusing on just a few journals, depending on the rank of their university, their sub-specialism, and the country they work in. The top ten journals represent a nexus of influence, judging by evidence of cross-citation (Sividas and Johnson, 2005) but these are a small number of the total. Marketing is a North American product[12] and the top ranking journals are dominated by US researchers, yet there are also distinctive European Marketing research agendas and a growing Asian influence. In short, many other academic disciplines can look to their top ten journals for a widely agreed global research agenda. In Marketing, the top ten journals are immensely influential but, given the scope of the field illustrated by the range of specialist journals, it is hard to say that they truly reflect a global consensus on research priorities or theoretical approaches.

Wilkie and Moore's (2003) suggestion that the structure of influence emanating from Marketing journals is uneven and fragmented is disputed by other researchers (Sividas and Johnson, 2005). But analyses of influence depend on presuppositions about how influence can be gauged. A cursory perusal of articles across a range of Marketing journals suggests that there are constant challenges to the theoretical and empirical values of the leading journals. If academics want tenure in leading US (and many Asian) universities, they have to publish in the top eight ranked journals. They seek to do this by operating in the networks of the leading conferences which sponsor the journals. However, academics in many European and lesser-ranked US universities do not face such prescribed publishing criteria for tenure or promotion. They can publish in journals falling outside the ranking lists and the papers are judged on their own merits rather than measured against pre-set journal ranking criteria. The differing professional structures for academic Marketing outside the leading US universities is one of the factors which give Marketing its fragmented character as a knowledge developing, building and disseminating exercise. Nevertheless, it is a paradox of Marketing studies that it is at once fragmented and pluralist, and narrow and prescribed. The top university business schools and top academic journals operate in the same, hermetically sealed, area with the same deep assumptions about the most appropriate scope and methods of the discipline. True, some academics in the top schools build careers researching beyond these confines, publishing research in psychology and sociology journals as well as Marketing ones. But the influence of the top schools and journals is palpable. One area in which this influence is manifest is in the curious preoccupation with defining Marketing studies.

## Marketing Definitions

The American Marketing Association (AMA) is a key component of the institutional infrastructure for Marketing studies. The AMA is probably the most high-profile academic and trade association for the discipline, and is highly influential in setting the tone for Marketing studies with its periodically updated definition. It is a reasonable place to start asking the question: of what does modern Marketing consist? The 2008 definition is as follows:

> Marketing is the activity, set of institutions, and processes for creating, communicating, delivering and exchanging offerings that have value for customers, clients, partners and society at large. (AMA, 2008)

The AMA definitions (see Box 2.2 below) locate Marketing firmly as a managerial activity, rather than as a social or statistical science or field of scholarship. The AMA is not only a society for academics in Marketing but also for professionals so it is, perhaps, no surprise that the managerial imperative is central to its definition. The American Marketing Association, then, represents the periodization of Marketing thought through its changing definitions of Marketing over 80 years. The AMA's periodic review of its definition reflects a desire to accommodate criticisms of prevailing strains of thought in Marketing, though the definitions keep the managerial emphasis.[13] Box 2.2 indicates the core managerial emphasis of AMA definitions, even if there are changes of nuance to accommodate new trends. Importantly, the AMA definitions reiterate the narrow managerialist idea of Marketing to the exclusion of social issues. Tadajewski and Brownlie (2008a, p. 4) argue that Wilkie and Moore's (2006) study of AMA Marketing definitions over the years highlighted a tendency for these to progressively 'eliminate marketing and society related issues from the definition of Marketing'. The wider social concerns of early Marketing theorists, then, have been relatively neglected under the managerial pressure for Marketing academics to create ever more effective targeting, segmenting, positioning, selling and profit-making techniques. The AMA definition, then, is a key element in the reduction of Marketing studies to an uncritical applied technique stripped of human and intellectual values.

In 1935, Marketing was defined in terms of a one-way flow from businesses to consumers. By 1985, the emphasis had changed slightly to reflect a two-way exchange process, encompassing intangibles such as ideas as well as tangible products, and not confined to business but to any kind of organization. In 2004, the notion of value was introduced and the emphasis on transactions changed to relationships. Marketing's role in creating value for society as well as for individuals and organizations featured in the 2007 definition. The assumption that Marketing is a discipline driven by, and grounded in, the priorities, values and interests of organizational managers remains, though, in all its definitions and also in the choice of article topics in the key AMA journal, the *Journal of Marketing* (Day and Montgomery, 1999; see Stewart, 1999).

---

## BOX 2.2

### AMERICAN MARKETING ASSOCIATION DEFINITIONS

**1935**

*As adopted by the National Association of Marketing Teachers, an American Marketing Association predecessor organization: [Marketing is] the performance of business activities that direct the flow of goods and services from producers to consumers*

**1985**

*[Marketing is] the process of planning and executing the conception, pricing, promotion, and distribution of ideas, goods and services to create exchanges that satisfy individual and organizational objectives*

**2004**

*Marketing is an organizational function and a set of processes for creating, communicating, and delivering value to customers and for managing customer relationships in ways that benefit the organization and its stakeholders*

**2007**

*Marketing is the activity, set of institutions, and processes for creating, communicating, delivering, and exchanging offerings that have value for customers, clients, partners, and society at large*

---

Definitions are a staple part of Marketing management texts and courses, yet other social science and humanities subjects tend to regard them with greater circumspection. The very act of defining is a disciplining process (Heilbrunn, 1996) which leaves open many unspoken alternatives (Derrida, 1979). Marketing's concern with definitions might be dismissed as insecurity about the legitimacy of the subject as a university discipline, but the preoccupation with definitions has persisted over the course of some 80 years. The cyclical re-evaluation of Marketing definitions (Baker, 2000a, p. 18; Gronroos, 2006) and scope (Day and Montgomery, 1999) is a distinctive and unusual feature of Marketing studies, reflecting perhaps the perpetual tension within the managerial Marketing project. Definitions secure the discipline within a delimited scope and reflect the interests and views of influential Marketing institutions. The AMA definition is but one – most trade and professional bodies have their own which tend to differ superficially but preserve the central managerial emphasis.

## Historical Influence and the Development of Ideas in Marketing Studies

Many Marketing textbooks assert that 'the marketing concept is a business philosophy that arose to challenge the previous concept. Although it has a long history, its central tenets did not fully crystallize until the mid-1950s' (Kotler, 1967, p. 17). Claims about the development of Marketing thought are, though, much disputed. In keeping with its 100-year presence as a university subject, Marketing studies has been characterized by many diverse styles and approaches. Important landmarks in popular Marketing thinking included the establishment of categories of Marketing activity, the 'functions' or elements of the discipline (Converse, 1930; Fullbrook, 1940); the alignment of Marketing with the growth in interest in management studies (Drucker, 1954); the popularization of the Marketing Mix as a shorthand for the demand management activities of Marketing managers (Bordern, 1964); and the competing paradigms of rational versus symbolic consumer motivations (Gardner and Levy, 1955), to name a mere few. That Marketing studies constitutes a substantial and diversified body of scholarship can hardly be disputed. Placing such developments into a historical context, however, has proved much more controversial. Explaining why some ideas have become more popular and widely accepted than others is equally problematic.

Claims of periodization in Marketing thought, such as Kotler's (1967) above, should be viewed with caution. For example, the often-repeated three eras schema (Keith, 1960) holds that organizational Marketing practice went through three evolutionary stages: production and then sales orientation before alighting in the era of Marketing orientation. This is not supported by a historical analysis of practice (Fullerton, 1988; Baker, 1976). The 'three eras' schema, repeated as fact in most popular Marketing management textbooks, has the rhetorical effect of producing the discipline as something progressive and unified, and tied to the neo-liberal order in the way that it matches perfectly the self-interest of organizations with the self-interest of citizens. The three eras myth might have been peddled as part of a personal agenda (Marion, 1993) but has become repeated so often as fact, perhaps because it reasserts the legitimacy of the Marketing concept. Consumer orientation is produced as the end point of a process, and signals the responsiveness of the Marketing discipline to consumer needs.

## Wroe Alderson and the Origins of Marketing

Some noted individuals have exercised considerable influence on the ways in which Marketing studies has been understood, but serious treatment of the work of these individuals has faded entirely from the pre-packaged Marketing studies which is presented in popular managerial textbooks and courses. Wroe Alderson was an early theorist in the development of the subject from microeconomics to the managerial discipline which it became in the 1950s. Alderson (1957, 1965), who published many of his ideas in a regular newsletter to business clients, felt that classical economics did not explain the ways in which markets 'cleared'. He looked at Marketing as an economic system driven by heterogeneous, and not homogeneous, consumers. Consumers had individual drives and needs and could not be expected to be satisfied with the same kinds of product and service as everyone else. Not only were all consumers not the same, according to Alderson, but their buying decisions were not motivated only by price or practical considerations. Economists assumed that markets 'cleared' with all goods sold, provided price was low enough and practical utility high enough. Alderson saw that fashions, trends and personal preferences, informed by individual difference and varying cultural background, all had a role in determining the demand for particular products and services.

Hence, Alderson saw that Marketing was needed as a new social science to understand the ways in which demand played out in different markets, and to help discover ways in which this heterogeneous demand could be managed. Alderson positioned his own theories on Marketing within the 'structuralist–functionalist' approach or 'paradigm'. His work, communicated in a famously inaccessible writing style (Brown, 2002; Wooliscroft, 2003; Wooliscroft et al., 2005), was superseded in popularity in the late 1950s by the much more direct and concrete managerialist approach of Kotler, Peter Drucker and others. Though Alderson's work is seldom cited in popular textbooks today, many academics still regard his ideas as relevant to the contemporary Marketing scene (Hulthén and Gadde, 2007).

Marketing emerged as a discipline, then, out of a sense of dissatisfaction with the conceptual frameworks provided by economics. The conflictual character of Marketing studies has been remarked on by Levy (2003), who understood it as an intrinsically contested field, given its status as an ideological and cultural phenomenon (Heath, 2007). Marketing is an area which realizes aspirations and influences the distribution of wealth and goods. It makes some people rich and content, but not others. An effective Marketing system delivers jobs, income and lifestyles. Little wonder, then, that the way markets and Marketing are thought of, talked about and enacted is a fiercely contested area subject to political sensitivity and impassioned argument.

## 'Layers' of Marketing Thought

Marketing practice itself, if not quite the oldest profession, must have a strong claim to be the next oldest. Barter, selling and persuasion were of course practised in ancient civilizations, and writing itself was possibly invented by Marketers (Brown and Jensen-Schau, 2008), while the invention of print and then broadcast media in the modern era provided new canvases of persuasion on which the Marketing folk could practise their arts. Marion (2006) argues that there are three layers to the discipline:

1.  **Marketing as practice.**
2.  **Marketing as a branch of knowledge.**
3.  **Marketing as an ideology.**

Layer one pre-dates the others. Layer two consists of the codified 'principles and tools' used by Marketers. For Marion (2006), these principles and tools are 'performative' in that they simultaneously describe and produce Marketing. This performative character places Marketing halfway between science and practice, 'conceptualizing and enacting market economy' (p. 247). Marketers in practice draw on the discipline's conceptual vocabulary (its 'tools and principles'), not only to *do* Marketing but to enact it, and by so doing, to legitimize both the practice and the practitioner of Marketing (Svensson, 2003; 2007). Layer three is Marketing's attempt to have its vocabulary and values shared by many, acting in a self-reinforcing way to affirm the ideology.

Arguably, there is a disconnection between layers two and three and layer one. Practice cannot be entirely controlled by the Marketing knowledge-producers, the academics, consultants and writers. While there is a well-developed professional infrastructure in Marketing, the professional bodies do not control entry to the profession to the degree which obtains in medicine, engineering or other technical and scientific disciplines. In any case, Marketing practice is generally too quick, too quirky, too rapid and too innovative to fall easily into the categorizations of Marketing professors. Marketing experts, after all, have no need of Marketing textbooks. Marion (2006) notes the example of Eastman Kodak, who created the cultural idea of amateur photography by making the technology available (citing Latour, 1987). This was cited as an example of Marketing defining and producing a cultural norm, not following self-declared consumer needs. As noted in the previous chapter, (Holt, 2004) technology, entrepreneurial vision and market resources enabled home photography to become a common practice. So layers two and three of Marion's (2006) scheme have a mutually reinforcing relationship which requires only a superficial engagement with layer one. One aspect of critical studies in Marketing history, then, is an attempt to pick apart the nature of the true relationship between these three layers and to answer the question: 'Why do we think of this thing in this particular way?' Marketing history, then, is a key element of critique in Marketing studies. But periodization of Marketing history can be a powerful way of inscribing particular Marketing ideas with legitimacy.

Wilkie and Moore (2003), acknowledging their debt to Bartels (1988), suggest that, since the early formalization of the subject as a topic of thought and scholarship, Marketing has evolved through four eras. They put the time before 1900 as an era of 'pre-Marketing' thought during which Marketing issues were intellectually embedded within economics. Of course, that does not imply that pre-1900 was, in a practical sense, a pre-Marketing era. Like other commercial topics, Marketing, and commerce in general, were often felt to be unworthy of intellectualization until the modern era, although the assumption that there has always been prejudice against Marketing practice and practitioners expressed in literature is wrong (see Stiener, 1976, in Tadajewski and Brownlie, 2008a). Writing was invented by Marketers (Brown and Jensen-Schau, 2008) and the need for products and services is universal. Commerce itself is not generally decried, except that in some cultures, the commercial class was considered to be lower in status to the intelligentsia and aristocracy.

Wilkie and Moore (2003) go on to argue that Marketing practice, research and education began to acquire its professional infrastructure of journals, trade associations and research bodies between 1920 and 1950. The period of 1950–1980 was the time when Marketing developed within the management science movement. Popular texts generally date the applied Marketing management approach from the 1950s (Kotler, 1967), although the ideas which informed it were much older (Baker, 1999). The fourth phase Wilkie and Moore (2003) see as a phase of fragmentation, with specialized research and practice sub-fields splitting off from, and forming a challenge to, the managerial/scientific mainstream. As we have seen, though, the managerial mainstream retains control of the major university business school Marketing departments, journals and professional societies and the evidence of a pluralist, reflexive and critical Marketing studies can generally only be found in a relatively small number of Marketing journals and academic departments which fall outside the mainstream.

Skålén et al. (2006) draw on Hollander et al. (2005) to offer a slightly different periodization of (American) Marketing thought to that of Wilkie and Moore (2003), from early Marketing thought (1900–1960) to Marketing management (1950–1985) followed by service management (1975 to present). These scholars feel that the historical evidence shows that managerial influence in Marketing was not a feature which appeared in the 1950s but, as this chapter indicates, was present from the very beginning of the discipline, even if it was conceived somewhat differently back then. But as Skålén et al. (2006) concede, periodizations are invariably arbitrary. In Marketing, they are sometimes used to promote particular, competing points of view.

## Nothing New in Marketing Studies

The ways in which the development and evolution of Marketing ideas are represented in the academic journals have been viewed with no little scepticism by scholars who see Marketing studies as a field which is open to the practice of recycling old theories as new. For example, papers reasserting a new era of Marketing responsiveness to customers regularly features in the top Marketing journals. Marion (2006) offers several examples, suggesting that 'Marketing orientation and "demand management" (p. 61) are denounced in favour of "customer centric" Marketing' (p. 56) in Sheth et al., 2000 (Marion, 2006, p. 256). The notion of 'customercentricity' was also posited in Deshpande (1999) as a renewal and re-invigoration of Marketing's commitment to, and sympathy with, customers. Marketing studies, like

Marketing practice, is about selling ideas, and Marketing academics have proved as adept at re-packaging old ones with a 'new improved' label as their practitioner colleagues.

Marketing ideas such as branding, targeting, positioning and segmentation are often assumed to be inventions of managerial Marketing but in fact were being practised long before Marketing was established as a field of thought and writing. As Baker (1976) pointed out, reinvention of the old is a time-worn technique of Marketing studies (Hollander, 1986) and also Marketing practice (Brown, 2001b). Marketing institutions, research styles and technology have evolved, but many Marketing practices claimed as new are far from new. Baker (2000a, p. 9) quotes Fullerton (1988) on the use of Marketing techniques by Georgian British pottery entrepreneurs Matthew Boulton and Josiah Wedgwood. They used market segmentation, product differentiation, prestige pricing, planned obsolescence, direct mail advertising and even product placement (in royal portraits), among other ways of creating interest in their innovative ware. Quickenden and Kover (2007), in a detailed historical study, show that Boulton, in particular, was very conscious of his market and, at the turn of the 1800s, was trying to use pricing differentiation to re-position his goods (silver plate and luxury ware) and expand his market to include middle-class as well as upper-class consumers.

In Hackley (2005a), the Marketing activities of Victorian entrepreneur Thomas Holloway, founding patron of the building now used by Royal Holloway, a college of the University of London, included branding, product placement (in stage plays and novels) and international advertising.[14] Not only were segmentation, targeting, positioning and product placement actively pursued by Marketing practitioners several centuries ago, but advertising promotion with persuasive rhetoric and visual imagery, often assumed to be a Western invention of the 1960s, was evident over 200 years before (McFall, 2004).

So, the periodization of Marketing studies into neat 'eras' of development, often glibly reasserted in popular textbooks, is hugely problematic. Historical examination of the topic serves to illustrate the de-coupling between Marion's (2006) layer one (Marketing practice) and layer two (Marketing principles) and the function of layer three (Marketing ideology and the assertion of periodization) to repair that de-coupling with a mythical representation of Marketing history. A factor in this de-coupling is the separation of Marketing practice from academic Marketing. Historical consideration of the development of Marketing thought through academic research and courses may be essential to a critical approach to the topic (Tadajewski, 2006b), but the institutional dynamics behind the success of certain ideas in Marketing and the failure of others are difficult to establish (see Peter and Olsen, 1983, for a discussion). The development of ideas, then, needs to be considered alongside the institutional and political forces surrounding the subject.

# CHAPTER SUMMARY

Chapter 2 has reviewed some of the historical research into Marketing's origins as a discipline of research, education and training. The subject was introduced to universities some 100 years ago in the USA but with rather a different character to that which it is known for today. The managerial style of Marketing studies with its emphasis on normative managerial prescriptions has evolved and become popularized under many influences but does not necessarily reflect the diversity of opinion in the field. The chapter explored the influence of some of academic Marketing's key institutions, its journals and its professional societies. Chapter 3 will go on to explore some of the critical implications of the rise of managerialism in Marketing studies.

# CHAPTER REVIEW QUESTIONS

?

1. Discuss how the evolution of Marketing studies as an academic discipline may have influenced the popular conception of what Marketing is.
2. Early Marketing theorists considered Marketing from a societal point of view as something essential to the general welfare of populations. But is it relevant to critique Marketing practice on the grounds of its sometimes negative social influence? Or is poverty the greatest evil?
3. Does intellectual critique of Marketing studies simply miss Marketing's practical point?
4. Should Marketing managers be concerned with the way Marketing knowledge disseminates from and through universities and academic journals?

## CHAPTER CASE

### The Internet Reverses Business Strategy Priorities: Building a Customer Base Before You Sell Anything

The new media and communications technology presents a challenge to the ways in which Marketing activities and processes can be conceived and poses a question about the continued relevance of classic Marketing concepts.

For example, 'viral' marketing has been widely regarded as the quintessential internet strategy since MSN Hotmail was initially popularized through emails. While email is still an important marketing communication tool, the internet has had even more radical effect on business strategy to the point where it has reversed conventional practice. Where once a business had to market its goods well to build up a customer base, now it can build up a customer base before it sells anything. YouTube is a good example – it is a free access website which allows anyone to upload their own clip of video for viewing by anyone else. It was launched in February 2005 by Chad Hurley and was backed by the same venture capital company that backed Google, Sequoia Capital. It has become enormously popular with thousands of people per day choosing to watch videos of, for example, a cat flushing a toilet or a girl speaking about her problems with her strict parents. YouTube claims that it shows 100 million videos per day.[15] Having achieved such a large client base, using it for fun, it is in a position to generate substantial revenue streams for advertising, sponsored links or 'branded' channels running off the same site. For new businesses or new products, the hard part is normally to get public attention so that enough people seek out the business and trail it. The internet is a flexible PR vehicle with huge potential volumes – anyone with an idea can cheaply create a site and wait for net surfers to discover it. If it becomes popular, it is immediately a commercial proposition because the volume of traffic means that clients will pay for their brand to appear on the site. Of course, internet strategies are essentially communications-driven, so any synergy that can be generated through press or TV stories is very valuable for leveraging interest in the site.

The economics of generating revenue through websites is simple. Every time we use a search engine, sponsored links and banner ads appear. If we click on them, the host site gets a fee. Not only search engines but any site can feature sponsored links with a fee structure generating revenue for every click. UK advertisers were expected to spend more on online advertising than on display advertising in newspapers in 2007[16]. Most of the £2 billion spend will be on search-engine advertising, and much of that on sponsored links. Google is the most popular search engine, but Microsoft's MSN and Windows Live Search engines are also used extensively. Microsoft has launched AdCenter[17] to manage all its online advertising. Hotmail and MSN users number some 10 million and Microsoft will use the data it has on these people to help advertisers target ads.

Internet advertising has become more popular as many young consumers no longer buy a newspaper or watch much TV but spend many hours online surfing websites or using email and messaging services. Every internet user leaves footprints that can assist profilers to target ads. Each website visited, for how long, and how each was navigated can all be logged and the information sold to advertisers wishing to target, say, music buyers, car enthusiasts or book collectors. The dynamics of the internet are changing and the sheer volume of traffic means that new business models are becoming viable. Many new web-based businesses crashed in the dot.com boom and bust of the 1980s because they failed to realize that they needed conventional advertising to build the brand before people would seek out their website. Today, such large numbers of consumers use the web to search for suppliers that search engine advertising can yield large numbers of inquiries without any prior brand-building activities.

## Case Questions

1.  To what extent is the internet changing segmentation priorities for Marketing strategy?
2.  Do classic Marketing principles account for new business models created by the internet?
3.  Do the strategic Marketing planning models which feature in the typical MBA syllabus have any relevance for internet-driven business strategies?
4.  The internet is a powerful example of the way in which new communication technology is changing the marketing landscape. Can you describe others?

### Notes

1 See www.hbs.edu/case/
2 Modesty forbids me from naming the incumbent.
3 See www.wharton.upenn.edu/huntsmanhall/timeline/1881.html;
    www.hbs.edu/about/history.html;
    www.bus.wisc.edu/students/why.asp;
    www.bs.cam.ac.uk/aboutus/ourhistory.html; and
    www.sbs.ox.ac.uk/MBA/School/ (all accessed 3 June 2008).
4 There are over 130 specialist marketing journals publishing refereed research papers, and more than that number of general management research journals that will publish papers about marketing. In addition, there are countless trade publications in marketing and related fields such as market and consumer research, advertising, and strategic marketing. See oase.uci.kun.nl/~driessen/journals.html for a list of academic research journals in marketing.
5 Marketing's leading academic journals are inclusive of all sub-specialisms, though the top-tier journals tend in practice toward exclusivity because of their role as ideologists of the marketing mainstream. The sub-specialist journals thrive because certain ideas are marginalized in the top journals. Top-tier journals, according to Sividas and Johnson (2005), include *Journal of Marketing*, *Journal of Marketing Research*, *Journal of Consumer Research*,

*Marketing Science, Journal of Advertising, Journal of Advertising Research, Journal of Retailing,* and *Industrial Marketing Management*.

6  For example, Witkowski (2005) points out that the *Journal of Macromarketing*, concerned with the effects of Marketing on society, was founded in 1981: the journal *Public Policy and Marketing* was launched in 1982 (p. 225). The *Journal of Marketing,* in contrast, was established in 1936 (See www.marketing journals.org/jm/).

7  See www.eiasm.org/index1.html

8  See www.cim.co.uk/home.aspx

9  With thanks to Pierre Mazzacano D'Amato MSc, PhD student of Royal Holloway, University of London who sources this information from the Association of Business Schools' (ABS) UK-based source: www.the-abs.org. uk/ and the American Marketing Association's (AMA) US-base source: www.marketingpower.com/

10  *See The EMAC Chronicle*, No. 3, May 2008, 'Marketing Landscape: A Pause for Thought', p. 5, www.emac-online.org

11  See www.marketingjournals.org/jm/

12  Though see Jones and Monieson's (1990) suggestion that early Marketing thought was influenced, and pre-dated, by German thinking of the historicist school.

13  Source: www.marketingpower.com/content2653039.php (accessed 11 April 2008).

14  Royal Holloway, University of London: www.rhul.ac.uk

15  A statistic reported in a story in *The Times* by Rhys Blakely: 'YouTube offers "branded channels" alongside the home-made videos', 23 August 2006, p. 49.

16  'You are the target', by Richard Fletcher and Mark Kleinmann, *The Sunday Times*, 13 August 2006, section 3, p. 5.

17  'Microsoft unveils new ads weapon', *The Times*, 14 August 2006, p. 33.

# CHAPTER 3

# MARKETING STUDIES AND MANAGERIAL IDEOLOGY

## CHAPTER OUTLINE

Chapter 3 explores the ways in which the evolution of Marketing studies may have circumscribed the forms of critique which are possible. In particular, Marketing's enormous success as a field of training, education, research, consulting and managerial practice has come about partly because the subject itself has been astutely packaged and sold as a managerial field. Addressing the 'intellectual' and 'political' dimensions in the typology of critique, the chapter discusses the idea of managerialism and its role in the critique of the ideological character of Marketing studies.

## Introduction: The Success and Wider Influence of Marketing Studies

'Managerialism' and 'managerialist ideology' are two terms which readers will not encounter in typical Marketing textbooks. But they are much-used (usually pejorative) terms in critical and cultural studies. Before exploring why they are used so often to refer disparagingly to Marketing studies, it might be useful to underline the huge popularity of managerial Marketing studies, in order to place in context the purported influence of managerialism within the field and in the wider world beyond.

## The Paradoxical Success of Marketing Studies

Whatever the limitations of the typical, managerial Marketing approach, it is amazingly successful as a subject of study, research and practice (Baker, 1999; Brown, 1995; Brownlie, 2006; Saunders, 1993), and as a cultural phenomenon. Perhaps a million students around the world are studying Marketing courses, and many more are studying courses with some Marketing component in combined degrees, sociological, cultural or media studies (Hackley, 2001a). The version of Marketing studies which has attained this popularity is the normative, 'how-to', problem-solving approach. The prescriptive strain in Marketing is deeply problematic yet it is a key component of its popularity. Thousands of students annually learn simple normative Marketing principles which can apparently be used as prescriptions for action in real Marketing situations.

## Marketing as Philosophy and Function

Following Drucker, Marketing is seen as a set of functions (initially set out by Converse, 1930) which together express a philosophy of business organization. Conventionally, Marketing studies is thought of as an applied discipline which consists of ways to make money (or win clients/market share/donations) by finding out what people want and selling it to them. The transactional view of Marketing is sometimes placed in a broader economic context of exchange. Marketing is seen as 'a social and managerial process by which individuals and groups obtain what they need and want through creating and exchanging products and value with others' (Kotler et al., 2005, p. 6; see also Bagozzi, 1975; Houston and Gassenheimer, 1987). Typical textbooks assume that this process can be managed by a class of trained professionals: the Marketing Manager. Marketing is cast as a category of work that is fundamental to any organization because it involves connecting the things the organization does with its markets, consumers and other stakeholders. At a strategic level, organizations need to adapt resources and skills to make the best possible fit with the demands of markets, provided, of course, that it is in their interests to do so (Borsch, 1958). The overall aim of Marketing is to establish strategies which will achieve a strong and sustainable competitive position (Hooley et al., 2003). At a tactical level, Marketing is designed to help consumers to recognize a brand amongst alternatives, to persuade some of them that one brand is different, and perhaps more relevant to them, than others, and to reassure consumers that it is going to do what it claims with a consistent quality (Ries and Trout, 1985). If Marketing techniques can achieve this in each product market which the organization serves, then each business unit of the organization should maintain its market share and revenue.

All these ideas are associated closely with the managerial priority in Marketing, the taken-for-granted assumptions which drive the field as a managerial discipline. Marketing in this vein is about transactions and value-creation (usually monetary profit) driven by the strategic influence of the organization and the operational decision making of its managers. Arguably, it depends for its plausibility on a naive realism, a sense that Marketing managers operate in an independent world of consumers. If a social constructionist perspective is taken (Berger and Luckmann, 1966) on the nature of social reality, then some of the deep assumptions of managerial Marketing seem much less secure. For example, on what grounds can we say that organizational managers make 'decisions'? Might they not respond intuitively to peer pressure, organizational controls, the political pressures of relationships with senior colleagues? The idea of a decision-making manager, returned to later in the book, seems important to the way in which managerial Marketing is constructed in text, yet there is little contextual detail about the social structures by which managerial action is constructed in organizations in typical Marketing textbooks.

## The Disconnection of Marketing's Managerial Research and Practice

When Marketing studies is discussed here, it is important to distinguish between the popular textbooks and courses and the esoteric scientific research enterprise of the discipline. To understand the wider influence of Marketing discourse, it is useful to appreciate the relationship between these two manifestations of managerial Marketing.

On the one hand, there is the impetus for a scientific Marketing studies, driven by academic research and underpinned by the Ford and Carnegie reports into American business education (Pierson, 1959). This enterprise, based on statistical modelling, has evolved into a major academic industry legitimizing management education and sustaining university business and management research. The argument for such research, as we saw in the previous chapter, is that it aims to generate scientific or universalized facts which, in principle, could be helpful to Marketing management to inform their decision making. It has become a self-referential industry of research which seems to justify the intellectual claims of Marketing studies as a university subject. The discourse of science confers power, and Marketing studies and practice are both as susceptible to its influence as any other field. It is hard to see the connection between the scientific research and managerial practice, yet relevance to practice is the justification for the research.

In contrast to the elusive and sophisticated scientific research, there is the normative, managerial version of Marketing, the folksy and anecdotal prescriptions for action which are couched in simple and easy-to-apply terms and which form the core curriculum of managerial Marketing studies. The scientific, or 'scientistic' (Willmott, 1993) branch of research in Marketing arguably has little or no connection with the popular managerial prescriptions of typical Marketing texts and courses. Scientific research in Marketing studies is highly esoteric and inaccessible to all but the most numerate practitioner. The normative concepts and tools of managerial Marketing, the Marketing concept, STP and so on, are not scientifically based but, rather, are consulting frameworks.

It has been argued that Marketing science, intellectually formidable though its research may be, has discovered no science of Marketing at all (Saren, 1999; 2000), in spite of periodic re-evaluations of Marketing and reiterations of its goals as a managerial science (e.g. Day and Montgomery, 1999; Hunt, 1991). The appropriateness of Marketing's scientific goals has been regularly challenged, for example by those who argue that Marketing practice is more art than science and Marketing studies more accessible to literary, historical and aesthetic forms of understanding than scientific (e.g. Brown, 1996, 1997; Brown and Jensen-Schau, 2008). Tadajewski (2006b: 168) cites Arndt (1985: 21), who argued that Marketing needed new forms of research and exploration, otherwise it would remain 'a one-dimensional science concerned with technology and problem-solving'. An intriguing feature of Marketing studies is that it has developed many new forms of research and exploration but has yet remained, in its most popular guise, a resolutely one-dimensional problem-solving discipline.

Marketing studies seems to have the ability to appeal in different guises to different audiences. One of the paradoxes of Marketing studies is that its popularity is based on a hugely successful brand image, a seductive, even Utopian (Maclaran and Brown, 2005) vision of socially beneficial wealth creation through consumption which, scientifically managed by the benign authority of brand Marketing organizations, satisfies needs and wants and, at the same time, optimizes the use of resources. This is, at best, an aspiration, or perhaps a Romantic ideal (Brown et al., 1998). Yet Marketing is also understood as a down-to-earth, practical, common-sense discipline, accessible to some simple yet ingenious models which are transmissible by text (e.g. Jobber, 2003). In this guise, influenced perhaps by Ted Levitt (Brown, 2005), Marketing writing has acquired a literary style which represents Marketing activity with a direct and common-sense appeal, immediately comprehensible to anyone through text.

## The Wider Influence of Marketing Discourse

Beyond the academic syllabus, Marketing concepts have become a common vocabulary in everyday working life. Since Kotler and Levy's (1969) paper called for the Marketing concept to be applied in non-commercial areas, the Marketing discipline has exercised an impressive influence over the management agenda of public, charitable and non-profit as well as commercial organizations. References to Marketing's key 'concepts and tools' are now heard in every field from legal firms to dentists, charities, hospitals, schools and government departments. The popularity of Marketing subjects in the curricula of great universities around the world is equally awe-inspiring[1]. The Marketing concept may not generate quite as many consulting dollars as once it did but Marketing discourse, arguably, retains a striking resonance in commercial and public life (Willmott, 1993, 1999). Marketing studies drives huge volumes of university student recruitment, management training and consulting, and academic and business textbook, journal and electronic publishing. Marketing is, in itself, a commercial and cultural force of nature. As Firat and Dholakia (2006) point out:

> The tremendous success of modern marketing cannot be overstated. Marketing has emerged as the principle mode of modern business relationships, and eventually as the mode of all relationships that all institutions have with their constituencies (or 'markets', as now widely used). (p. 124)

They go on to say that:

> In part, this success is due to the fact that the marketing concept captured the essence of modern culture and of democracy ... with institutions serving citizens' wishes. (p. 124)

The idea that organizations should be forced, by competition or, in the public sector, by regulation and target-setting, to serve the needs and wants of individuals in the most efficient way has wide appeal. The associated idea that Marketing organizations are tapping into the psychological, statistical and social sciences to seek ever-improved techniques of discovering and fulfilling those needs and wants through managerial action is just as powerful. Marketing is the management subject which articulates the ideal of organizations in the service of citizens more compellingly than any other. At the same time, it engages its students with shared experience as consumers. Marketing studies taps into our fascination with consumption as well as our need to understand our part in the all-embracing managerial imperative.

## Normative Marketing and the Marketing Concept

As we have seen, the core curriculum of Marketing revolves around what is widely regarded as its main idea: the Marketing concept. This places an organization's customers at the heart of its activities. In the much-cited words of management guru Peter Drucker (1954):

> Marketing is not only much broader than selling, it is not a specialized activity at all. It encompasses the entire business. It is the whole business seen from the point of view of the final result, that is, from the customer's

point of view. Concern and responsibility for marketing must therefore permeate all areas of the enterprise.

The Marketing concept is ideological in character (Marion, 2006; Whittington and Whipp, 1992). It is something that is meant to be done, rather than reflected on. Marketing authors have written of the 'adoption' of the Marketing concept (e.g. Baker, 1974) as if it is a matter of converting the doubters to accept the ideology as passion rather than reason. It has become commonplace to hear organizational rhetoric about serving customers. The key assumption of Marketing management is that, through its constellation of applied concepts, models and axioms, the Marketing concept offers not only an organizational ideology but a practical manifesto for sustained competitive success. Most importantly, this organizational ethos is positioned as something which will benefit the whole of society by improving distributive efficiency and promoting wealth creation.

## Marketing Studies as Marketed Commodity

A particularly noticeable issue for university students studying Marketing as part of general degrees is that it is very reliant on all-embracing general textbooks which purport to cover every major area of Marketing but cite very few primary authors in the text. Other social science or humanities subjects tend to assume that students will read the original works of a wide range of scholars. The dominance of mass-marketed megatexts[2] (exemplified by the works of Philip Kotler) for over-taught Marketing courses represents a massive publishing industry (Hackley, 2001a)[3] and points to the extent to which Marketing has itself become a commodified product (Brownlie and Saren, 1995; Holbrook, 1995), packaged and sold for maximum return in programmes taught by colleges, universities and professional bodies and training organizations to thousands of students. This commodification is not complete or total: it is continually negotiated, resisted and compromised by the natural curiosity of students and the intellectual energy of Marketing teachers (Hackley, 1999). It does, though, mean that critique in and of Marketing studies has to fight for intellectual space with a commercial behemoth, the ideologically driven managerial Marketing project upon which student numbers and publishers' revenues (not to mention academics' jobs) are so heavily dependent. One of the aims of this book, incidentally, is to try to bridge a gap between the kind of Marketing course which is boiled down to a relatively narrow and uncritical diet of easily learned techniques designed for applied Marketing management, and the kind which are oriented around original research and social scientific scholarship.

Most strikingly, the distinctively North American idea of managerial Marketing studies with its neo-liberal ideological baggage of individualism, free markets and aggressive consumption (Witkowski, 2005) has captured the imagination of the elites in Asia, post-communist Eastern Europe

(Fox et al., 2005), Africa, the Middle East and the Indian subcontinent, judging from the huge traffic in international students who come to the West to study Marketing in business and management degrees. In some areas, there has been a reaction against the poor cultural fit of the American Marketing management model, for example in Mediterranean Europe (Cova, 2005) and Scandinavia (Gronroos, 1994). In others, there has been a striking reaction of 'techno-orientalism' (Jack, 2008, citing Morley and Robins, 1992) whereby Asian cultures have turned the tables to compete with, and often beat hands down, Western firms in technical Marketing expertise. The individualism implicit in managerial Marketing, with all its neo-liberal undertones, has been adapted to the less individualist cultures of Asia with remarkable results. Not only are Asian countries able to deliver levels of Marketing excellence in service and quality which far exceed those of the West, Asian elites have also adapted the ethos of extravagant individual consumption to fit the norms of hierarchical and group-oriented cultures (Chadha and Husband, 2006).

# Managerialism

So many students of Marketing aspire to be organizational managers that it will seem odd that the idea of management itself is in any way a problem. But the notion of 'managerialism' is hugely problematic in management studies for two main reasons. One is that the way the manager is represented in typical Marketing studies fails, for many students, to reflect organizational reality. The second, more difficult, issue concerns what some see as a cult or ideology of managerialism which carries implicit and unquestioned values and beliefs. Marketing studies is seen by many to be an ideological vehicle which promotes a one-sided managerialist way of looking at the world. This has implications far beyond the function of Marketing.

Marketing studies, then, is a subject which, in its most popular guise, is founded on particular preconceptions about the role, power and status of organizations and their managers in capitalist economies. A rather narrow idea of managerialism (Morgan, 1992; Skålen et al., 2006) pervades much Marketing theory and teaching and, in the view of critical theorists (e.g. Tadajewski and Brownlie, 2008a; Willmott, 1999), leaves limited space for critical perspectives. Managerialism is a term which broadly describes the ideological tone of discourse on economics and organization in advanced industrial nations. According to Enteman (1993), managerialism replaced socialism and capitalism as the pre-eminent ideology of our time since it acts to justify business activity at the expense of all other forms of relationship and economic organization. It is sometimes regarded as a dangerous ideology in that it assumes that both social policy and organizational activity are determined not by the political process but by technocratic managers, and thus risks eliminating the interests and needs of individual citizens.

It is manifested in, for example, the spread of managerial values through government agencies and public and non-profit services, a phenomenon sometimes called the New Public Management. Marketing is usually deeply implicated in the propagation of the New Public Management (Cousins, 1990; Laing, 2003). A major part of this is the use of Marketing techniques by government and state-sponsored agencies to achieve ends which are considered politically or socially desirable by the ruling party. For some, 'social Marketing' activities can redeem the discipline by using the tried and tested Marketing techniques of persuasion to promote socially beneficial ends (Gordon et al., 2007; Saren and Hastings, 2002). For others, this is a highly dubious position, given that social Marketing is itself a political act which carries and promotes the power inequalities and neo-liberal values of the prevailing state authority (O'Shaughnessy, 1996; Witkowski, 2005, citing Brenkert, 2002). Marketing techniques, then, are increasingly co-opted by states to encourage ostensibly socially beneficial behaviours. Examples would be 'social Marketing' campaigns that encourage safer driving, healthy lifestyles and environmental protection. However, far from redeeming Marketing from criticisms that it has negative social effects, the 'social Marketing' movement could make things worse by appearing to legitimize the technocratic model of Marketing practice which draws such criticism in the first place.

## Self-doubt and Self-reflection in Marketing Studies

Criticisms of Marketing studies, then, need to be located within the fact of its resounding success as a cultural phenomenon (Firat and Dholakia, 2006). They also have to acknowledge two other issues. One is that the academic Marketing journals regularly feature self-critical papers. For example, Arndt (1985) called for 'paradigmatic pluralism' in the research methods and intellectual traditions upon which Marketing academics draw. Brown (1995) wrote of Marketing's 'mid-life crisis', which was expressed in many papers published in the academic research journals characterized by critical self-examination and doubt about its values and priorities. An influential Scandinavian school of relationship Marketing oriented around services has evolved out of criticism of the dominant, product-oriented North American Marketing management 'paradigm' (Gronroos, 1994, 2006; Gummesson, 2002a). Thirty-one years after Arndt's (1985) call for Marketing studies to embrace a wider range of research methods and intellectual approaches, Brownlie (2006) makes the same appeal, writing of the possibilities for a critical Marketing which is not narrow or prescriptive but draws on 'the wider social sciences' (p. 506).

In a multi-authored series of reflective pieces, Bolton (2005) appeals for a 'Marketing renaissance' which improves thought and practice in the field. This, she argues, can be achieved through greater 'horizontal vision' so that academic Marketing researchers make creative intellectual connections to generate new theory and thereby 'advance the science and practice of Marketing' (p. 1). Appeals for new ideas and theory, then, are common to all the academic Marketing groups, but precisely what they mean by 'new theory' can be very different. For example, it is clear from Bolton's (2005) example of a story from medical research that her vision of academic Marketing is modelled on natural science, in keeping with the *Journal of Marketing*'s stated aim of generating rigorously verified, universalized facts to improve Marketing management practice. Brownlie's (2006) appeal for Marketing studies to engage with wider social scientific theory is based on a quite different vision of the field as an interpretive social science engaged with wider, non-managerial intellectual values and which is sensitive to political issues of equality, identity and power. In yet another contrast, Gronroos (1994) and Gummesson (2002b) are concerned that the North American Marketing management paradigm does not reflect the European mentality or the relationship-oriented Marketing environment of post-industrial Europe. Therefore, their appeal is for a different tone of management education and practice.

As the examples above show, many Marketing academics are sensitive to the criticisms the discipline attracts. While repeated and sincere calls for renewal and re-appraisal seem to be blithely ignored by the typical textbooks, they are evidence that there is a great deal of debate and self-criticism in the discipline. Then again, one lesson of contemporary Marketing is that customers shape products and Marketing studies is a business with massive demand. Its customers, students, educators, publishers, universities and colleges, government agencies and, indirectly, Marketing employers, influence the tone of the typical Marketing studies taught course. A critical Marketing studies discipline which releases intellectual creativity and opens up space for new ideas, then, cannot simply be imposed by decree. It has to be enabled by its constituencies, and facilitated by its institutions.

The second issue, related to the first, is that, for all the intellectual disdain focused on Marketing, the discipline was founded on the laudable social aims of improving the efficiency of Marketing distribution and applying research evidence and ethical criteria to the education, and subsequently improving the practice, of Marketing management (Tadajewski and Brownlie, 2008a; Wilkie and Moore, 2006). Wealth creation is the universal imperative in the neoliberal era and poverty the greatest evil but Marketing studies originated not only to promote and develop techniques to increase the power and profitability of Marketing organizations, but also to take a critical account of the effects this essential activity would have on society and individuals. This societal perspective has been increasingly marginalized (Witkowski, 2005), or so it seems to those who see Marketing activity as a one-way street of environmental destruction and corporatist power. The one-way-street view is sometimes mobilized in anti-global and anti-brand movements in which Marketing activity is directly and deeply implicated (Klein, 2000). In turn, Marketing studies, in so far as it promotes and underpins Marketing activity, is implicated in criticisms of Marketing practice. But, even in the light of such vehement and widespread criticism of Marketing practice and values, the attractions of Marketing careers and Marketing courses clearly remain compelling for a great many people, judging from the evidence of booming university student recruitment and vibrant professional bodies.

Critique of Marketing, then, needs to be placed in a wider context of its extraordinary popularity as a management field of training, research and education. Nevertheless, its success in itself is not reason enough to ignore the barrage of criticism of its intellectual standards from other fields. Neither is it a reason to ignore the widespread discontent toward the prevailing norms in the subject from Marketing academics themselves.

## The Cultural Status of Marketing Practice

One defence to some of the criticism levelled at Marketing is that it results from prejudice. It is fair to say that Marketing, selling and the commercial trades in general are sometimes looked down upon as inferior professions, and therefore attract unfair criticism. Dixon (1979) has argued that this prejudice is not as culturally embedded as people sometimes think. In fact, snobbery toward the commercial trades and professions is rather a modern phenomenon. According to Dixon (1979), Marketing practice itself has not historically attracted the prejudice sometimes attributed to it today. Marketers add value and supply activities which are necessary to life and material happiness and this view has been reflected in ancient literature. The criticisms Scott (2007) alludes to in Chapter 1 no doubt reflect a sincere intellectual appraisal by non-Marketing academics but might also betray some intellectual prejudice against the study of Marketing, as opposed to a prejudice against Marketing as practice. As we will see later in the book, the very idea that management ought to be studied in universities has, in some parts of the world, met with stiff and prolonged resistance from other intellectual communities.

So it is not easy to dismiss criticisms of Marketing as mere cultural prejudice against commercial activity per se. However, it is important to acknowledge that the idea which is a given in typical texts and courses – the idea of the manager who controls resources and serves customers – is not uncontested. This idea of the manager is central to the way that typical Marketing studies texts construct their subject matter, but few of them give any more than superficial attention to examining the idea and role of the manager in organizations in spite of its centrality to the popular idea of Marketing studies.

Most typically, today, Marketing is understood as an applied, vocational subject at the interface of business and education, oriented toward managerial training and organizational problem solving, rather than toward social scientific and human inquiry for its own sake. This managerial orientation, or, more precisely, the way that the idea of managerialism is played out in Marketing studies, is a key part of the global popularity of Marketing in particular and management and business studies in general. Marketing's presence, in remarkably similar forms, in taught university programmes and training courses around the world, is possible because of its positioning as a managerial problem-solving discipline concerned with techniques rather than values. At the same time, this managerial problem-solving orientation hinders the acceptance of Marketing studies as a legitimate university subject and intellectual discipline by non-management fields.

The role of critique, and what forms critique can or should take in such an idealized scheme, are difficult to establish. There is no single model for critique and there are no set criteria for critical analysis. As an ideal, critique liberates thinking and empowers a refreshed creative engagement with a subject matter. The rationale for this book is that critique, in whatever form, has an indispensable role to play in Marketing research and education, and in its engagement with practice. To this end, the book is an exploration of some of the meanings of critique in Marketing, and of some of its possible implications. Critique of Marketing studies implies a critique of managerialism since Marketing is widely considered to be a vehicle for managerial ideology.

## Neo-liberal ideology and Marketing studies

For Witkowski (2005), the North American, managerial problem-solving character of popular Marketing studies carries with it a 'legacy' of neo-liberalism.

> When modern marketing first emerged as a separate discipline around 1900, its theoretical foundations were based in large part on classical and neo-classical economics ... Like its parent disciplines, marketing assumed the existence of private enterprise, competitive firms, the rule of law, and the free international movement of goods, services and capital. Marketing theory also adhered to the philosophies of individualism and utilitarianism. (p. 222, citing Bartels, 1988, and Wilkie and Moore, 2003)

For Witkowski (2005), these values characterize what is known as 'neo-liberalism' and underpin Marketing's managerial ideology of consumer satisfaction, at any cost.

In academic management studies, managerialism refers to the supposed interests and values of organizational managers and the prioritization of these in the way that a discipline is conceived and taught. In Marketing education, students are typically, and implicitly, asked to play the role of managers in addressing case studies and engaging in presentations or problem-solving projects and exercises. The universal 'we' is invoked in conventional Marketing textbooks in a way which deflects closer examination of the complexities and paradoxes of the managerial role and assumes that the interests and values of students, citizens and managers directly coincide (Hackley, 2003a).

Managerialism, moreover, springs from an idea that management is a generic set of skills and techniques which can be applied to any sector of organizational activity, hence many MBAs teach 'general management' principles which can then be applied by graduates to any industrial, government or non-profit sector. So, much of academic Marketing studies is couched in terms of prescriptions for managerial action. This gives rise to a paradox: many Marketing academics feel sincerely that they are engaged in a politically and ethically neutral exercise of seeking solutions to management problems, for the ultimate betterment of organizations and citizens alike. But many more cultural theorists, historians and sociologists insist that Marketing studies and the conduct of Marketing management are deeply political matters because they are sites of ideology which promote particular interests and values as if they are universal, even if Marketing academics choose to ignore the political implications and antecedents of their work.

The question of whether management competence can be taught in classrooms as a generic skill is a complex one. Setting aside for the moment the difficult question of the role and nature of management education, it is possible to say that, for many academics of other intellectual fields, managerialism is a key matter which separates Marketing and all of the functional management studies subjects[4] from the ostensibly open and unbiased spirit of inquiry which guides research and scholarship in literature, psychology, sociology, history, linguistics, maths, physiology, chemistry and so on. The imperative of managerialism is seen to distort priorities and shape findings to suit a narrow and misconceived agenda: the interests of managers, as they are reconstructed, imagined and represented by academics.

This is all the more perplexing when one considers that academic Marketing is widely criticized for lacking a sense of managerial reality. There is a perceived gulf between academic Marketing and the lived realities and discourse of practising managers, evidenced by repeated claims of a 'weak linkage' between Marketing scholarship and Marketing practice. Yet managerial relevance is claimed to justify a great deal of academic

Marketing research. Managers themselves do not necessarily feel that academics are right when they insist that their research is relevant to practice. Saren (1999, p. 30) notes that the AMA (American Marketing Association[5]) Task Force in 1984 reported that Marketing practitioners felt that the work of Marketing academics had little relevance for them, partly because the field had failed to develop strong theories (in the *Journal of Marketing*, 1988), and such claims about the lack of relevance for practitioners of the work of Marketing academics are regularly repeated in the academic journals (Brown, 2007; Katsikeas et al., 2004; Piercy, 2002a; Wensley, 2007).

Managerialism, then, is a relatively unexamined foundational concept driving much academic thinking in university business and management schools. Managerial research and scholarship are driven implicitly by a sense that they should be about and for management, however that category is defined. Since there are no practising managers publishing any more in the top Marketing and management academic journals (Brown, 1995), the only way managers can express disagreement with academics' claims about the managerial relevance of their research is by not reading it – an option most managers exercise freely. But then again, academics could argue that just because managers do not engage with the academic journals, it does not necessarily mean that their work could not be relevant in principle. There are Marketing academics, for example, who have acknowledged that the subject may have failed as a managerial discipline (King, 1985) but argue that the blame for this lies with the nature of management as well as academics.

# Managerialism and Power

Skålen et al. (2006) see managerialism not in terms of a relatively benign process of organizing and directing material human resources but as a discourse of power and domination. The tools, techniques and vocabulary of Marketing management can be seen in terms of a 'governmental' rationality which frames human subjectivity. Skålen et al. (2006) argue that Marketing has always been fundamentally a managerial discipline and that its key doctrine of consumer orientation, extended across every employee in a service marketing era, creates a sense of self-management (Foucault, 2000) through which employees as well as consumers orient themselves and their thinking around a neo-liberal set of values about the primacy of markets and marketized relationships. Managerialism in Marketing discourse is the ultimate control mechanism. Under its influence, employees manage themselves because they have internalized the values of consumer orientation.

Managerialism, then, is a key issue of which to be aware in taking a critical approach to Marketing studies. It has many possible implications in Marketing studies, but the central issue for a critical approach is that being aware of some of the implicit assumptions embedded in managerialism is essential if we are to ask penetrating questions about the taken-for-granted aspects of typical forms of Marketing studies. The notion of managerialism as an ideology of neoliberalism was outlined above and the implications of this will be explored throughout the book. Another, more prosaic criticism of managerialism in Marketing studies is that the way the Marketing manager is represented and portrayed in typical texts and courses simply doesn't square with organizational reality.

## Ideology and Critique

However, there is a case that critique in Marketing can serve to support, rather than undermine, the Marketing world-view. As we have seen, Marketing, insofar as it is produced through published writing, incorporates criticism as a regular feature. Is it possible that this criticism, far from undermining the unquestioned acceptance of a Marketing order of things, serves to reinforce Marketing ideology?

Marion (2006) draws a distinction between two meanings of ideology. One, associated with Marxism, refers to ideology as a distortion of truth. The other (sometimes called ideology with a small 'i') refers to a set of beliefs which are widely taken for granted and unquestioned. Ideologies can confer legitimacy on, that is, offer tacit support for, particular societal norms and power structures. Marion (2006) cites anthropologist Dumont (1977) to elucidate the second version of ideology as sets of beliefs so important to social structures that they are unquestioned. In this sense, ideology is not a distortion of an absolute reality but, rather, one manifestation of social reality.

Ideological analysis has been used in Marketing and consumer research – for example, in Hirschman (1993), who investigated the dominance of masculine ideology in academic consumer research. Hirschman (1993) cites Eagleton (1991) on ideology as the ways in which a particular 'world-view or value and belief system of a particular class or group of people' is reproduced through various strategies (p. 538). These include universalization, instrumentalism and normalization (Eagleton, 1991). Universalization is a strategy whereby the values of one group (Marketers) are represented in terms which assume that they are good for everyone. Instrumentalism means that the character of relationships is defined by the Marketing system, so, for example, human happiness is equated with consumption. Normalization is the ideological strategy of presenting particular values and beliefs as if they are to be entirely taken for granted as a good thing.

For Marion (2006), Marketing has an ideological character in that it carries a set of relatively unquestioned beliefs (in the operation of markets, consumer orientation, the satisfaction of needs and wants, etc.) which provide legitimacy for marketing professionals and for the market economy. Marketing concepts and doctrine also incorporate criticism, to legitimize Marketing ideology. Therefore, critique in Marketing is a never-ending part of the process of legitimization of Marketing ideology. However, critique is also potentially powerful in revealing inconsistencies and flaws in Marketing's ideological world-view, especially given that Marketing science has not produced any solid facts or theory but is, rather, a set of normative concepts and ideas which cannot stand up to verification in any scientific sense.

For Marxist thinkers, ideology critique has the end of emancipating workers from the false ideology of markets. On the other hand, ideology critique has been adapted in academic studies of Marketing (Hackley, 2003b, following Alvesson and Deetz, 2000).

Hackley (2003b) draws attention to previous work on ideology in Marketing:

> Marketing discourse in general has been noted for its ideological character by many authors. Seen from a critical management studies perspective marketing is said to constitute its objects, consumers, workers and managers, and in so doing reproduces broader social relations of power and authority (Brownlie et al., 1999; Morgan, 1992). Firat (1985) noted ... that marketing research's mimicry of natural science by 'accepting temporal/contextual facts and truths as universal and eternal truths' (p. 143) made the field ideal for exploitation as an ideological vehicle. (p. 1327)

As Marion (2006) claims, the idea of ideology has not been used very much in research in Marketing studies. However, it is far from unknown and has given rise to some impassioned debates about the use of the term, focusing on its association with neo-Marxist critical theory.

## Critical Theory and Marketing Research

In Chapter 4, the use of critical theory is discussed at more length. For the present, it is important to make one point. Hackley (2003b) suggests that the use of critical theory concepts such as ideology in the investigation of Marketing issues is a matter of intellectual integrity rather than a critique of capitalism. Other authors, notably Hetrick and Lozada (1994), have argued that a purist interpretation of critical theory concepts means that they should imply critique not merely of Marketing but of capitalism itself. Murray et al. (1994), on the other hand, argue that this need not be so. They suggest that a critical agenda in Marketing and consumer research can retain an intellectual and moral integrity focusing on power, inequality and social issues within a market system.

The assumption made in this book is that critical theory is, as Bradshaw and Firat (2007) suggest, a central enabling position underpinning critique in Marketing studies. The virtue of critique in this vein is intellectual – it is instructive and corrective to look at received ideas stripped of their implicit assumptions, and neo-Marxist critical theory offers an analytical vocabulary with which to deconstruct and critique Marketing studies. Critical theory offers a radical intellectual take on Marketing studies but it cannot entail a value position on social theory. What it can do is to point to the power dynamics underlying knowledge structures and thereby bring intellectual insights to Marketing studies which are hidden behind the implicit values and relations of mainstream managerial Marketing studies.

Marketing is, as we see from the variety of research in the academic journals, nothing if not varied, eclectic and quirky. But there seems to be a centrifugal force, emanating from Marketing's key institutions and linked with its apparent role as a metaphor for neo-liberalism, which pulls most of its textbooks and courses around an established set of precepts. Philip Kotler's many texts list the 'key concepts' of marketing including needs, wants, demands, markets, exchange, transactions and relationships, value and satisfaction, and products (services, offers, experiences). Kotler positions these 'key concepts' at the centre of his managerial Marketing scheme. Taxonomies, in natural as in social science, are invariably provisional, but they create a sense of solidness for a field of thought and Kotler's taxonomic impulse draws on his detailed knowledge of labour economics and sociology. Stephen Brown (2005) writes of his long-held suspicion that Kotler's vision of marketing as the means of both wealth creation and wealth distribution was inspired by the work of Karl Marx, and his suspicion was confirmed when he interviewed Kotler to discover that his PhD and early publications did indeed make extensive use of Marx's theories. The idea that more effective Marketing management will increase social welfare by creating (and democratizing) wealth, distributing goods and services more effectively and exhorting organizations that their best interests are aligned with those of the private citizens whom they serve is a powerful one. But a Marketing studies without the conceptual tools to investigate this profound claim is a discipline which cannot reflect adequately on itself. This lack of critical self-reflection, or reflexivity, in Marketing is one thing which opens it to charges of being a vehicle of managerial ideology.

Such a charge links with ethical criticisms of Marketing practice in the sense that an ideological stance implies a taken-for-granted and unquestioning attitude toward things. If Marketing studies is an ideological vehicle for managerialism, then it is little wonder that the field attracts such vehement criticism for its standards of social responsibility and its attitude to environmental sustainability. So the intellectual, political and ethical levels of critique can be intimately connected in the context of particular criticisms of Marketing studies and its role in management education and practice.

## Marketing and Power

Finally, the ideological aspect of managerial Marketing studies needs to be understood in light of the evolution of the discipline as a business in its own right. Marketing knowledge is packaged and sold as a commodity (Holbrook, 1995). Marketing ideas can be worth millions in consulting fees to astute gurus who know how to sell them. Some of these prescriptions find their way into textbooks which generate serious sales revenue from the thousands of students studying Marketing as part of university and college courses. Marketing is, arguably, the most powerful recruiter to university courses of all the booming business and management subjects (Hackley, 2001a). MBA courses, MScs in Management and Business, BA and BSc degrees typically have marketing subjects as the most heavily subscribed courses. So, in the world of university education, marketing is a commodity which generates revenue in competition with other subjects. The Marketing discipline is also a valuable commodity for academics, for academic authors and publishers, and for management consultants. For critical management scholars, Marketing's role as a commodity goes even further since it brings the discourse or language of the market into many public services and areas of citizenship.

There is another sense in which Marketing can be said to exercise a political influence. People working at every level in call centres, hospitals, charities, law firms, government and universities are familiar with the insistence from their senior managers that they behave in a more 'customer oriented' or 'service oriented' way. Exactly what this behaviour entails is often a site of intense negotiation in which management and employees find the limits of their power to define working roles and practices (Gamble, 2007). Some argue that the language of Marketing has reached deeply, not only into organizational life but also into non-organizational life, especially through consumption but also through the way that government and social services are defined and 'delivered'. For example, many charitable and non-profit organizations now recruit people with a commercial Marketing background to deploy techniques like segmentation and positioning. Not only has Marketing language crossed into new professional areas, it has even affected individuals who have nothing to do with Marketing management. As patients, students or recipients of government welfare, we are now encouraged to see ourselves as consumers. For critically inclined scholars, the language of Marketing (customers, service, value, etc.) has become a language of power which translates all relationships into commercial relationships.

---

## CHAPTER SUMMARY

Chapter 3 has reviewed some viewpoints on the suggestion that Marketing studies in its popular form constitutes a vehicle for managerial ideology. For a subject of study in universities, this is a serious charge since it implies a lack of intellectual and also moral independence on the part of academics in the field. Whether the charge is fair or not, a cursory glance at any popular Marketing management or Marketing principles textbook will show that they do not deal in critical concepts of cultural analysis, such as ideology, and therefore are not equipped either to refute the charge of managerialism, or even to acknowledge it. Leaving aside the cultural and critical studies perspectives for the present, Chapters 4 and 5 return to a managerial perspective and focus on more functional levels of critique, in order to further ground the subsequent analyses in a context of Marketing's managerial concepts and techniques.

---

## CHAPTER REVIEW QUESTIONS

1. Is intellectual critique necessarily political?
2. What is managerial ideology and is it relevant to Marketing practitioners? Is it relevant to Marketing students?
3. In what sense might the intellectual, political and ethical levels of critique in Marketing studies collide?
4. Is it important to regard Marketing studies as an applied, managerial discipline rather than a field of cultural and social study? If so, why?

---

## CHAPTER CASE

### Astroturfing PR Strategies

'Astroturfing' is a term used by Democrat US Senator Lloyd Bensen to describe fake grassroots publicity campaigns.[6] The explosion of web-based public communications fora, such as blogs, chat rooms and general interest websites, has created an opportunity for unscrupulous lobbyists who want to manipulate public opinion on consumer and political issues. Some public relations (PR) firms have posted their own content promoting a particular view without attribution, so it appears to be from a disinterested commentator. The UK *Times* newspaper reported that an apparently home-made video ridiculing US politician Al Gore's views on global warming and posted on the YouTube video website was, according to the US *Wall Street Journal*, produced by a PR company retained by oil company Exxon Mobil. Sponsored links to the video were placed anonymously on Google. Astroturfing has some commonality with 'guerrilla', 'buzz' and 'viral' Marketing, in the sense that the aim is to create a self-perpetuating word-of-mouth impetus on a particular issue.

## Case Questions

1.  The idea of propaganda is not considered in typical Marketing manage-ment textbooks but, as in the case example, the use of public relations as a Marketing tool is difficult to appreciate in any other terms. Is it fair to argue that Marketing studies' role as a vehicle of managerial ideology obscures this role? Does it matter?
2.  Is it right to use public relations in this way even if the motives are not personal gain but the promotion of particular values?
3.  Marketing is often regarded with suspicion and distrust. Does the use of techniques such as those above undermine the integrity of the disci-pline? Might they have damaging effects?

**Notes**

1   To get a flavour of the academic reach of the discipline, look at the extent of academic resources on the main professional websites. At the time of writing, (2008) the UK Chartered Institute of Marketing (www.cim.co.uk/cim/index.cfm) boasts 'some' 50,000 members and students world-wide. The American Marketing Association (www.marketingpower.com/) claims 'nearly 40,000 members and a huge range of resources for training and networking both for practitioner and academics. Academic associa-tions also boast significant memberships as indicated on sites such as the American Association for Consumer Research (www.acrwebsite. org/index.asp), the UK Academy of Marketing (www.academyofmarketing.info/), the European Academy of Marketing (www.emac-online.org/associations/emac/index.asp), the Australia and New Zealand Marketing Academy (www.anzmac.org/), the Marketing Science Institute (www.msi.org), the Academy of Marketing Science (www.ams-web.org/displaycommon.cfm?an=19) and many others indicate.
2   See, for example, the 942-page Jobber (2003) *Principles and Practice of Marketing* retailing at £40; Brassington and Pettit (2006) *Principles of Marketing* at 1264 pages and £43; Kotler et al. (2007) *Principles of Marketing* at £45; Dibb (2005) *Marketing Concepts and Strategies* at 878 pages and £40 (as of May 2008); there are many more examples.
3   Stephen Brown has described these as 'Big Fat Books About Marketing' in his 1995 masterpiece, *Postmodern Marketing* (ITBP, London).
4   I am thinking mainly of Human Resource Management, Organizational Studies, Management Studies, Strategy, Accounting and Finance, and also sub-areas such as Business Economics, Leadership, Entrepreneurship Studies and so on, besides Marketing.
5   See www.marketingpower.com/
6   'Slick lobbying is behind penguin spoof of Al Gore', Chris Ayres, *The Times*, Saturday 5 August 2006 p. 42.

# CHAPTER 4

# THE MARKETING MIX AND THE CHALLENGE OF CULTURAL BRANDING

---

### CHAPTER OUTLINE

Chapter 4 returns to more functional issues, though with a critical agenda, in focusing on the techniques of managerial Marketing. The chapter reviews the Marketing Mix in the light of functional standpoints in order to try to connect a critical Marketing studies perspective with the managerial mainstream approach. In particular, the chapter opens up challenges to the managerial approach based on alternative ways of understanding how Marketing occurs as a socially constructed and symbolic phenomenon based around consumption.

---

## Introduction: Marketing Management or Culture?

Marketing practice is conventionally concerned with revealing or creating consumer needs and wants and matching those to the capability of the firm. The consumer orientation of Marketing has, according to Skålen et al. (2006), been the principle thread of Marketing studies for the past 100 years. But consumer orientation in practice can be construed in many ways. Typical managerial formulae like the Marketing Mix are open to the charge that they simply do not adequately explain the activities of Marketers or the socio-cultural basis of consumption.

For example, how might Marketing academics and practitioners conceive of trend-spotting exercises such as 'coolhunting'? 'Coolhunting' has become a catchphrase referring to the need for Marketers to find out what is 'cool' in order to orient their brand planning in the best way to make the brand appear cool too (Southgate, 2003). Conversely, brands can be regarded as cool in themselves and therefore enhance the prestige and salience of, for example, movies in which they are placed or celebrities who are photographed using them. The 'CoolBrands programme'[1] promotes brands that it regards as high performing. Its list of 'Britain's Coolest Brands 2006' includes Asahi Beer (marketed in the UK but made in Japan), *Arena* magazine, Chanel, Canon, Alfa Romeo, Blackberry, Beck's, Diesel, First Direct, Gaydar.co.uk, O2, Chivas Regal, Revlon, Hitachi, Goldsmith's (the London University College), Nokia, Storm, Sony, yell.com and many others. But what theories can be deployed by academics in conceiving and investigating such an obtuse yet apparently key area of Marketing practice as seeking out trends in cool? And what, if anything, is the connection with the static notion of a Marketing Mix?

## Madeleine Objects and the Meaning Possessions

The Marketing management approach implicitly assumes that consumption can be managed, or at least influenced by, using organizational power and resources. But others have written about consumption as a self-generating activity through which individuals impose cultural meaning on objects. An old photograph; your first bicycle; your first car; a tattered toy bear; a cardboard suitcase – such objects can evoke powerful feelings of nostalgia or reflection, but they are not only present in museums. McCracken (2005) discusses the power of what Proust called Madeleine objects. These are objects which can evoke rich meanings, memories or associations. McCracken suggests that Madeleine objects have many powers: they can 'cut away time and place and transport us'; sometimes they 'grab at the senses and make the world drain away' and they can be a 'cut on the surface of our reality, a hole through which culture comes spilling into life' (pp. 119–20). Madeleine objects are not well understood: they defy neat theorization. But, clearly, if a brand could evoke such power, it would be a great marketing advantage.

Holt (2004) suggested that some 'iconic' brands, like Coca Cola, Harley Davidson, Volkswagen and Budweiser, resolve contradictions in cultural identity. Coca Cola was shipped to American troops during the Second World War and became part of an 'identity myth'– consuming Coke was a ritual of national solidarity. In time, Coke became a supra-national brand icon, consumed in many cultures which looked to America as an inspiration. Coca Cola marketing exploited the identity myth that evolved around the brand. Iconic brands have benefited from becoming part of the cultural history of their time. They acquire a meaning that transcends the product. But do iconic brands like Coke emerge by accident, opportunism or design? Do brands make culture, or does culture make the brand?

One dimension of cultural branding is that iconic brands (Holt, 2004) are imbued with rich cultural meanings. These may not have the power of a Madeleine object but nevertheless can evoke associations which give the brand a strong cultural resonance for many consumers. Many current university students will, when they grow older, recall their Nike trainers, their iPod or their FCUK T-shirt and the adventures they had while these brands were part of their life. Brands can become part of culture and therefore part of the experience and memories of consumers. Cultural branding strategy seeks to imbue brands with meaning by making them part of cultural life, but Marketing management's 'normative' body of theory seems to fall considerably short in explaining the power of consumption and the role of Marketing in promoting it on a vast scale. Kotler et al. (1999, p. 4) assert that 'marketers manage demand and build profitable customer relationships', but Holt (2004) suggests that the marketing managers behind iconic brands are riding a cultural wave which they can neither control nor predict. In other words, customers can be exploited, but not managed.

We will return to the challenge cultural branding poses to the Marketing management approach later. The following will review the well-known Marketing Mix from a functional perspective before the chapter returns to consumer culture issues.

## The Marketing Mix

Of all the acronyms, aphorisms and general clichés of the Marketing canon, the Marketing Mix, a term coined by Bordern (1964) and popularized as the 'Four Ps' by McCarthy (1960), is probably the most well-known of all. After over 40 years, it remains a ubiquitous teaching device in Marketing education at every level, in spite of waves of criticism from many quarters. It consists of the main variables that can be changed to alter the marketing offer. McCarthy's (1960) framework places these variables under the headings Price, Promotion, Place or Physical Distribution and Product.

For Kotler et al. (1999, p. 97), the Mix is the 'set of controllable tactical marketing tools that the firm blends to produce the response it wants in the target market… [it is] everything the firm can do to influence demand for its product'. The Mix elements are blended to create a differential advantage for the brand by *positioning* it in a carefully defined market space. Positioning refers broadly to the characteristics, tangible and symbolic, of the brand in relation to its competitors (Ries and Trout, 1985). The Mix is generally treated as a simplistic cause–effect mechanism in typical texts, leaving aside the highly problematic issue of exactly how much control over Mix variables a Marketing manager might actually have.

## The Marketing Mix and Consumer Value

In spite of its back-of-the-envelope character, the Mix has been subject to some more sophisticated theorizations. For example, Holbrook (1999) sees it as a vehicle for optimizing positioning, and therefore maximizing consumer value.

> One way to view the positioning problem for a brand is to conceive it as directed towards attaining an *optimal location* in a *market space*, where this market space represents the perceived positions for the set of competing brands in the relevant product category ... the prescription for success is to appeal to a target segment whose needs and wants are not being satisfied by the available array of competing offerings. In other words, we can attain *differential advantage* for our brand by locating its perceived position closer to the idea point of a target segment than the perceived locations of other available offerings. Accordingly, we should design all communicative aspects of the *marketing mix* for that brand (the product itself, the list price, the channels of distribution, the advertising and sales pitches – in short, the Four Ps of product, price, place and promotion) to achieve perceptions of the brand that will place it in an optimal position relative to its competitors. (Holbrook, 1999, p. 2, citing Woodruff and Gardial, 1996, p. 124, original italics)

Holbrook (1999) argues that the optimal positioning for a product is achieved where consumer value is maximized for the segment of interest. Value, therefore, is a foundation of the marketing concept, since the generic idea of marketing as exchange (Bagozzi, 1975; Houston and Gassenheimer 1987) is predicated on the assumption that, in an exchange transaction, each party obtains increased value through the exchange. Holbrook (1999) notes that some dimensions of consumer value can be conceived as other-oriented, such as the implied status of owning and displaying a Gucci watch, or self-oriented, where consumer choice is governed by subjective and experiential criteria of fun, beauty or instrumental efficiency. These typologies are not necessarily mutually exclusive – they might well be combined in the consumption of the same marketing offer. This conceptualization is important as consumer value is sometimes seen one-dimensionally in terms of 'need satisfaction' or even 'customer delight'. A closer examination of the complexities of consumer value generates deeper insight into exactly what sort of marketing offer constitutes a differentiated value proposition for the consumer. Many product management initiatives make use of positioning maps or other conceptual tools based on visible criteria such as product features, price, warranties and so on, but neglect to use a viable framework for examining in detail exactly what the consumer is getting subjectively from the exchange.

The positioning metaphor is often conceived in terms relative to other offerings in the marketspace, rather than relative to the perceived value accruing to consumers. Most importantly, the mix elements are interdependent in the sense that they can all signal the positioning of the product or service. They are also variable within the same offer: the mix components can, in principle, be altered to respond to differing market and competitive conditions. Differing mix combinations can be used for the same product in different markets. The same model of car, for example, often carries a different price, specification and even name in different international markets. This is especially important where a product sells across international borders and revenue maximization is contingent upon differing competitive conditions and marketing environments in each national market.

## Adaptations of the Marketing Mix

In response to some of the criticisms of its limitations as a managerial conceptualization (see, for example, Brownlie and Saren, 1992; O'Malley and Patterson, 1998), the alliterative Mix has, in some literature, been extended and adapted to include a fifth P, People (training, skills, etc.), a sixth, Processes (such as Just In Time production or JIT, benchmarking, Total Quality Management, outsourcing and so on), and others. In retailing, a P can be added for Presentation of merchandise, while in services marketing, Participants, Physical evidence and Process have been added (Booms and Bitner, 1981, in van Waterschoot, 2000, p. 226). The Mix formulation has also been adapted into a version which reflects the customer, rather than the Marketing manager, perspective, entitled the four Cs of consumer orientation (or 'customercentricity' – Deshpande, 1999). In the customer-oriented version of the Four Ps, Product equates to customer needs and wants; Price is the subjective cost (or 'opportunity cost') to the customer; Place/Physical distribution refers to the convenience and ease with which the customer can acquire the product, while Promotion is anything to do with customer communication (Kotler et al., 2007, p. 99).

## Managerial Implications of the Mix

The detailed exposition of each element in Table 4.1 will be found in any introductory Marketing textbook. The table indicates how the Marketing Mix offers educators a neat shorthand with which to refer to numerous general issues in Marketing management, some of which might, in principle, be influenced by the Marketing manager, depending on the organizational politics and resources obtaining. There is a try-it-and-see character to the Mix,

**Table 4.1**  Marketing mix decisions

| Price | Product | Promotion | Physical distribution |
|---|---|---|---|
| Psychological? | Core, | Advertising | Exclusive, |
| Market based? | augmented, | (press, TV, | intensive, |
| Cost based? | extended. | posters, sales | selective. |
| Skimming? | Tangible/ | promotion). | Direct, |
| Penetration? | intangible. | Public relations, | intermediated. |
| Loss leading? | Product range | personal selling, | Operational issues: |
| Positioning? | brands: | sponsorship, | perishable? |
| Credit terms? | family | e-commerce, | Obsolete in a day? |
| Differential? | brands, | WOM, viral, | Where is the |
|  | extended | e-marketing. | market? |
|  | brands. |  |  |

although it offers infinite opportunities for experimental research to measure the demand response to changes in an independent variable, in the hope that such a change might happen in other markets too. Most importantly, the Mix has become associated with the discursive and concrete style of classroom management education. A discussion based on this style might help to illustrate, by contrast, some of the critical positions, while also linking them to the typical Marketing management curriculum.

However the Mix is conceived, the decisions made on each element have a number of implications. Moreover, Mix decisions are not only interdependent in their effect; they are also mutually contingent. For example, a low price will not usually fit with a prestige distribution outlet, because high-end retailers will only want to stock items with a large profit margin. On the other hand, an item that is priced against prestige competitors will normally have to be discounted in order to sell in low-price outlets. There are retailers who specialize in selling designer brands at discount prices, such as TK Maxx,[2] but while the brand owner will appreciate the extra sales and profile generated by such discounted sales, they cannot risk too many items being sold in this way or the brand image of exclusive quality may suffer in the long run. Even so, luxury brand manufacturers are astute in managing their various market segments by differentiating the brand for those prepared to pay premium prices while maximizing revenue, and exposure, by allowing cheaper versions to be sold at discount as well (Chadha and Husband, 2006).

## Price

The relationship between Mix elements and Marketing outcomes is not always obvious. The population of many countries is ageing, because of lower birthrates and longer life expectancies. Many of these older citizens, sometimes called 'the grey market', are active consumers with money to spend. One organization, Saga (see www.saga.com.uk), has taken market segmentation as its primary strategy, aiming a range of products and services exclusively at the over-50 age group. Saga originally sold holidays and it is now a large tour operator, but it also publishes a magazine that reaches a million households, sells medical, car and household insurance and other financial services, runs popular radio stations, and acts as an intermediary for a range of retail sales and other services. While the over-50s are active consumers who compare prices and look for good value, price is often not the main consideration in their purchasing, so this sector can be very profitable provided the service quality is excellent. It is a very large market segment in which price is not the key variable across a range of products and services. In other circumstances, as Torsten Veblen (1899) suggested, there is an incentive for some consumers to pay as high a price as possible when buying prestigious items because the high price adds to the sense of exclusivity.

Price does not necessarily only refer to the sticker on the product. The availability of credit is an important component of pricing. Credit terms on a relatively low interest rate over three, four or five years can add 20 per cent or more to the margin, with only an administrative cost involved. Offering extended warranties for consumer electronic or other high involvement goods can also add considerably to margin. Some UK electronics retailers were accused of making 100 per cent profit on their product warranties and little on the products themselves. Many consumers have had the experience of buying a new laptop or TV and then being put under some pressure by the salesperson to buy the warranty as well. Motor car retailers have a complex system of financing deals which are central to their margins.

## Pricing and Brands

One consideration can override all others with regard to pricing. Consumers will pay higher prices for strong brands than for weak ones. Branding is the key to creating a quasi-monopolistic position and super-normal profits for manufacturers. Brand considerations will cause consumers to cut short their information search and opt for the reassurance of a trusted brand. A higher price in this case may be part of the reassurance, with consumers rationalizing the higher price with the logic of 'you get what you pay for'. In this sense, a strong brand creates a quasi-monopoly for the producer, since there are significant barriers to entry for rivals, the barriers to entry being (1) copyright over the established brand and (2) the very large promotional costs needed to break into the market. A strong brand gives producers control over many important features. For example, a strong brand can dictate terms to retailers, say, by demanding more shelf space or a more prominent shop position than rivals, or by squeezing the retailer's margin because the brand can guarantee high-volume sales. A strong brand can also influence retail price, although price control is against fair competition laws in most countries. Nevertheless, if a supermarket wishes to discount the price of a strong brand to attract more customers into the shop, the brand manager might threaten to withdraw supply because of the risk of diluting the brand's perceived quality positioning. On the other hand, in some national markets such as the UK, the retailers are so powerful that they can charge even strong brands a premium fee just to stock them.

Price, then, may be a key variable in the Marketing mix but it is not necessarily under the control of the Marketing manager. It is often dictated by production costs, variable costs, taxes and competitive issues. From an ethical standpoint, market-based pricing, or charging according to what the market will bear, seems problematic. Then again, product managers have a duty to shareholders and revenue is needed to reinvest in new products. There is, though, clearly a thin line between market-based pricing and profiteering or exploitation of a dominant market position.

## Product

Levitt's (1960) article 'Marketing myopia' suggested that products are only products (or services) to manufacturers: to consumers, they are bundles of benefits. A car provides travel, comfort, safety, fun, perhaps prestige and status. In the famous comment of one global cosmetics firm CEO, 'we don't sell cosmetics – we sell hope'. Another, allegedly the CEO of a drill-making company, averred that his firm didn't sell drills but holes. The logic of this is that subjective benefits are what ultimately interest many consumers. According to Levitt (1960), conceiving of products in this abstract way helps manufacturers to think in terms of the potential threat from alternatives. Levitt (1960) argued that the US railway companies did not realize that they were in the transport business and failed to react to the increasing threat from road and air travel. He argued that the 1950s Hollywood movie business did not realize that it was in competition with TV in providing entertainment, and consequently lost large numbers of cinema customers until the business recovered in the next decade. Increasingly, car manufacturers have begun to differentiate their vehicles on grounds not only of practicality, economy, power and performance, but also fun, entertainment and status.

Products can be conceptualized according to Kotler et al.'s (2007) 'levels' of product, consisting of the core product (the fundamental benefit, such as personal travel), the actual product, consisting of the whole packaging, design, components and service elements, and the augmented product, which is whatever can be added to the actual product to make it special. So, for example, a core product car might be four wheels, a seat, a steering wheel and an engine: the actual product might be a Ford Mondeo, and the augmented product could be a Mondeo with sunroof, extra powerful engine, leather seats, alloy wheels and so forth. Some augmented products go further than consumers require. '3G' mobile phones have been marketed on the assumption that consumers will want to access websites and download content to their phones. Many phones also incorporate video cameras pointing to the user to facilitate live video conferencing.

New products and new innovations are sometimes considered two different things. A new product is usually a variation on the existing products available. There are many new mobile phones coming on to the market every week but most of them are variations on the basic theme. A new innovation, on the other hand, is something that has not been seen before, at least not in that particular context. The Segway[3] vehicle is a recent innovation which has no identical rivals. The personal computer, the hand-held calculator, the digital watch and the flatscreen TV were all significant innovations for the manufacturers who first brought them to the market. They were quickly followed by many imitators who improved on the original designs, added newer technology and reduced production costs by producing on a greater scale. It was once thought that radical new innovations could assume a two-year lead over the rest of the market. This is no longer the case as rapid technology transfer, internationally mobile finance and global labour markets mean that a new innovation can be closely copied within weeks. Where intellectual copyright is owned, it takes an army of lawyers to enforce, and sometimes even that is not enough: many developing countries are ingenious at reproducing copies of existing brands on a scale that is very hard for the copyright owners to police. Even where intellectual copyright laws are policed, ingenious manufacturers can often quickly make close copies which may not infringe copyright but which serve the same purpose as the original. Intel successfully branded a generic commodity, the microchip, and achieved market dominance for a time. But AMD focused on providing cheaper alternatives and have now overtaken Intel in a number of high-quality chip markets.

## Brand Stretching, Brand Extensions and Multibrand Strategy

Many manufacturers extend successful brands across related product markets (line or brand extensions) and across entirely new markets (brand 'stretching'). Some feature the family brand (for example, Heinz[4]) on many of their products. Others take a different view. Rather than using a powerful family brand to extend products and services under the same brand, they adopt a multi-brand strategy. Unilever[5] and P&G[6] are well-known for this, supplying scores of products which have individual brand identities and do not trade prominently on the family brand name. Saga has become a powerful family brand. As mentioned, from its origins as a supplier of specialist holidays for the over-50s, it has extended the Saga brand into insurance and other financial services.

In recent years, some brands have found that consumers will accept many variations on the original theme. In 1996, KitKat, estimated to be the world's number 2 chocolate bar after the Mars Bar,[7] introduced the orange flavour with the orange wrapper in addition to the traditional red wrapper and milk chocolate flavour. Today, there are at least 28 flavour variations of KitKat available across the world, including about 15 flavours produced for Japanese customers alone. In addition, there are scores of temporary, 'limited edition' combinations of novel flavours and formats such as KitKat chunky, two and four fingers (with a three-finger KitKat in development), KitKat cubes, balls and many more. Tradition and continuity is important for many brands, and some brands' consumers are quite conservative in what they will accept as an authentic brand representation. But KitKat have found that their customers recognize and accept the brand in many forms that are far removed from the original.

Brand line extension is a popular strategy in the cigarette market. Philip Morris Company's[8] Marlboro cigarette brand, the biggest-selling cigarette brand in the world, according to some sources,[9] has extended its brand across more than ten sub-brands of cigarette, serving different markets. The online dictionary Wikipedia estimates that in Canada, locally produced Marlboro Reds are the best-selling and Marlboro Lights are unavailable, while Marlboro Menthol Lights are estimated to be the best-selling brand smoked by African Americans. The second-largest cigarette manufacturer in the world, R.J. Reynolds,[10] also produces numerous brands some of which, such as Camel, are extended across more than 20 lines.

Yamaha[11] has stretched its brand across audiovisual products, motor cars and motorbikes and musical instruments. Brand stretching is also popular in the cigarette business, as it is in the fragrance and fashion businesses. Tobacco companies, for example, have got around advertising restrictions while simultaneously getting into new markets by stretching the cigarette brands into other products. Apparel branded with cigarette brands such as Camel and Marlboro are sold, sometimes through branded stores.[12] Some cigarette companies have set up independent firms to handle non-cigarette marketing of the brands.[13] Brands have become cool and many people act as free mobile advertising poster sites for manufacturers by wearing T-shirts and other clothing with the brand name featuring prominently. French Connection achieved great success for a time with its controversial advertising campaigns and FCUK T-shirts, which were a very common sight in the UK for several years. The added attraction of this form of advertising for manufacturers is that consumers pay them for the privilege.

Hyper-brand extender Virgin,[14] on the other hand, features the family brand in many unrelated areas such as airlines, train companies, retail stores, cars, mortgages, credit cards and personal loans, mobile phones, wine, balloon flights, books, bridal gowns, cosmetics, drinks, holidays, jewellery, computer games, radio stations, restaurants, lingerie, incentive schemes, lifestyle centres and more. These are separate businesses which only have the brand in common. Other manufacturers, such as Kellogg's, combine a family brand policy across many of its products with independent lines which do not feature the family brand name.

# Physical Distribution

Getting the offer to the customer involves far more than the logistical effort of getting the product or service to its end user. It is a key mix variable in many respects. Considerations include the perishability or durability of the product. For example, a newspaper must be delivered within hours, a banana within a few weeks, while a car can sit on the dockside for months before delivery to its final customer. Another consideration is the degree of control the brand owner requires over the marketing effort at the point of sale. A third consideration is cost.

Distribution channels might be long or short depending on the commodity being sold. A short distribution chain can mean selling direct to the consumer via a catalogue or website, a method with which Dell computers has become associated. Other brands are sold via direct mail or telesales, or even through retail stores owned by the manufacturer. Selling direct to the end user can be useful in the book business, and with fashion and household goods among many other products and services. A direct-to-consumer distribution approach gives the manufacturer full control over price, margin and merchandising. On the other hand, a long distribution chain uses one or many intermediaries (wholesaler, retailer) before the offer reaches its end user. This can be easier for the manufacturer, since there is no need to set up the elaborate and expensive marketing apparatus for direct sales through catalogues, websites and so on. There are expenses incurred though in paying off the intermediaries. Every link in the chain will require a profit margin, reducing the margin to the manufacturer. In addition, there might be relatively little manufacturer control over such issues as merchandising, shelf space, local advertising or price. This control is often key to the brand and relinquishing it can risk dilution of the brand identity. Franchising is a popular alternative, especially in service markets, where the manufacturer supplies the market through franchised stores and so retains control over all aspects of marketing while it doesn't have to bear the business costs.

Using intermediaries might have many advantages. Local distributors have local marketing expertise and well-established stores with a regular high volume of customers. On the other hand, intermediaries have to be managed and motivated with incentives and price negotiations. And each brand is in competition with others. Apocryphal stories abound of salespeople plying distributors with gifts to retain their goodwill (and their orders) or even sabotaging rivals by, for instance, surreptitiously re-arranging the shelf or freezer to put rival brands at the back and out of sight. Walls, the UK's number 1 ice cream brand,[15] thought of a good way of popularizing their ice cream in the UK many years ago – they gave retailers a free fridge bedecked with the Walls logo. The presence of rival brands in the same fridge was no doubt subtly discouraged.

Disintermediation, the policy of reducing the links in the distribution channel, is popular in some markets. The manufacturer eliminates links in the chain by, for example, establishing its own retail outlets, establishing a website with retail interface for direct selling, or setting up a personal sales force to establish direct links with retail outlets.

The distribution outlet, like all the other elements of the mix, has an important communicative dimension. Distribution channels can be categorized in terms of an exclusive–selective–intensive continuum. A product that is positioned as a prestige purchase will need a distribution outlet that suits the positioning, so, for example, Gucci[16] or Louis Vuitton[17] products are normally sold in highly specialized outlets in prestige shopping areas: in other words, exclusive outlets fit the exclusive positioning of the product. Specialized items like sportswear are often sold in selected outlets that group such items together and offer some specialist expertise to help the consumer make a choice, like sportswear or shoes, though it must be said that many non-specialist outlets are appearing which seek to undercut the prices of the specialist retailer. Items that are high volume and low margin, such as chewing gum, are sold wherever a retailer will sell them. This intensive distribution is possible because it is assumed that these items, usually bought on impulse, do not need to have their brand image reinforced by that of the retail outlet.

## Merchandising and the Marketspace

Merchandising is a term that usually refers to the marketing effort going into the sale at point of purchase. The point of sale can be very important for sales volume, regardless of how compelling and persuasive the advertising and the offer might be. For instance, some department stores have in-store promotions, give-aways, free trials, even in-store advertisements on video screens to steer consumers toward a particular brand. In the world of confectionery and cigarettes, brand owners try to get their product shelf space in the 'golden arc', the area an arm's reach either side of the serving counter in the CTN (confectionery/tobacco/newsagent) style outlet. Chocolate bars, potato crisps, sweets or candy and chewing gum are often bought on impulse, as an afterthought. The brands within easy reach of the consumer as she pays for her other items will sell the most.

Merchandising also refers to the way products are presented in the retail setting. This can mean window displays, shelf space (more shelf space normally equals more sales) and the arrangement of displays in the store. Many retail stores undertake detailed analysis of the way consumers wander through the shop and browse the displays in order to maximize sales per square foot or retail space. Supermarkets often assume that most customers will come into the shop for bread and milk, and most customers will naturally want to walk to the left. Therefore, shops are designed with an entrance to the right and the bread and milk in the far left corner, so customers have to walk through the whole store to get the main items they wanted. As we wander past the shelves stacked with attractively packaged goods, listening subconsciously to the piped music that slows our blink-rate and lulls us into a sense of hazy well-being, smelling the baking bread odour that is carefully funnelled back into the store, we are all-too-inclined to put more items in our baskets. This, of course, is the whole point of retail store design: the entire environment is a marketing strategy and little is left to chance in the retail marketspace.

Merchandising often begins before we enter the store because the architecture of retail environments has been regarded as hugely significant since the beginning of the century. Retail environments set the scene for consumption and the early retail entrepreneurs (Marchand, 1998) knew that the awe-inspiring architecture of flagship retail stores and corporate headquarters played a key part in the effort to legitimize big business and promote consumption. Retail architecture today can be no less evocative, even to the extent that some of it evinces past times in nostalgic 'retroscapes', especially common in the global 'Irish' pub phenomenon, clothes retailing, and tourist attractions in which consumption experiences are built around historical events (Brown and Sherry, 2002). If the architectural environment captures the consumers' imagination, then the sales effort is already half accomplished.

## Promotion

It would be an oversimplification to assume that promotion is always tactical because it is an element of the Mix. As we have seen previously, any mix element has the potential to be strategic in its effects in certain circumstances. This is especially true of promotion because successful campaigns can have powerful and long-term effects on entire markets. For example, the iconic advertising campaign for Levi Strauss 501 jeans in the 1980s was said to have increased sales in the entire global denim jeans market by 600 per cent (Hackley, 2005a). Given this potential to inspire consumers on a huge scale, advertising and promotion, or, to use the American term, marketing communication, has been described as the most important source of sustainable competitive advantage for organizations (Schultz et al., 1994, p. 47). Seen as such, marketing communication clearly reaches into the strategic area in its implications.

Another reason for the importance of communication in marketing is its flexibility. Communication can support a wide range of marketing objectives.

Two major advertising trade associations, the American Advertising Federation (AAF[18]) and the UK Institute for Practitioners in Advertising (IPA[19]) are referred to in Hackley (2005a) in a discussion of the many objectives marketing communication can achieve. The AAF conducted a survey revealing that many CEOs realized the value of advertising but, nevertheless, cut the advertising budget in times of economic downturn. The AAF produced a major advertising campaign in which they demonstrated how iconic brands were inconceivable without advertising. The value of advertising within marketing tends to be downplayed by marketing professionals because they are not communication professionals. But, as the AAF campaign demonstrated, most major consumer brands owe a great deal to the image that advertising, in all its forms, built and sustains.

There is a large academic literature debating whether promotion and advertising (often collectively named marketing communication) persuades or reassures, convinces or reminds, sells or publicizes (see examples in O'Shaughnessy and O'Shaughnessy, 2004). These questions go to the core of the distinction between Marketing as management science, and Marketing as culture. Marketers with a product to sell need to make potential buyers aware of the offer and they need to do this in a way that attracts interest. Anyone who has worked in selling will confirm that public recognition of the brand is a powerful advantage. Salespeople who are supported by high-profile advertising find that their task, while never easy, is far harder without that brand recognition.

Typical textbook treatments take it that the design of persuasive promotional messages is usually targeted consciously at a consumer who realizes that the communication has a marketing motive. As we see in many examples throughout this book, this is only part of the story. Communication comes in a huge variety of forms. It can be implicit, explicit, symbolic, visual, aural, tactile, mediated, non-mediated, personal or impersonal. Any of these can apply to promotional communication. A track and field athlete wearing the sponsor's logo on a baseball cap during a post-meet TV interview is implicitly promoting that brand to the viewers and symbolically linking it with values of competition, success and the exciting world of modern media. A financial services advertisement for an investment product in a serious newspaper might go into explicit detail about the product qualities and the risk attached to owning it. Some public telephone companies in the USA make callers listen to a sales message before they are connected. Sales staff in many retail outlets are trained to encourage customers to buy more by asking them if they would like additional items to go with the intended purchase. 'Would you like to supersize that?' has become a familiar request in some fast-food outlets. Some magazines carry print ads with inserts of perfume samples or skin cream so that consumers can experience the sensation of the product through the advertisement. Moreover, promotional methods can be used to publicize each other element of the Marketing Mix. For example, the

London advertising agency DDB Needham has created a long-running and successful campaign which promotes the price competitiveness of Volkswagen cars (Hackley, 2005a).

The 'promotional mix' in managerial texts refers to the armoury of communication tools available to Marketing and includes public relations, press and poster advertising, TV, radio, brochures, trade exhibitions, cinema, hand-delivered flyers, telesales, direct mail, SMS text messaging, email spam and so on. Personal selling is a form of promotion, as salespeople persuade, communicate offers, create goodwill and build relationships as well as take orders, but 'promotion' is more commonly identified with mediated communication. Promotional messages can be carried on commercial radio and television broadcasting, in print media as classified ads in the local press to full-page glossy ones in style magazines, on outdoor media such as roadside billboards and public plasma displays, 3D media displays, in cinema advertising, on the backs of parking tickets and theatre programmes, on promotional hot air balloons, airships, mugs, pens, labels, internet sites and T-shirts. A medium is any channel of communication: a media 'vehicle' is a particular advertising context, such as a radio or TV show interval, a particular newspaper or magazine, or a specific roadside billboard site. The basic task of Marketing communications is to crystallize some aspect of the brand in a creative way and then to communicate that to as much of the target audience as possible within the available budget.

Many new Marketing communication initiatives do not so much communicate an offer to consumers as insert the brand into everyday experience. Ad-wraps[20] is a new concept in outdoor promotion. Car owners can go to the ad-wraps website and enroll. If they fit the profile required, their car will be wrapped with vinyl material carrying advertising. Car owners can be paid up to £200 Sterling per month, depending on the nature and length of the contract. Ad-wraps carry out spot checks on the vehicles and install a GPS tracker on many of them so they can tell advertisers at all times where their advertising is being displayed. The concept is striking because sponsored cars are rare enough to be head-turners. The typical driving route and social circle of the driver allows access to difficult-to-target consumer segments.

Another example is that of outdoor advertising in Glasgow subways which achieved a significant rise in brand awareness for Singaporean beer brand Tiger. The UK Outdoor Advertising Association (OAA[21]) reports that both prompted and unprompted awareness of the Tiger posters was measured at up to 70 per cent among the 18–24 year-old target audience. 58 per cent of respondents agreed that they were more likely to drink Tiger beer as a result of seeing the posters. The subways in major cities are powerful advertising sites since they are used by millions of commuters daily all year round. Many urban subway users are young, and subway posters offer a welcome visual distraction from the routine of regular travel.

A final example of the reach of communications in Marketing practice concerns the rise of the internet both as an advertising medium and as a source of new business models. According to research by the European Interactive Advertising Association (EIAA), UK consumers lead Europe in online consumption,[22] with expenditure reaching almost four times as much as the average online expenditure of French consumers, the lowest spending nation in Europe. The research indicated that holidays and travel tickets are the most popular online purchase. Other popular online purchases are books, CDs, electrical goods, insurance and clothes. The demographic of internet Marketing users is also changing with more female consumers increasing the amount of time they spend on the internet in relation to time spent watching TV or reading newspapers and magazines. This growth in online activity seems to be part of a general trend. Online advertising, with its combination of multi-media appeal, instant response capability, measurability and huge coverage, is assuming greater weight in Marketing matters. The capability of classic Marketing principles in conceptualizing the impact of new media in Marketing remains to be seen.

## The Marketing–Media–Branding Complex

The efficacy of differing media channels and vehicles is difficult to disentangle. Branding, marketing, advertising and promotion are often treated as separate and distinct disciplines. There are good reasons for this, one of which is that they tend to be organized professionally along separate lines. Being a Marketing professional or a brand manager usually implies a managerial role in a company, while being in advertising, direct mail, PR or merchandising usually implies a different career structure, professional associations and networks and differing qualifying examinations. Nevertheless, historical treatments of these topics show how intimately they are related – indeed, they show that they must be properly understood as parts of a whole Marketing–media–branding complex.

Danesi (2006) draws a distinction between propaganda, publicity, public relations and advertising, but he notes that modern consumer culture as we know it really began when branding, the naming of commodities, joined with advertising and new hybrid techniques of persuasion evolved from the advent of mass communications technology at the turn of the century. The aim was ultimately to sell products but this is not necessarily achieved by persuading individual consumers to buy. Increasingly, brand planners seek 'presence': that is, they wish to make their brand visible in the consumer's environment in plausible and persuasive contexts. Mediated entertainment provides the perfect context for brand presence. Danesi (2006) maintains that:

> the integration of brand image with pop culture has, actually, always been the implicit strategy in big brand marketing [since] major brands and the

media formed a partnership early in the twentieth century. The 'content' of the entertainment-artistic world has since become increasingly more 'branded'. Brands are now being showcased in one form or other in movies, TV programmes and other cultural domains. 'Brand placement', as it is called, has become the most effective (in terms of reaching customers) of all the branding strategies ever devised. (p. 92) (see also Tiwsakul et al., 2005)

## Brand Meaning and Visual Culture

The emotional texture of brands has been noted since the 1950s (Gardner and Levy, 1955). But emotions, like everything else, have a social dimension. To put this another way, our most visceral responses are, to some extent, socially conditioned. Marketing a brand entails many practical tasks of management and organization but, at a cultural level, Marketing has to engage with the meaning of a brand (Schroeder and Salzer-Mörling, 2006). As McCracken (2005) avers, much Marketing activity is the attempt to persuasively influence this meaning by means of, for example, publishing narratives about the brand through public relations activities, managing customer relations to generate positive emotions towards the brand, and trying to elicit the desired consumer response from visual brand cues.

The use of visual imagery in branding takes countless forms and includes logos and other brand marks, websites, packaging, colour and product design, advertising, promotional brochures and so on. Schroeder (2002, p. 4) suggests that:

> marketing is fundamentally about image management ... A key characteristic of the twenty-first century economy is the image. Brands are developed based on images, products are advertised via images, corporate image is critical for managerial success. (also citing Chajet, 1991; Firat et al., 1995; and Willis, 1991)

The interpretation of imagery is culturally located and in this, brand Marketing imagery is a constituent part of visual culture.

# Non-Commercial Applications of the Marketing Management Approach

The Marketing management approach has, as noted, permeated the non-profit and public sector as well as the commercial sector. The Mix elements can be seen at work in many different settings, applying the logic of Marketing management to all manner of commodities. For example, *The Times Higher Education Supplement (THES)*[23] has reported that American universities now adapt commercial marketing techniques to recruit students. Boston's Northeastern University placed a billboard inside the stadium of the local baseball team, the Boston Red Sox. The American Council on Education, representing 1800 US colleges and universities, plans a $4.5 million TV advertising campaign on behalf of its members. After some resistance to marketing in universities, it is now accepted as part of the natural order of things in Higher Education. It is estimated that four-year private colleges in the US spend over $2000 to recruit each student. The *THES* reports that many universities market-test new degrees. While the US university system seems ahead of that of the UK as regards its marketing, it has become common even in the UK for universities to hire marketing consultants to conduct re-branding exercises, to the consternation of some academics. Many UK universities now need a range of income streams and offer consultancy, conference, accommodation and other services on a commercial basis. A further example is seen as marketing principles are increasingly applied in the marketing of political parties and electoral candidates (Peng and Hackley, 2005).

So the extension of the generic Marketing concept is predicated on the assumed relevance of Marketing's normative concepts, whatever the context. The website of the *Journal of Business-to-Business Marketing*[24] lists the following topic areas covered by that journal in business-to-business contexts: relationship management, buying behaviour, buyer–seller relationships, segmentation, marketing strategy, ethical marketing, legal issues, the 'business marketing mix' areas including products, services, managing innovation, pricing (including negotiating), industrial logistics and supply-chain management, packaging, direct marketing, promotion and personal selling, advertising and internet marketing. The ethos of this journal seems to be that while the context is different, the concepts are just as relevant as in any other sphere of application.

## The Marketing Mix and Brands Revisited

The preceding section gives a flavour of the kind of practical management discourse typically applied through the vehicle of the Marketing Mix. The Mix and branding are often treated in different sections of Marketing courses, and even as separate courses with their own differentiated textbooks, but as Holbrook (1999) indicates, the two ideas are mutually contingent. A brand has to be carefully managed through the tools of the Mix while the rationale for the Mix is to create a strong brand.

## Brands and the mix

The discourse of the Marketing Mix produces managers as controllers of resources and managers of demand in a very literal and concrete sense. It also produces readers as co-managers in a process of projective identification. The manager is a heroic figure, a cult figure, and his (this is a patriarchal discourse) problems are ours. Mastering this discourse in itself can be a useful part of management education for the power such rhetoric confers, regardless of the practical effectiveness of the techniques.

A different vocabulary, though, is needed to understand brands as cultural artefacts. Brands can be conceptualized not only in managerial terms as names, marks of difference that assist recognition, transform consumption experience and evince reassurance of quality and origin (Feldwick, 2002) but also as key cultural signifiers. As such, brands constitute a symbolic vocabulary through which we articulate and negotiate social status, lifestyle and identity (Holt, 2004; Belk, 1986). Holt (2004) suggests that understanding brands demands:

> ... a cultural historian's understanding of ideology as it waxes and wanes, a sociologist's charting of the topography of contradictions the ideology produces, and a literary critic's expedition into the culture that engages the contradictions. (p. 49)

This complexity of approach reflects the idea of brands as 'cultural, ideological and political objects' (Schroeder and Salzer-Mörling, 2006, p. 1). Conceiving of brands as cultural objects resonates with our intuitive sense that brands, and brand logic, inform our everyday experience as social beings in significant and far-reaching ways (Bradshaw et al., 2006; Klein, 2000; McCracken, 2005).

The managerial Marketing approach tends to reduce the success of brands to the selection of Mix elements. But many brands operate also by association with popular culture. The Mix elements are present as incidental facts about the brand but do not have the decisive role in creating brand success. Many brands are located within popular culture, obtaining visibility within media entertainment to create an association with celebrity and produce a sense of normalization for the brand (Hackley, 2005a; Tiwsakul et al., 2005).

The conventional Marketing management curriculum places this element of brand strategy in a minor supporting role, yet Marketing as a whole is increasingly media-driven. Media exposure generates the breadth and depth of visibility which give brands a persuasive presence in the market.

The management of brands, then, is hard to explain simply in terms of the demand-management mechanics of the Marketing Mix. To be sure, brands have to be delivered to consumers: they have to have a price, they have to be promoted. What's more, there must be something there that constitutes the product or service, a bundle of attributes and benefits that are acceptable to consumers as a Mercedes car, a Parker pen or a Nike running shoe. But a consideration of brands as cultural phenomena shows that the Marketing Mix operates at an undeniably important but largely operational level. Mix decisions are necessary for Marketing: the mix framework is not sufficient to understand brand Marketing in all its symbolic complexity. For that, we must consider brands, and Marketing, as cultural phenomena.

## General Criticisms of the Marketing Management Approach

The Marketing Mix is the central plank of the Marketing management approach inspired by Philip Kotler. Managerial Marketing in this common-sense and simplistic vein has, as we have seen, been criticized on many counts. For example, according to Gummesson (2002b) and others involved in the Scandinavian Marketing group (e.g. Gronroos, 1994), the Kotlerian vision of Marketing management lacks theoretical integration, focuses disproportionately on fast-moving consumer goods (fmcg) consumer marketing to the neglect of industrial and services marketing, and emphasizes transactions controlled by Marketing professionals while neglecting the systemic exchange-oriented approach adopted by some earlier theorists (including Alderson). Instead, Gummesson (2002a, 2002b) promotes relationship Marketing as a 'new paradigm' for Marketing which takes account of the service orientation of many enterprises in post-industrial economies and accommodates the logic of customer retention as opposed to ever-increasing sales (but see O'Malley et al., 2008 for a critique of the relationship metaphor of marketing).

Others have indicated that the US-inspired paradigm for Marketing management neglects the needs and interests of small firms (Carson, 1993), and plays down the creative and entrepreneurial character of Marketing in favour of a mechanistic, bureaucratic approach (Carson, 1993; Carson et al., 1995; Hackley and Kitchen, 1997). The relative neglect of the entrepreneurial perspective and the concomitant neglect of qualitative forms of everyday understanding in small business Marketing are also remarked upon (Carson et al., 2001; Hills, 1994; Mumby-Croft and Hackley, 1997).

Views of relationship Marketing conflict – as noted previously, some commentators have claimed that relationship Marketing is a new paradigm replacing the transactional Marketing management paradigm in post-industrial economies (Gummesson, 2002a, 2002b). Others have argued that relationship Marketing is a dimension of Marketing management which focuses on differentiating the brand through enhanced customer service (Doyle, 1989). Berry (1983) wrote that:

> relationship marketing is attracting, maintaining, and – in multi-service organizations – enhancing customer relationships. Servicing and selling to existing customers is viewed to be just as important to long-term marketing success as acquiring new customers. (pp. 25–8)

On this view, rather than a new paradigm, Relationship Marketing (or RM) can be seen as the attempt to retain existing customers by establishing lines of communication, value and trust between providers and consumers.

Yet, in spite of these criticisms and many more, the mainstream Marketing texts and courses remain relatively unchanged and topics such as entrepreneurship, innovation, service management, marketing communication and branding are typically taught, not as central components of Marketing management logic, but as entirely separate sub-disciplines.

---

## CHAPTER SUMMARY

Chapter 4 has reviewed the Marketing Mix concept from a functional perspective and offered a descriptive account of some of its managerial implications. Functional and also intellectual dimensions of criticism were indicated, including the challenge which cultural branding poses for the implicit claims and legitimacy of managerial Marketing as a problem-solving, demand-creating technique. Chapter 5 continues the review of managerial Marketing concepts with an account of some issues in strategic Marketing.

---

## CHAPTER REVIEW QUESTIONS

1.  The managerial 'school' of Marketing (Sheth et al., 1988), reflecting the interests, value and priorities of organizational managers, remains the dominant discourse of texts and courses about Marketing. It is particularly identified by a 'normative' thrust, a tendency to offer prescriptions or rules-of-thumb for managerial action which ought to apply in a wide

range of circumstances. Does the Marketing Mix offer a coherent basis for action for a typical Marketing manager? Give reasons for your answer.

2.  Brand extensions and brand 'stretching' show that the Marketing Mix elements can be subordinate to a strong brand. List four global brands and describe, from your own knowledge, their mix elements. Can competitors duplicate these elements? By doing so, might they duplicate the success of the brand?

3.  Describe what you understand by cultural branding and evaluate the extent to which it maps onto the Marketing Mix approach.

---

## CHAPTER CASE

## Iconic Brands and Marketing Management

### The top 25 global brands by value[25]

1.  Coca Cola
2.  Microsoft
3.  IBM
4.  GE
5.  Intel
6.  Nokia
7.  Disney
8.  McDonald's
9.  Toyota
10. Marlboro
11. Mercedes-Benz
12. Citi
13. Hewlett Packard
14. American Express
15. Gillette
16. BMW
17. Cisco
18. Louis Vuitton
19. Honda
20. Samsung
21. Dell
22. Ford
23. Pepsi
24. Nescafé
25. Merrill Lynch

## Case Questions

1. Reflect on this list of key global brands. To what extent might each of them constitute an 'iconic' brand? Explain your reasons.
2. Discuss how the success of each brand might be explained, or not, by classic Marketing management principles.
3. How important are the Marketing Mix elements in the success of these brands? Are other factors important too?

### Notes

1 Source: CoolBrands programme, www.superbrands.uk.com, in *Sunday Times* promotional insert, 24 September 2006.
2 See www.tkmaxx.com/index.asp
3 See www.segway.com/
4 See www.heinz.com/
5 See www.unilever.com/ourbrands/
6 See www.pg.com/en_US/products/all_products/index.jhtml
7 en.wikipedia.org/wiki/Kit_Kat
8 See www.philipmorris.com/
9 See en.wikipedia.org/wiki/Marlboro_(cigarette)
10 See www.reynoldsamerican.com/
11 See www.yamaha.co.uk/
12 See www.tobaccofreekids.org/adgallery/index.php3?Type=7
13 See www.ash.org.uk/html/advspo/html/brand.html
14 See www.virgin.com
15 See www.unilever.co.uk/ourbrands/foods/Walls.asp
16 See www.gucci.com
17 See www.louisvuitton.com/
18 See www.aaf.org/ (accessed 17 September 2006).
19 See www.ipa.co.uk/
20 See www.ad-wraps.co.uk/drivers/myadwrap.htm (accessed 10 September 2006).
21 See www.oaa.org.uk (accessed 17 September 2006).
22 See www.eiaa.net/news/eiaa-articles-details.asp?lang=1&id=85 (accessed 17 September 2006).
23 Source: 'US uses ads to sell academe', by Jon Marcus, *Times Higher Education Supplement,* 21 July 2006, p. 11.
24 See aux.zicklin.baruch.cuny.edu/jbbm/editorial_posture.htm (accessed 21 July 2006).
25 Source: Business Week Online website, bwnt.businessweek.com/brand/2005/, 'The Top 100 Global Brands Scoreboard', data provided by Interbrand (accessed 20 July 2006).

# CHAPTER 5

# THE STRATEGY DISCOURSE AND MARKETING STUDIES

---

## CHAPTER OUTLINE

Strategy and Marketing studies discourses coincide in many respects. A critical Marketing studies has to evaluate the way in which strategy discourse is used, especially given that strategy is sometimes implicated along with Marketing studies in accusations that it is intellectually trivial and ideologically driven. As a discourse of organizational power and control, strategy rivals Marketing in reach and influence. The chapter continues the review of functional Marketing concepts from Chapter 4 in order to frame the overall critical perspective of the book in terms of the prescriptive Marketing studies of typical texts and courses.

---

## Introduction: Marketing and Strategy in Common

Many models of practice commonly found in the curricula of Marketing courses and among the pages of Marketing textbooks are also found in strategy courses. Product portfolio models such as the Boston Consulting Group growth/share matrix (BCG), the General Electric matrix (GEC) and the Product Life Cycle (PLC) and growth strategy models like Michael Porter's Five Forces, his equally well-known generic competitive strategies, and H. Igor Ansoff's (1965) 'product/market expansion grid' are among the frameworks which populate the strategic Marketing and strategic market planning chapters of most managerial Marketing textbooks and courses (e.g. Kotler et al., 2005). In addition, the concepts of targeting, segmentation and positioning are also common between Marketing and strategy texts and courses, as are the models of organizational and market analysis such as familiar mainstays of business courses at every level, the SWOT and PEST analyses.

Management strategies are formed within many sets of tensions. One of the most commented upon is between creative flexibility on the one hand, and formal bureaucracy on the other. Marketing orientation is supposed to entail responsiveness to markets and customers, but if the organization is operating to a carefully devised strategic plan, then managers might be reluctant to be creative or spontaneous, preferring instead to go by the book. 'Strategy' in management usually connotes ideas like unity of purpose, long-term goals, the provision of significant resources, planning and organization. Kotler's original formulation of Marketing management as planning, analysis, implementation and control binds the Marketing function into a planning, and strategic, approach.

In management books, strategy is typically distinguished from tactics in that strategic decisions are normally of longer-term import and therefore command greater resources and more detailed planning than tactical decisions. In common with most things in management, there are few clear demarcations between strategy and tactics in practice. Ostensibly tactical decisions on, say, price or distribution, can also be strategic in their implications if they are pursued on a long-term, corporate-wide basis. On the other hand, an essential feature of strategy is flexibility – if a stratagem doesn't get the desired results, it should be revised in short order. The Marketing Mix, as we saw in the previous chapter, is described by Kotler as a toolbox of tactical weapons. Yet, it is also clear that these ostensibly tactical tools can have strategic implications.

Intuitively, organizational strategy and Marketing seem to go together (Hooley et al., 2003, 2008; Piercy, 1998). Marketing, according to Drucker (1954), is the primary orientation of the successful, outward-looking and customer-satisfying organization. It therefore requires substantial resources and top-level support, and it delivers long-term value to shareholders. A business strategy is, on the face of it, worthless without a Marketing element, while Marketing activity is made possible through the resources that the business strategy makes available. Yet Marketing and strategy tend to operate as two disciplines in many university departments, with different textbooks and separate departments and courses.[1] The two fields pursue differing intellectual agenda. Some have argued that the Marketing field has given little attention to debates in the world of competitive strategy (Day and Wensley, 1983). On the other hand, others have suggested that strategy has benefited from developments in Marketing (Biggadike, 1981).

Wensley (1996, p. 162) suggests that the principles of Marketing strategy are 'to achieve persistent success in the marketplace over the competition' while business strategy is more concerned with the integration of functional areas within the firm (p. 163). On the one hand, business strategy takes in the big picture. On the other, Marketing strategy defines the firm's activities. There is a view among some strategy academics that Marketing should be regarded as a junior discipline. It is seen as tactical and operational, focused on the product-market level and feeding into corporate objectives and values. This view is sometimes illustrated with a herringbone schematic in which each market offer, with its own action plan for each element of the Marketing mix, dovetails into a product market plan, a business plan, and a corporate plan. The organization is conceived as separate strategic business units based around distinct offers with their particular markets, brand managers and product development programmes.

For others, Marketing is so fundamental to the organization's purpose that it ought to be known as 'strategic Marketing'. This is the Marketing ethos applied throughout the organization with a strategic scope and vision (Doyle, 2001). Kotler (1988) quotes a 'Marketing planning manager' saying that:

> ... the marketing manager is the most significant functional contributor to the strategic planning process, with leadership roles in defining the business mission; analysis of the environmental, competitive, and business situations; developing objectives, goals and strategies; and defining product, market, distribution and quality plans, to implement the business strategies. (p. 35)

In this passage, strategy is identified with planning. Marketing in organizations, by implication, is formal and bureaucratized, in keeping with the Marketing management planning model. In turn, this implies that organizations work to a kind of rationality in which Marketing opportunities are spotted, analysed, market-tested, and put into action with control mechanisms ensuring constant feedback, all within a corporate-level strategic vision. Strategic Marketing planning models are said to 'help managers think in a structured way and also make explicit their intuitive economic models of the business' (MacDonald, 1999, in Baker, 1999, p. 50). Strategic Marketing planning is conceived here as a lexicon of concepts without which Marketing action might be intuitive and chaotic. One might argue that intuitive and chaotic Marketing seems to serve some organizations very well indeed. Marketing success can be, and no doubt often is, achieved without any use being made of formal planning concepts. Indeed, strategic market planning can be seen as a sterile paper exercise which has little connection with the reality of organizational behaviour (Mintzberg and Waters, 1985; Mintzberg, 1994). Nevertheless, they remain part of the conventional business and management curriculum and a major focus for the attention of academic researchers in the field.

One aspect of the two disciplines seems hard to separate. According to the textbooks, the first step in strategic Marketing planning is to ask what business/market the organization is in. Asking and answering this question is supposed to lead to a detailed evaluation of the organization's strengths, weaknesses, resources, capabilities and how these might be aligned with external market opportunities. So the answer to the question establishes clear parameters for organizational activity from which spring coherent goals and plans.

The 'what business are we in?' question echoes Levitt's (1960) ideas about the importance of defining the organization's scope of activity in terms of the sets of consumer needs it satisfies. This definition should normally be based on an assessment of what the organization's skills and resources equip it to do – in other words, on its basic or 'core' competencies (Hamal and Pralahad, 1991). Above all, a strategy has to be achievable and therefore must fall within the resources and capabilities of the organization. However, management must also have the imagination to conceive of markets and products that may not yet exist. The 'what business are we in?' aspect of strategic planning can be expressed in terms of the organization's 'mission' and articulated in a 'mission statement'. The mission statement is a device to crystallize strategic thinking and distil it into a simple paragraph or phrase, and then to communicate the strategic vision throughout the organization (Hackley, 1998b), at least in principle.

The strategy discourse, like that of Marketing management, is intended to be persuasive of the idea that organizations, markets and consumers are subject to rules and forces which, discovered through social scientific investigation, enable some degree of control to be exercised over them by a class of professional managers. Many find these discourses imperfect but worthy attempts at management education. Others regard them as self-referential and empty management babble. The popular strategy discourse, as it is used in Marketing management textbooks, focuses on a concrete reified world of management action, inviting the reader/student to project their own identity onto that of the problem-solving manager.

At this point, it might be worth going back to some issues raised in possibly the most popular management book of all before going on to review some of the key concepts of the strategy discourse. These issues are not generally part of the formal Marketing strategy curriculum but do illustrate the 'success factors' mentality of much strategic Marketing research.

## Peters and Waterman's Distillation of Organizational Excellence

No doubt it is harder to devise a winning strategy and put it into action than it is to pick out general similarities between apparently successful organizations. Many business gurus have made their name by distilling the elements of successful organizations into strategies that might be applied in other contexts. Peters and Waterman's *In Search of Excellence* was derived from a consulting study of 43 of the top 500 Fortune 500 companies in 1982. They induced eight main themes that characterized excellent management in these highly successful companies.

**Table 5.1**  An adaptation of Peters and Waterman's eight success factor themes[2]

1. **A bias for action**, active decision making – 'getting on with it'.
2. **Closeness to the customer** – learning from the people served by the business.
3. **Autonomy and entrepreneurship** – fostering innovation and nurturing 'champions'.
4. **Productivity through people** – treating rank and file employees as a source of quality.
5. **A hands-on, value-driven ethos** – a management philosophy that guides everyday practice, with management showing its commitment.
6. **Sticking to the knitting** – staying with the business that you know.
7. **Simple form, lean staff** – some of the best companies have minimal HQ staff.
8. **Simultaneous loose–tight properties** – autonomy in shop-floor activities plus centralized values.

The book still sells quite well, although the authors readily admit that what succeeded in 1982 might not succeed in 2010, and in some cases didn't succeed in 1983. The themes in Table 5.1 cohere somewhat with the Marketing philosophy with regard to the closeness to the customer and autonomy/entrepreneurship. The 'loose–tight properties' could support quick responses to consumer and market conditions well-supported by the centre's ethos, reward systems and resources. The book has been invoked as support for the Marketing philosophy, although it was not positioned as a Marketing book. Its appeal lay partly in the fact that its main success factors seemed to be relevant to any kind of organization. Another reason for its popularity was its concrete, non-technical writing style.

Peters and Waterman generalized in everyday language, across very different businesses and markets. The academic literature tends to adopt a more technical vocabulary, and makes use of finer distinctions between, say, business strategy and Marketing strategy, and between strategy and tactics.

If organizational strategy is, at least in part, about creating a sustainable differential advantage for a brand, it should be remembered that the ideas of strategy are competing against each other for PR coverage, consulting dollars and textbook sales in much the same way. Peters and Waterman were employed at one of the top US consulting firms of the time, McKinsey, and this gave their work some credibility. This and other consulting organizations in the area have featured largely in the popularization of key Marketing and strategy ideas (Hackley, 2001a). Massachusetts, USA, is the home of McKinsey's, the Boston Consulting Group, and of course Harvard Business School, which is famous for the case study approach to management education. This is a Marketing exercise par excellence, with a veritable production line of management ideas produced and sold on a massive scale over 50 years. For Gramsci (1971), ideologies have a centre of formation which seeks to control and promote the ideas from which it derives its power and authority. If Marketing and strategy have a centre of formation, then Boston, MA would seem to satisfy some of the criteria for that description.

A descriptive outline of some of the most well-known Marketing strategy concepts follows.

# Concepts of Marketing Strategy

## Positioning, Segmentation and Targeting

Segmentation, targeting and positioning (Biggadike, 1981; Hunt, 1994; Wensley, 1999; Wind and Robertson, 1983) are perhaps the most significant concepts of managerial Marketing and strategy. Put simply, a Marketing plan has to have an idea of the consumer group of interest (segmentation), it must have an idea of how to communicate the offer to them and deliver it to them (targeting) and it must have an idea of how the offering is to be described, differentiated and branded (positioning).

### Positioning

Positioning is sometimes defined as the set of associations, tangible or intangible, emotional or symbolic, linked to a brand. This set of associations defines the brand in relation to, and differentiates it from, its competitors. Brand planners are used to using the idea of positioning in a very abstract way with regard to the consumers' perceptions and preconceptions that distinguish the brand from others. This notion of positioning is in the mind of the consumer (Ries and Trout, 1985) and brand planners seek to influence the consumers' perceptions to a degree that would not be possible by relying only on word-of-mouth recommendations, repeat custom, conventional advertising and PR.

Strategic planning writers, in contrast, tend to use the term to refer to the more concrete attributes of the brand in relation to competitors, such as its tangible features, price, distribution channels and the levels of service provided (Hooley, 2000, p. 207). The brand, or the idea of the product that is the brand, is something that seems to transcend its component parts.

Positioning 'maps' are often used in the brand planning process to articulate the main aspects of the brand, its characteristics, 'personality', target consumers, buying opportunities and so forth. Brand positioning strategy can be based on relatively subjective judgements informed by market or consumer research data. A new brand, for example, might be positioned in a 'gap' which is not served by existing market offerings. Alternatively, a brand might be positioned against existing competitors with the aim of taking sales off them. For example, Guinness was, for many years, the only dark 'stout' beer available on draught in many UK bars, until Murphy's, another dark stout beer, was launched in the UK. A clear and advantageous positioning is something that can be achieved over the long term but positioning is nevertheless a nebulous and variable notion. For example, the impact of public opinion on positioning is such that a negative PR story could seriously damage a brand's position.

For example, Cadbury's is a global market leader in chocolate confectionery with many strong brands. The company has been innovative in its marketing communications with a ground-breaking sponsorship deal with popular UK TV drama *Coronation Street* and web-based initiatives including games and competitions. In June 2006, the company received a major setback when more than a million units of Cadbury's chocolate products had to be recalled because of the risk of salmonella infection from a leaking pipe in one of their factories. The affected brands included 250g Dairy Milk Turkish, Dairy Milk Caramel and Dairy Milk Mint bars, the Dairy Milk 8 chunk, the 1kg Dairy Milk bar, the 105g Dairy Milk Buttons Easter Egg and the Freddo bar.[3] Cadbury's claimed that the incident cost it £20 million but one commentator feels that this was a conservative estimate because it 'doesn't take into account mid-term damage to sales and the lasting damage to brand image'.[4] The author goes on to suggest that Cadbury's can recover the damage because it is a well-loved brand in the UK and this trust can be fully restored with about £20 million worth of advertising and a 'major longer-term public relations initiative aimed at restoring the trust once synonymous with the brand'. This appears to have been the case with a recovery in sales for Cadbury reported in mid-2008,[5] helped by some high-impact advertising campaigns.

If a positioning strategy appears to be declining in effectiveness, then a brand might be re-positioned through, for example, an advertising campaign designed to appeal to new user segments or to encourage new usage occasions. One way of re-positioning a product to attract new buyers is to focus on a hitherto under-served usage opportunity or market segment. For example, the breakfast cereal Kellogg's Cornflakes[6] created one advertising campaign for the UK which promoted consumption of its cereal in the evenings or as a snack at any time.

Positioning, then, is a way of conceptualizing the brand as consumers understand it so that policy has a coherence and continuity of theme. Since brand equity has begun to be accounted for in balance sheets, preserving the integrity or 'essence' of the brand is of great importance, alongside the use of intellectual property laws to police its use. Of course, it is an inexact activity in brand planning; some would argue it is a spurious one since consumers and culture bestow meaning on brands. But positioning offers a management vocabulary which preserves a sense of control and this in itself serves a political purpose in organizations.

### Segmentation and Targeting

Segmentation refers to the way that consumers and potential consumers can be profiled, categorized and sorted into groups in order to 'target' them with marketing initiatives. Directing marketing effort where it is most likely to succeed is intended to optimize the efficiency of the marketing budget. Market segments have to be viable in the sense that they must have the necessary disposable income, the segment must be large enough to sustain the required level of sales, and it must be accessible. In principle, any characteristic that is shared by a group can be used as a segmentation variable. Demographic segments are probably the most well-known, with variables such as age, sex, income and geographic location being useful for grouping customers for particular brands.

The importance of segmentation can be overplayed. Defining consumer groups carries risks – the definition may be too narrow, or it may simply be misconceived. Who is in a better position to decide on the appeal of the brand than consumers? Can brand managers decide in advance to whom their brand is most likely to appeal? Getting segmentation wrong could mean misdirecting the marketing effort and ignoring potential consumers.

Some argue that segmentation is an important aspect of strategic Marketing science while others question its coherence and practical value (see, for example, Saunders, 1995; Wensley, 1995, 1998). Brand image is the key element for competitive success, but conventional segmentation theorists ignore the influence of non-consumers. Owners of prestige cars know that many people who have never owned them and never will, know very well that ownership signifies prestige, success and glamour. Wearers of Rolex watches no doubt enjoy the fact that many non-consumers will recognize the brand they wear. The brand image is dependent on a cultural idea of the brand and, in turn, this cultural presence cannot be generated by targeting Marketing effort exclusively at narrowly defined groups. Television advertising campaigns promote the brand to a general audience but that Marketing effort is not wasted if the cultural meaning of the brand is sustained through such campaigns because buyers are buying that cultural meaning. The notion that Marketing activity which leaks across the boundaries of the desired market segment into the world of the non-segments is wasted is clearly wrong because brand building is a generalized activity which involves creating meaning. Clearly, it is possible to exaggerate the role of positioning and segmentation. Brands are more important to some people than to others. Then again, it is possible to define oneself by anti-brand positioning: a paradox that reflects the huge influence brands wield in social life (Hackley, 2005a).

Brands are used not only for their practical utility but also for symbolic purposes, to communicate a desired or aspired personal identity (Elliott and Wattanasuwan, 1998). 'The consumer is engaged on a symbolic project, where he/she must actively construct identity out of symbolic materials, and it is brands that carry much of the available cultural meanings' (Davies and Elliott, 2006, p. 155). The difficulty for consumers is that some identities may be regarded by others as authentic, and some not. In any in-group, there are authentic members and members who, in the view of other members, lack that authenticity. This is perhaps most evident in the choices around personal style. For example, many women will spend a month's wages or more on a Gucci or Prada handbag because of the sense of authenticity designer brands confer in the view of other members of the group. Even a fake bag will be preferred to a non-designer brand. Consumers have to contend, though, with the ever-changing nature of brand fashion within which they orient themselves and work up a sense of social and individual identity. It seems possible that strategy and Marketing management discourses exaggerate the extent to which these disciplines own techniques to control such culturally and psychologically based matters.

Market segments are naturally not static entities, and segmentation strategies have a time limit. For example, MTV (Music Television) revolutionized the worlds of pop culture and the music industry when it was launched 25 years ago.[7] MTV remains hugely successful and reaches vast audiences, though with content considerably supplemented to the non-stop music promotion videos it originally featured. 'Reality' shows like *The Osbournes* and *Laguna Beach* charted a new direction for MTV programming. MTV is suffering some impact on advertising revenues, though, because of the wider trend for young consumers to spend more time on the internet than on TV viewing. This important audience is increasingly difficult to target with segmentation strategies since they engage less with conventional media than the previous generation. MTV remains an important brand but is facing increased competition as websites operating on broadband such as YouTube, MySpace and Google expand into promotional pop videos and other forms of video content.

In the USA, a new and lucrative target market segment has emerged – not teens (teenagers) but tweens. Tweens, standing for pre-teenagers from about 8 to 12, is a demographic group with an estimated spending power of some $59 billion annually[8] in the USA alone. The tweens spend their parents' money not on toys but on CDs, iPods, designer clothes, cosmetics, DVDs, Disneyland holidays and cinema visits. In the 1950s, Elvis Presley was credited with creating the idea of the teenager in Western culture, with movie stars such as Marlon Brando and James Dean also promoting the teenage years as a time of rebellion, assertiveness and independence. A huge industry of movies, records and clothes was opened up by this cultural shift. Today, the teenage demographic has fragmented into many differing interest groups, some of these indistinguishable from adults, but the tweens has emerged as the next major force in Marketing. Like the teens of the 1950s and 1960s, the rise of the tweens has been reflected in the media. The Disney TV channel shows many popular shows starring tweens such as *The Suite Life*, about twin pre-teen boys who live in a hotel, and *Hannah Montana*, about a pre-teen with a secret life as a pop idol. Consumer, religious and parent groups have expressed concern that the trend leads to premature sexualization of children since tween Marketing often shows them behaving and looking like young adults.

This raises concerns about the ethicality of segmentation and positioning where vulnerable groups, such as children or the poor, are bombarded with Marketing initiatives suggesting that a particular identity positioning, signalled by the ownership and display of certain branded goods, is important, aspirational or necessary to their happiness and peer approval.

## Strategic Planning Models

The strategic planning models of SWOT, PEST, BCG, Ansoff and Porter are, essentially, consulting frameworks which have sold well and retain their place in the textbooks and curricula of managerial Marketing. They epitomize the practice-based discourse and translate easily into classroom teaching. The strategic market planning process boils down to three questions: an analysis of the organization's current situation, the expression of its desired and feasible goals and an elaboration of tactics and strategies to achieve the goals, along with an account of the resources required and scenario plans of different environmental events which might impinge on the ideal plan.

Asking the primary strategy question of 'what business is the organization in?' (Levitt, 1960) leads to a thoroughgoing analysis of the organization's operating environment, including factors such as internal strengths and weaknesses and external opportunities and threats (SWOT) and a consideration of the political, social-legal, economic and technical factors which might impinge on the business (PEST).

**Table 5.2**    The 'three questions' approach to strategic Marketing planning

| Question | Implied response and typical models |
| --- | --- |
| Where is the organization now? | Analysis of the organization's current situation: SWOT, PEST; product portfolio models |
| Where does it want to be in five years? | Setting objectives within the resources and skills capabilities of the organization |
| How does it get there? | Strategies for growth; Porter's generic strategies; Ansoff's matrix |

One important issue concerns the competitive structure of the market in which the organization operates. Strategies for success in an oligopoly (between three and ten or twelve suppliers), duopoly (two suppliers) or monopoly may be very different to those in a highly competitive market with many suppliers. For example, a duopolistic or monopolistic supplier would be likely to have much more control over price than a supplier in a very competitive market. In a market with many suppliers, price elasticity of demand is likely to be higher than in a market with fewer competitors. That is, a small change in price is likely to result in a large change in demand if there are many alternatives for consumers to choose. A strong brand can create a quasi-monopolistic position in the sense that consumers will not regard alternatives as equally desirable, so they will be prepared to pay a higher price for the strong brand even though other brands are not really inferior. The motor car market is an example of this – prestige brands such as BMW and Mercedes are generally more expensive than Ford, Mitsubishi or Citroen, even though they don't always score more highly on tests for safety, reliability or owner satisfaction. A brand is central to competitive strategy because a strong one generates higher long-term profitability than a weak one, even after accounting for the Marketing expenditure.

Another competitive factor to consider is entry cost. Some markets, for example the UK detergent market, are dominated by major suppliers with big Marketing budgets. A new entrant must be prepared to make a large investment just to have a chance to compete against the incumbent players. This is called a 'barrier to entry' to a market. Other barriers to market entry include protectionist import policies such as quota limits or tariffs designed to make it more difficult for foreign manufacturers to gain entry to the domestic markets. Another barrier to entry may be the ownership of intellectual property rights or raw materials. For example, Microsoft owns the intellectual property rights to the Windows operating system and alternative operating systems have found it almost impossible to gain a foothold in the consumer market. De Beers, the South African diamond company, owns the rights to the most fertile diamond mines in the world.

## Where Do We Want To Be and How Do We Get There?

Once a detailed analysis of the current situation has been undertaken, the planners are in a position to think about the possibilities for the future. The question 'where does the organization want to be?' implies that the analysis of the organization's strengths, weaknesses and the environment in which it operates will suggest objectives it can achieve within the limits of its resources and skills. These might be articulated in terms of sales growth rates, market share, financial returns or other criteria. The 'planning gap' refers to the distance between the current and desired positions. Say, for example, that an organization is currently holding the fourth largest market share in a product market that is declining in size defined by unit sales. The senior management decide that market leadership is an achievable five-year aim. The planning gap refers to the sales growth needed to close the gap between the current and desired positions.

'How do we get there?' refers to the best method or methods for getting from the current to the desired position. Economist Michael Porter's work has provided much of the vocabulary for articulating strategic planning. Most well-known are his generic strategies for growth (market leadership, cost leadership or innovation). Porter distilled commercial growth strategies into just three possible alternatives. The firm could set out to be the lowest cost producer, achieving sustainable competitive advantage by being the lowest price supplier. This might be achievable if the firm held an advantage in labour or operating costs, or could achieve economies of scale in raw materials acquisition. Alternatively, it could become the market leader, if, say, it could take advantage of its network of supplier and distributor relationships to become the dominant supplier. Finally, if the firm had strengths in market research and product research and development, and enjoyed the structural flexibility to nurture and support new ideas, it might be the first to the market with new product innovations.

Ansoff's product/market expansion grid is another well-established framework for planning growth (Ansoff, 1965). This, like Porter's generic strategies, is a simple rationalization of sales-led growth. A firm might grow by generating greater sales in existing markets with existing products; it might grow by generating greater sales in existing markets with new products; it might grow by entering new markets with existing products; and it might grow by entering entirely new markets with new products. A phrase that has become popular in this context is 'organic' growth. Firms can generate growth from within, 'organically', by increasing sales and revenue.

Alternatively, organizations can grow through mergers and acquisitions. Lateral (or horizontal) mergers or takeovers entail buying into an organization that is in essentially the same market, such as when an estate agency buys into another estate agency. Vertical mergers or takeovers entail buying into an organization operating at a different level in the chain of supply. For example, a wholesaler might buy a retailer, or a retailer might buy into a raw material supplier. There can be economies of scale or scope in mergers and takeovers – for example, if two firms merge, they might be able to operate with just one head office. Half the administrative staff could be laid off to save on variable costs, and the excess office space sold. Of course, mergers and acquisitions are not Marketing activities as such, but they are invariably driven by Marketing considerations in the sense that revenue and profit, or efficiency and effectiveness in the case of non-profit organizations, are usually the motives.

## The BCG Matrix

The Boston Consulting Group and its models of product portfolio analysis, used to decide which market offerings should be kept, invested in, 'harvested' or divested, have become standard fare in strategic Marketing planning approaches (especially the 'BCG Matrix'[9]). The drawback with the BCG matrix is that there is seldom enough information to compile detailed accounts of relative market share for each of the firm's products or services. The matrix divides market offerings into four categories which, in turn, are placed in two categories of market. The market might be growing or declining. The market offering of a particular firm might hold a large market share or a small one. A large market share in a growing market is called, in the BGC terminology, a 'star'. A market offering that holds a relatively large share in a static or declining market is called a 'cash cow'. A small market share in a rising market is called a 'question mark'. A small market share in a declining market is named a 'dog'.

The matrix is supposed to assist in making decisions about which market offerings the firm should invest in (especially 'stars' and 'question marks'), which it should milk for cash ('cash cows') and which it should cease to provide ('dogs'). The popularity of this matrix in Marketing texts remains, but its impracticality as a management tool has resulted in relatively little use for it in organizational contexts. Many organizations do not even have the accounting sophistication to know which of its products are profitable and which are not, let alone being able to work out their relative market share and market growth rate. Moreover, many organizations supply particular combinations of market offerings because of issues other than relative market share. For example, branding issues can lead to decisions where multibrand or family brand strategies are deployed. In some markets, for example the motor car market, many components must be provided as spares, whether or not they are profitable to supply in themselves.

## The Product Life Cycle

The product life cycle (Cox, 1967; Day, 1981; Levitt, 1965) may be outmoded but also retains its place in the Marketing literature (Hooley, 1994, in Hackley, 2001a, p. 81) as does the diffusion of innovation model (Rogers, 2003). The PLC relies on a biological life-cycle metaphor to conceive of a new product or service sales cycle in terms of four main phases. The first, 'Introduction', is when Marketing costs are high and sales growth is slow. The second, 'Growth', sees sales increasing rapidly as knowledge spreads about the product. During this phase, profitability is likely to be high because the brand is charging a premium price. 'Maturity' represents a plateau of high sales and steady profits as growth ceases. New entrants have come into the market but the advantage of being the first results in a high plateau of sales. 'Decline' represents a reduction in sales as competition eventually erodes the advantage. The life cycle model suggests that sales will decline until they no longer sustain profits. In some variations of the PLC, 'obsolescence' is added as a fifth phase. The PLC suggests various possibilities for Marketing interventions at each stage. For example, during the maturity phase, Marketing costs can be minimized, although many firms seek to preserve this phase through tactical Marketing interventions such as short-term price reductions, 'special' offers or 'new improved' formulations. The management of the decline phase is important, since to make a brand obsolete too soon can stifle potential sales.

The PLC has perhaps lost much of its credibility as a consulting tool since sales patterns can fall into virtually any configuration, therefore it is impossible to tell at which stage of the PLC a particular brand might be at any given time. Historical sales data cannot be extrapolated to predict the sales cycle because past sales patterns are not necessarily an indication of the future. The structure of the market could change with new entrants, new innovations or new technology, or through fluctuations in raw material availability. Moreover, the length of each phase, if indeed a particular brand's sales fall into such phases, cannot be estimated.

Rogers' (2003) diffusion of innovation model uses a normal distribution curve to illustrate the phases through which a new market innovation might diffuse through a population. It is based on assumptions about the motivation of buyers. 'Innovators' are the consumers who like to be the first to own new innovations. In many cases, new innovations attract premium prices and the innovators are so highly motivated that they are prepared to pay this premium price. The next group of consumers to enter the market are called 'early adopters'. They are quick to take up new market innovations but not as highly motivated as the innovators. During this second phase of diffusion, the price may be reduced somewhat to entice more consumers. The subsequent phases are driven by the 'early majority', 'late majority' and 'laggards' in turn. By the time the laggards enter the market, the innovation is no longer new, price has fallen substantially and there are many competitors.

The PLC and the diffusion of innovation models are useful teaching devices since they conceptualize differing market conditions for new products and new innovations and lend themselves to speculative discussions on alternative managerial actions for each phase. Their drawback as consulting tools is that they are highly generalized and may not map onto any given situation. Moreover, managerial decisions are contingent upon many factors that are not considered in these models.

# Challenges to the Marketing Strategy Discourse

The foregoing descriptive, if sceptical, account of strategy discourse in Marketing illustrates the sense of engagement which this approach elicits. Presented as a technical management problem, Marketing becomes an intellectual challenge. Its uses in management education seem self-evident, though its presence in university curricula is more controversial. Taking it at face value, what can be said about the functionality of this discourse, and the technical effectiveness of its tools and concepts for creating long-term competitive advantage for organizations?

## Strategy or Serendipity?

Strategic Marketing ideas suffer from the same credibility flaw as the Marketing Mix. They might all be useful pedagogic or consulting devices for encouraging students/managers to think in a commercial, market-focused way, but do they offer adequate explanations of organizational success? Can such broad-brush frameworks possibly account for the multitude of situational variables which may occupy management expertise (Hackley, 1999)? Or is there a tendency for the strategy discourse to be used to rationalize that which has already happened? 'Strategy', after all, is a seductive word. Every manager would like to learn of a template for success, and management consultants and academics are always willing to sell them one, but linking the strategic cause with the market effect is far from easy.

Strategies are embedded within a cultural context. Holt's (2004) thesis of cultural branding suggested that 'iconic' brands resolve contradictions of identity in particular cultural and historical contexts. If Holt is right, is it plausible that the manager of an iconic brand set out to do just that, to resolve a contradiction in social identity? Or is it more likely that the brand became iconic through a series of historical accidents? Perhaps these accidents were underpinned by astute business policies, but the brand's status could not be attributed to Marketing strategy alone. There are uncontrollable elements to organizational action and much of the Marketing activity Holt describes seems reactive and intuitive. Brand managers exploited unexpected trends which evolved within particular social and historical forces by, for example, sending free crates of Coca Cola to frontline US troops when they learned of the significance Coke held as a symbol of home for those troops. Just how much control is organizational management able to impose on such complex variables as identity and culture? Given this difficulty, it is tempting to ask just how much of the strategy discourse is a matter of rationalizing that which has already happened.

The strategy literature, and indeed also the mainstream Marketing literature, tend to reduce promotion and 'Marketing communication' to a supporting function (Hackley, 2001). But the idea of the brand seems intimately bound up with communication as its essence lies in public perception. Consequently, it is no surprise that many brands seek to locate themselves within popular culture by obtaining visibility within media entertainment (Hackley, 2003d; Tiwsakul et al., 2005).

The conventional curriculum ignores this element of brand strategy, yet Marketing as a whole is increasingly media-driven.

## Strategy or Rationalization?

Strategy discourse has been frequently sprinkled with the philosophic sayings of wise ancient generals like Sun Tzu. It is a male discourse (Chalmers, 2001) which produces male power in organizations. Some, equally wise but pacific philosophers have observed that life must be lived forwards but can only be understood backwards.[12] There is always the risk with strategy talk that it relies on rationalization rather than on genuine forward planning. There may seem to be a logic to action when it is analysed retrospectively, even though, while it was happening, few could see any logic to it at all. How many successful entrepreneurs will say that when they began, some people thought they were crazy? Surely the most difficult thing in organizational strategy is to spot an opportunity no one else can see?

Levitt's (1960) 'Marketing myopia' promoted the idea that Marketing orientation could preclude organizational failure. Yet there are many examples of managed Marketing failures and accidental successes. For example, Viagra started life as an embarrassing and unwanted side-effect before it was realized that the side-effect had a huge market (Letiche, 2002). Penicillin is another well-documented accidental innovation. Other innovations simply failed because technology and consumer tastes moved on, like vinyl records.

But being sceptical about strategic panaceas is not to suggest that pursuing and discussing organizational strategies is a futile endeavour. Far from it. Many organizations have immense resources and capabilities in Marketing. They exert huge power, most obviously in the choices, and the limits to those choices, that result for consumers. They must make decisions about action and the decisions clearly have far-reaching implications. To make these decisions in an ad hoc or careless way would, on the face of it, be an irresponsible use of the resources they have. Moreover, Marketing decisions usually have to be accountable: they must be justified to someone who controls the resources. Yet, while many organizations have similar resources, they often succeed by differing degrees. There is much at stake in finding out the difference between success and failure. Large organizations are often driven places because of the intense pressures they face. They have demanding stakeholders who all have high expectations of performance. Managers, shareholders, customers, and the economy in general depend on the performance of organizations. Everyone has a master, and the pressure to raise the level of performance is intense. Consequently, the strategy industry of books, theories and consulting ideas thrives even in the most economically advanced nations. There is much pressure for public and private organizations to achieve ever higher levels of efficiency and effectiveness. Strategy debates are deeply implicated in this effort.

At a most basic level, it seems entirely plausible to say that organizations which work to some kind of collective purpose are more likely to succeed than those which have no such purpose. Organizations which devise strategies do so to achieve sustainable competitive advantage in the long term. At least, this is the logic of management strategy. On the other hand, human social activity develops through moment-by-moment encounters, and of course much action is driven by habit and convention, not to mention the need for power and control.

Some ethnographic studies reveal chaotic organizations full of people trying to resolve complex personal conflicts and pursuing short-term personal goals, and getting by at odds with management rather than working in unity with it (e.g. Watson, 1994). How can such an organization be said to have a strategy when it is an entity containing diverse and, often, mutually antagonistic groups? In classic sociology, the conflicts between management and workers are often highlighted – in some work, the rivalry of different groups of managers is evident. The idea of strategy, and the unproblematic lines of control and command that it can imply, must contend with the reality of organizations. Directives from senior management may be negotiated, resisted, misinterpreted or simply ignored. Strategy, therefore, cuts across issues of organizational structure, employee motivation, skills, training and culture.

The rhetoric of strategy is part of organizational discourse through which individuals make their claims for power and control (Knights and Morgan, 1991). 'Strategy' cannot easily be explained as something that stands apart from the people who make it. Indeed, it may be wrong to identify strategy with planning at all: 'emergent' strategy evolves through and in the interactions of organizational members (Mintzberg and Waters, 1985). It is not something that is planned or made explicit, yet much of the strategy discourse is about planning for success. This contradiction between strategy and planning is just one of the many contradictions that obtain within the strategy dialogue.

## Marketing and Strategy as Practice

The core Marketing curriculum epitomized in typical texts has changed little in the 40 years since Kotler (1967) defined it. Practice is something that is necessarily ongoing (Pomerantz and Fehr, 1997, cited in Svensson, 2003, p. 4). Many textbooks exclaim that the business environment is ever-changing and increasingly complex, yet the Marketing thinking they describe seems not to have changed all that much in response to this complexity (Hackley, 2003a). Many of the consultants' strategic Marketing planning models still found in modern texts have been disregarded by most organizations since their heyday in the 1980s. Another issue with the way Marketing management is typically conceived in its texts and courses is that it treats language merely as a vehicle that reflects and expresses social reality. This ignores movements in social and cultural studies that acknowledge the role language plays in *making* social reality.

The relatively few ethnographic studies of how people construct and negotiate Marketing work in particular situations tend to undermine the coherence of this social representation. As we have seen in many examples in this chapter, Marketing work is part of a complex social field and is actualized in ways that, on the face of it, owe little to the packaged models peddled in mainstream courses (Ardley, 2005; Hackley, 1999, 2000; Svensson, 2007). The heterogeneity, situational specificity and lack of consensus which surrounds Marketing practice might be better explained by the idea of Marketing as a social construction (Hackley, 2001a; Hirschman, 1986, following Berger and Luckmann, 1966). Whatever characterizes Marketing practice in different settings, it is something that is talked and written about a lot as well as done. This implies that it needs no fixed point of correspondence in the world because it exists in interaction. Marketing is what we say it is. A fixed 'it' of Marketing agreed upon by all is not necessary for communication on the topic to take place. And one thing we know about practical Marketing management is that the textbook rules for success are made to be broken. So it may be revealing to study the way we use the idea of Marketing as a point of reference for our talk, writing and theorizing, as Brown (2005) and others have indicated by their focus on Marketing writing, discourse and ideology (see also Morgan, 1992: Willmott, 1999).

Marketing probably needs more work which studies actual Marketing activity in its organizational context in a way which can be understood by practical people and less attempts to offer speculative generalizations about procedures and processes for competitive success.

---

## CHAPTER SUMMARY

The main premise of many Marketing textbooks[13] and taught courses[14] is that strategic Marketing principles and techniques can give an organization some influence over an operating environment characterized by change, complexity and uncertainty. Marketing is conceived as a discipline that suggests the best possible kind of managerial action in a wide range of circumstances. The rationale for this 'normative' style is that deploying Marketing concepts and techniques will reduce risk in an unstable operating environment. Of course, it is hard to dispute that we cannot control the world as much as we might like and that most forms of action benefit from some preparation and planning. This is as true for a family dinner as it is for the international launch of a new motor car brand. While it may seem grandiose to speak of one's strategy for a forthcoming dinner party, the principles of analysis and planning can be applied to any context. But do they reflect organizational practice, or merely the post-hoc rationalization of practice?

Chapter 5 has offered a functional outline of the way that the strategy discourse is typically played out in Marketing textbooks and courses, along with some sceptical reflections about what this discourse offers Marketing studies in terms of its intellectual weight, its ethicality and its functional effectiveness. In particular, the chapter reviewed perspectives which position the strategy discourse as a repertoire of gender, power, managerial ideology and organizational politics. Chapter 6 returns to some more theoretical issues in discussing the role of research in Marketing studies and Marketing practice.

---

## CHAPTER REVIEW QUESTIONS

**?**

1. Choosing a selection of ideas from the strategy discourse, examine their implications in terms of functionality, ethicality, intellectual robustness and as managerial ideology.
2. Does segmentation always make practical sense in strategic Marketing? Analyse the likely target segments for five brands of your choice. Can these segments be adequately defined? Can they be targeted? Are the segments likely to change?
3. Evaluate the implications of a strategic Marketing studies which is based on practice rather than on hypothetical consulting frameworks. What is the value of the strategic market planning frameworks for management education?

---

## CHAPTER CASE

### Strategic Partnerships Generate Rapid Growth in the Mobile Phone Industry

The Caudwell Group[15] is a private company which was sold to venture capitalists Doughty Hanson & Co and Providence Equity Partners in September 2006 for £1,460,000,000 Sterling. It was founded by brothers John and Brian Caudwell in 1987 in Stoke-on-Trent, Staffordshire, England. Midland Mobile Phones, as it was then called, took eight months to sell its first batch of 26 phones. The group now sells an estimated 26 phones every minute. It generated turnover of more than £1,000,000,000 Sterling in 2000 and was twice named the UK's fastest growing company (in 1996 and 1997). The Caudwell Group's rapid growth has been generated by lateral and vertical strategic partnerships supported by three over-arching principles: (1) an incentive-driven human resources strategy (2) extensive strategic investment in IT systems and (3) market-leading customer service levels. This strategy has been possible because each company in the group has had an ethos of sales-led growth, generating the cash and market power to negotiate new partnerships at each level of the group's development.

The group expanded from retailing into wholesale distribution, logistics and mobile accessories and insurance, and now employs some 8000 people worldwide. One of the group companies, Dextra Solutions, has the following statement on the Caudwell website:

> We pride ourselves in offering a complete customized range of product and service solutions, ensuring each customer is able to differentiate product and packaging options without compromising on price or market positioning, whilst maintaining competitive advantage. We deliver to 33 countries with a 72-hour service guarantee within Europe and 4–5 day service worldwide.

Dextra Solutions is Nokia's largest accessories distributor worldwide and the largest in Europe for Motorola and Sony Ericsson. In 2006, it will distribute over 11 million accessories to high street retailers such as Tesco, Asda, Orange and O2.

Other Caudwell Group firms include LSG (Lifestyle Services Group), which provides insurance, identity protection, credit protection and information security services for businesses; Phones 4u, the high street mobile phone retailer which is the UK's largest distributor of mobile phone airtime, offering customers access to a number of airtime suppliers including Vodafone, O2, Orange, T-Mobile, Virgin and 3; Cornerstone Resourcing, a recruitment business; the Mobile Phone Repair Company with a turnover of £16 million annually and which receives over 3000 handsets a day; Caudwell Logistics which supplies warehousing, transport, IT and security services to the Caudwell Group and other customers; Policy Administration Services Limited, which handles mobile phone insurance policies and claims and fulfillment for the Phones 4u company; and 20:20 logistics, a 'value added' distributor and the UK's largest distributor of mobiles phones.

......................................................................................................................................

## Case Questions

1. What, in your opinion, were the defining factors in the success of the Caudwell Group strategy?

2. Mobile telephone technology is developing constantly: what new opportunities do you feel will be available for businesses in the next 10 years?
3. Can the Caudwell Group's growth be adequately explained by the conventional MBA vocabulary of strategic planning?

## Notes

1 Warwick Business School in the UK is an exception, with its department of marketing and strategy, reflecting the views of senior academics like Robin Wensley and Nigel Piercy regarding the close relationship between the two fields.
2 See www.businessballs.com/tompetersinsearchofexcellence.htm (accessed 5 August 2006). See also www.tompeters.com
3 See news.bbc.co.uk/1/hi/uk/5135962.stm – 'Cadbury's bars face more testing' (accessed 2 September 2006).
4 Source: Stefano Hadfield, writing in the *Independent* Media Weekly, 7 August 2006, p. 15.
5 Source: 'Dairy Milk recovery continues to sweeten Cadbury's sales', business.timesonline.co.uk/tol/business/industry_sectors/consumer_ goods/article 4169782.ece, Financial Times Online, 19 June 2008 (accessed 11 July 2008).
6 See www.kelloggs.com/cgi-bin/brandpages/product.pl?product=449& company=3
7 Source: Dominic Rushe, 'MTV struggles to keep the attention of its young audience', *The Sunday Times*, 20 August 2006, p. 9.
8 Source: LA Notebook, Chris Ayres, *The Times*, 22 August 2006, p. 15.
9 Porter works for Harvard Business School and Peters and Waterman worked for McKinsey's. They, and the Boston Group, are all located in Massachusetts, USA. Philip Kotler, too, was once at Harvard, so you could say that marketing, and strategy, are American cottage industries. Of course, this implies that there are significant cultural presuppositions buried within managerial marketing, of which the major exponents themselves may be unaware.
10 Ray Croc created the McDonald's empire from a small hamburger store; Akio Morita, CEO of Sony, invented and marketed the original Walkman in spite, according to legend, of negative market research results; Bill Gates, Richard Branson and Henry Ford, widely though their entrepreneurial achievements differ, need no introduction from me.
11 Research in marketing and entrepreneurship is itself an academic specialism with a journal and several collected works.
12 This aphorism is variously attributed to Søren Aaby Kierkegaard and Johan Wolfgang von Goethe.
13 A textbook authored as 'Cranfield School of Management' (2000) and called *Marketing Management: A Relationship Marketing Perspective*

(London, MacMillan) used this very cliché (on p. 283). I also cited it on page 72 of my book *Marketing and Social Construction* (2001a).

14  The largest business school in Europe, the Open University, offers the module 'Marketing in a Complex World' on its MBA (see www.open.ac. uk/oubs/qualifications/qualifications.htm#MBA).

15  See www.caudwell.com (accessed 11 July 2008). The group was bought out in September 2006.

# CHAPTER 6

# RESEARCH, THEORY AND RESISTANCE IN MARKETING STUDIES

---

## CHAPTER OUTLINE

Chapter 6 moves from an examination of the practice-oriented discourse of the previous two chapters to consideration of the roles of theory and research in academic Marketing studies. It reviews academic debates about the methods, scope and purpose of research in Marketing studies and draws a distinction between three main categories of research. 'Marketing research' refers to managerial research conducted by academics according to their model of the most appropriate methods and aims of practical, problem-solving research in the field. 'Research in Marketing' refers to academic Marketing studies research which is 'pure' rather than 'applied', undertaken out of intellectual curiosity for its own sake. Finally, there is market research conducted by practitioners. The chapter reviews debates about the relevance of research in Marketing studies to practice and education and the ways in which they might feed into a critical Marketing studies discipline. The final theme of the chapter is resistance, concerned with the ways in which ideological norms of research in the field have been resisted and opposed by alternative ideas of science and research.

---

## Academic, Practical and Managerial Marketing Research

A discussion of research in Marketing studies needs to refer to a question about the scope and axiology or purpose of the discipline. For some management academics, then, Marketing is simply a managerial problem-solving discipline. For others, it is a social scientific and humanistic field of study oriented around the processes and practices of markets, including not only the study of organizational management but also the social study of consumption and consumers, public policy and so on. Many academics would argue that this is a false distinction: the managerial study of Marketing and the social study of Marketing need not be mutually exclusive, and each can be as usefully explored with any intellectual tradition of research.

There is sometimes a distinction drawn between Marketing research and research in Marketing (Wensley, 1995, 2007). Although each refers to academic Marketing research positions, one leans toward the managerial orientation and the other toward research in academic Marketing studies, which is conducted out of intellectual curiosity for its own sake.

---

### Marketing research

#### Primary aims

To solve the problems of managers and to assist them in decision making, especially with regard to decisions that occur in the interface between the organization and its publics, such as other businesses, clients, government bodies and regulatory agencies, consumers and other stakeholder groups.

#### Primary audience

Organizational managers.

#### Most common methods

The statistical analysis of questionnaire surveys and the thematic analysis of qualitative data sets from focus groups, interviews, observation or other qualitative data-gathering approaches.

### Research in Marketing

#### Primary aims

To explore consumption and Marketing phenomena in both 'pure' and 'applied' research and scholarship in order to generate insights, ideas and methods to enhance knowledge and contribute to theory.

#### Primary audience

Academics, scholars, researchers, policy makers.

#### Most common methods

Uses similar research approaches to marketing research though informed by more detailed, explicit and eclectic theoretical influences.

---

**Figure 6.1    Distinctions between Marketing research and research in Marketing[1]**

## Marketing Research

The 'Marketing research' category is often defined in terms which place it at the heart of the Marketing concept, as an activity which generates market and consumer information without which the organization cannot become Marketing or consumer oriented. One professional market research society uses this definition:

> Marketing research is a key element within the total field of marketing information. It links the consumer, customer and public to the marketer through information which is used to identify and define marketing actions; and to improve understanding of marketing as a process and of the ways in which specific marketing activities can be made more effective. (ESOMAR,[2] in Malhotra and Birks, 2006 p. 6)

This, then, reflects a managerial orientation, focusing on the problem-solving requirements of managers. Many market research businesses evolved from advertising agency research departments. They tend to be highly pragmatic in their use of research methods. While the rhetoric of science and quantification is as powerful in the practitioner field as in the academic, there is also an acceptance that qualitative or interpretive approaches to consumer and market research have equal validity. The larger Marketing research agencies offer a full range of quantitative and qualitative research expertise. Smaller agencies tend to specialize in particular approaches. For example, one UK-based agency[3] specializes in using insights from the academic discipline of semiotics to interpret research findings for strategic Marketing purposes. Another small agency specializes in ethnographic research for Marketing.[4] Other agencies specialize in particular industry sectors, such as book Marketing,[5] media research,[6] business-to-business Marketing[7] or internet-based Marketing research studies.[8] Other agencies, such as Euromonitor,[9] conduct large-scale general business intelligence research for a wide range of practical uses.

While the professional field of Marketing research retains sophisticated quantitative approaches to opinion research, experimental research and surveys, it has also moved towards methods which reflect a desire to articulate and generate insights into the consumer experience. Questionnaire surveys and other objective methods generate indirect information on consumer attitudes, behaviour, likes and dislikes. Experiential consumer research, in contrast, has become more closely associated with subjective and interpretive methods designed to get not at the expressed values and attitudes of consumers but at their subjective experience of consumption phenomena. This qualitative emphasis on getting at what lies beneath the surface is reflected, for example, in the qualitative methods research unit at leading UK agency MORI.[10] To get at these insights, the emphasis is placed on a creative yet empirically grounded interpretation of qualitative data. Advertising agencies have been particularly advanced in adopting data-gathering techniques consistent with the 'experiential' approach, using ethnography, depth interviews, observation and other approaches taken from anthropology (Hackley, 2001c; Hackley and Tiwsakul, 2006) to generate insider perspectives on brands and consumption that they can turn to the strategic Marketing purposes of their clients.

The emphasis on 'experiential Marketing' is reflected in the changing priorities of global Marketing organizations. For example, Proctor and Gamble announced a diversion of cable TV advertising 'spend' to new media to reflect their 'experiential' Marketing approach.[11] They want their brands to feature as meaningful artefacts in the landscape of peoples' daily lives. One way they try to gain this understanding is by sending senior executives to live with consumers to see first hand what brands mean in ordinary lives.

## Varieties of Marketing Studies

The research in the Marketing category encompasses a variety of differing visions on the scope, aims and methods of research in Marketing studies. Typical Marketing management texts suggest that to study Marketing is to bring all the accumulated wisdom of the arts and social sciences to bear on a topic that engages us on many levels. It is certainly true that academic Marketing studies has drawn on a very wide range of intellectual traditions for inspiration and methods. These include sociology, economics, statistics, anthropology and psychology (for a review, see Baker, 2000c). The subject matter of Marketing is porous at its edges, so its theoretical scope is practically without limit.

That Marketing studies lends itself to a great variety of research approaches is evident from a small selection of published work: Marketing phenomena have been investigated not only from the predictable theoretical vantage points of cognitive psychology, economics, statistical and administrative science and sociology but also from literary studies (Stern, 1990), poststructuralism (Shankar et al., 2006; Skålen et al., 2006), art history (Schroeder, 2002), critical theory (Murray and Ozanne, 1991; Murray et al., 1994), historical analysis (Bartels, 1988; Brown et al., 2001), existential phenomenology (Thompson et al., 1989), anthropology (Belk et al., 1988; Peñaloza, 2000), feminism (Caterall et al., 2000, 2005; Fischer and Britor, 1994), rhetoric (Tonks, 2002), postmodernism (Brown, 1995; Firat and Venkatesh, 1995), creative non-fiction or literary journalism (Hackley, 2007a) and dramaturgical theory (Moisio and Arnould, 2005) to mention but a few examples.

What is more, it would be quite mistaken to suppose that this apparently eclectic body of work lies on the fringes of Marketing because it has no solid managerial implications. Far from it. These authors would maintain that the intellectual traditions they draw on generate insights which have profound relevance for Marketing management, as can be seen by the overtly managerial implications, for example, of socio-cultural research in branding (see Brown et al., 2003; Holt, 2004; O'Reilly, 2006).

Yet, the eclecticism and intellectual breadth of research in Marketing studies is not evident from typical textbooks or courses, nor from the top Marketing journals, as we have seen. Marketing studies has been particularly criticized, even within the critical glass house of management and organization studies, for not incorporating critical perspectives into mainstream teaching and research. Progress in developing a significant element of critique has been slow (for example, see Morgan, 1992 and 2003, making the same call for action a decade apart), though the widespread discontent with the status quo among many academics is reflected in the recent growth of interest in Critical Marketing from research scholars (see, for example, Brownlie et al., 1999; Saren et al., 2007; Tadajewski and Brownlie, 2008a). Accounting and Finance, for example, is often cited as an example of a subject which, in its university courses, has moved away from a purely mechanical, instrumental approach to embrace critical traditions from other disciplines (Burton, 2001), but this credit is not usually given from disciplines outside business and management schools.

Perhaps some management disciplines do incorporate critical perspectives but not to an extent that grants them true intellectual independence, at least not in the opinion of many academics from other fields. After all, there is clearly a danger that critical work in management studies might serve not to question and interrogate extant management practices but, set within the ideological parameters of the study of management, to confer a spurious intellectual legitimacy on the field. Academics from other disciplines who assume that this is invariably the case give insufficient credit to the sincerity and openness to criticism and change of both management academics and practitioners. Nonetheless, a critical approach has to acknowledge the putative role of university business and management departments as apologists and public relations officers for big business. On the other hand, it would seem odd for academics working in the field of management education to ground their intellectual work in a rejection of capitalism. Then again, in a critical education, it can be intellectually instructive to look at directly opposing viewpoints. Management education does attract criticism for its narrow vocationalism and instrumentalism, a tendency from which disciplines such as history or literature are assumed to be immune. But every field of study is subject to its political influences.

## Theory in Marketing Studies: Art or Science?

The role of theory in Marketing studies is a longstanding and continuing source of debate and controversy within the discipline (Fisk, 1971). Detailed consideration of the philosophy of knowledge issues in research in Marketing studies is beyond the scope of this book, but interested readers might wish to refer to texts which deal with these issues, such as Burrell and Morgan (1979), Hackley (2001a, 2003b), Hunt (1992), and Lee and Lings (2008).

One persistent source of disagreement concerns the psychological, cultural and historical status of Marketing practice. Is it science (Hunt, 1992) or is it art (Brown, 1996)? Much research in the field springs from deep assumptions about how Marketing practice can be categorized, the role of academics in management education, and also philosophical debates about the status and nature of scientific practice. There are sharp division within the academic Marketing field on these very issues.

Typical Marketing texts tend to address such deep and complex debates by ignoring them entirely. As we have seen, there is very little theoretical material included in the typical managerial texts and courses promoting a 'normative', problem-solving approach. Some argue that this is the only possible orientation for managerial Marketing because, in spite of 100 years of effort, the discipline has not developed any viable theory of its own (Saren, 1999), in spite of some serious attempts (Hunt, 2002; Sheth et al., 1988). Others have pointed out that, while Marketing research papers cite theoretical sources from many other fields including psychology, economics, sociology and cultural studies, the reverse is seldom true (Burton, 2005, citing Baumgartner and Pieters, 2003): papers in other fields rarely cite Marketing studies. Part of the reason for this might be because Marketing's use of theory from other disciplines often distorts the original theories to fit them into Marketing's managerial scheme (O'Shaughnessy, 1997). Still others (Biggadike, 1981; Charnes et al., 1985) suggest that Marketing does not get the credit it deserves for its theoretical contributions to other branches of management studies, such as strategy, or that research in Marketing studies is marginalized out of intellectual snobbery towards management studies in general. Finally, theory has been apprehended in Marketing as an intellectual battle of oppositions, which must be won or lost (Anderson, 1983, 1986; Hunt, 1990, 1992, 1994; Kavanagh, 1994). An alternative view is that theories in Marketing should be understood as contributions to a pluralist understanding of complex subject matter (Arndt, 1985) with different intellectual visions of Marketing studies not in competition but co-existing side by side. As we have seen, the variety of theoretical approaches in the academic journals is testimony to the pluralism of research in the field, though the legitimacy of varieties of research in Marketing remains hotly contested and the top journals and typical texts and courses remain dominated by a 'scientistic' (Willmott, 1999) mode of research.

Saren (1999, p. 30) notes that the AMA (American Marketing Association[12]) Task Force in 1984 reported on the reasons for the relative under-development of theory in Marketing and its concomitant neglect by Marketing practitioners (in the *Journal of Marketing*, (1988) Special issue 24). Research in Marketing, some argued, had been misdirected and misapplied, and had lost its relevance to Marketing practice. Some suggested that academics were too concerned with quantitative sophistication, others that quantitative Marketing research wasn't sophisticated enough. Still others pointed out that, for all the pieties of the Marketing research textbooks, remarkably few Marketing innovations genuinely evolved from research.

## Uses of Theory in Marketing Studies

The ways in which Marketing studies have co-opted theory are open to considerable criticism. The field claims to be more outward-looking and eclectic in its uses of theory from other disciplines (Deshpande, 1999) and in the ways these are used and it has been suggested that this willingness to use other theories has inhibited Marketing from developing its own (Day and Montgomery, 1999). Yet, there are those who feel that some of this judicious borrowing of theory is not merely excessive but dysfunctional (O'Shaughnessy, 1997). Marketing has, it is alleged, played fast and loose with some of the work of other scholarly disciplines, not only appropriating old theory and presenting it as new, but twisting it into distorted forms to fit the Marketing agenda. Clearly, there is scope for a more thoroughgoing intellectual critique of Marketing studies which focuses on the integrity with which theories are used.

Gronhaug (2000) refers to the use many Marketing texts make of sociological concepts such as the family life-cycle, roles, status, culture, reference groups, norms, social class, relationships and networks, though most of these occur in the discussion of consumer behaviour. Foxall (2000) makes similar points about concepts such as decision making, information processing, behaviour, perception, learning, attitude, dissonance, problem solving, lifestyle, segments, needs and wants (cited in Hackley, 2001a, p. 131). As noted above, O'Shaughnessy (1997, p. 677), discussing the use research in Marketing has made of concepts from philosophy and psychology, suggests that Marketing's conceptual borrowing constitutes 'illicit grafts with dysfunctional consequences'. Certainly, the uses popular Marketing textbooks make of ideas like needs, wants, behaviour and self-actualization often seem somewhat glib with no reference to their sociological, historical or etymological sources.

It has been argued that the managerial genre of Marketing artificially limits the scope of the subject in order to privilege its status as a management technique (and also to sustain the cult status of the manager) and play down its interdependence with other disciplines. In addition, managerial ideology in Marketing studies risks overstating the extent to which consumer demands can be controlled, and understating their dependence on exogenous economic and cultural forces. The insularity of research in Marketing, at least in its mainstream courses and top journals, has been commented upon critically (Brown, 1995; Firat, 1985). While theories from other disciplines are invoked in Marketing studies, there is a noted tendency for engagement with other disciplines to be relatively superficial (O'Shaughnessy, 1997).

## Philosophical Standpoints in Academic Marketing Research

Within academic research in Marketing, there have been prolonged debates about the most appropriate philosophical basis to adopt. For some, a realist scientific approach is seen as having the most powerful integrity. Others prefer a relativist perspective (e.g. Hunt, 1990, 1991, 1992; see also the review in Kavanagh, 1994). Holbrook argued that all science involves interpretation (Holbrook and O'Shaughnessy, 1988; see the discussion in Hackley, 2003b, pp. 11–15; see also Lee and Lings, 2008; Hirschman and Holbrook, 1992) and therefore an interpretive, rather than a statistical and realist, model of research is needed. In particular, Holbrook argues that a subjectivist, experiential perspective can be fruitful, both as an end in itself and as a source of strategic managerial insights. This view reflects a view of science not only as incremental progress based on steady and methodical observation and analysis, but also as creative leaps of insight and intuition. Holbrook has also argued in favour of the virtues of 'pure' as opposed to 'applied' research in Marketing. Not only can research which is creative generate unexpected outcomes (a cursory study of almost every major scientific discovery illustrates the dialectical character of discovery and verification) but it might also be a more appropriate model of creative Marketing practice (Hackley, 2003b; Hackley and Kitchen, 1997). As we have noted earlier, while much Marketing practice is characterized by careful observation, measurement and incremental change, many striking Marketing innovations had no need of formal research at all. Holbrook's perspective (explained in papers such as Holbrook and Hirschman, 1982) reflects the importance much innovative Marketing activity has placed on quirky insight, unconventional information and an understanding of the subjective consumer experience.

The question of which research approach is the most appropriate for studying Marketing phenomena cuts across issues about scientific method. Attempts to apply scientific standards to academic or professional research in Marketing have not been confined to the statistically inclined. Sociologists, anthropologists and cultural theorists (such as Emile Durkheim, Claude Levi-Strauss and Pierre Bordieu) have maintained that their approach to research is as rigorously scientific as that of any natural scientist. Psychoanalysis, according to Freud, was science too. Yet all of these examples involved theoretically informed interpretation rather than (or as well as) experimentation and empirical testing of hypotheses.

In Marketing studies, the dominant model of research is experimental and hypothesis-testing, developed through rigorous statistical analysis. This model of research often induces a hypothesis from previous, speculative research or empirical investigation to form a statistically testable hypothesis, for example in managerial research into the Marketing 'orientation' of organizations (Narver and Slater, 1990). More generally, this is part of a large-scale enterprise engaged in seeking out empirical generalizations, or, if you prefer, countable facts, which inform the body of factual knowledge that Marketing managers might, in principle, draw upon to make their decisions (Day and Montgomery, 1999). The use of sophisticated techniques to draw statistically significant inferences from large samples of questionnaire surveys or other measurement instruments is also a big part of the market research and opinion polling industries.

Alternative models of 'interpretive' research have evolved, based mainly on smaller samples of qualitative data (especially interviews and observation) rather than on large-scale surveys or controlled experiments. Many of these approaches have endeavoured to grasp the consumer experience of Marketing interventions. Since the 1980s, researchers have built a significant body of research using interpretive theory to analyse qualitative consumer data sets (Hirschman, 1986; Hirschman and Holbrook, 1982; Holbrook and Hirschman, 1982). Collectively, the interpretive research approach in Marketing and consumer research has been labelled Consumer Culture Theory or CCT (by Arnould and Thompson, 2005). Tadajewski (2006b) has argued that CCT and the interpretive influence in Marketing can actually be traced back much further, to the work of motivational researcher Ernest Dichter (e.g. 1947, 1949, 1955, 1979). Dichter used an eclectic mix of theoretical influences in his methods to uncover the hidden and unconscious motives behind consumer behaviour. These influences included economic geography, political science, psychoanalysis and psychology (Tadajewski, 2006b, citing Fisk, 1971, Newman, 1958, and Mittlestaedt, 1989, 1990).

Marketing studies boasts no great scientific discoveries. There are no benchmark studies to give form to the debates about scientific method in the field. Arguably, the field has contributed quite a lot of useful research to the sociology of consumption which is informed, and often enriched, by an acquaintance with the material practices of Marketing and management. But the debates continue largely in a political vacuum in the sense that no studies seriously critique the role of power in the influence of Marketing ideas. Intellectual critique abounds in the field's monographs but much of this is conducted on the sterile ground of philosophy of science. There is a need for theory debates in Marketing studies to engage with the sociology of scientific knowledge, informed by historical accounts (such as Tadajewski's, 2006b) of how political influence informed the way particular ideas in Marketing came to be regarded as accepted and taken for granted, while others were discarded by the mainstream as irrelevant.

## What is Theory in Marketing For?

Theory itself can be conceived in very different ways. Hackley (2005a) suggests that the meaning of theory may differ depending on the level and scope of explanation sought, which may be psychological, social or cultural. These, though, are interpenetrating categories. For example, some theory seeks to explain and/or predict individual behaviours, such as Icek Ajzen's theory of planned behaviour (Ajzen, 1991, 2002), which has been used in Marketing and consumer research studies (e.g. Notani, 1998) to try to link self-expressed attitudes (toward, say, a consumer brand or product) with actual purchasing and consumer behaviour.

Moving from the individual, a theoretical framework might seek a more social level of explanation, for example where one's gender might influence the way advertisements are processed, drawing on sociological theories of gender and social identity. Marketing journals carry a great many research studies which seek cause and effect in consumer behaviour, but an alternative theoretical approach might seek what Hackley (2005a) calls a cultural, rather than social, level of explanation. In a cultural (or socio-cultural) perspective, the nexus of stimulus–attitude–behaviour are not seen as separated and sequential processes but, rather, are understood to be formed mutually. For example, Ritson and Elliott (1999) took an ethnographic approach to understand how adolescents used their knowledge of advertisements in their everyday interaction with friends and associates. In this research, Ritson spent a prolonged time in UK schools as a teacher, using this access to speak informally to adolescent students about advertising in their own school environment, giving a high order of ecological validity to the research.

In the cultural perspective, 'attitude' or 'behaviour' does not exist separately from its context of realization. Clearly, research studies in Marketing can have profound differences as regards epistemology (the nature of knowledge and what can be known) and ontology (the nature or essence of the Marketing phenomena which are studied). Marketing academic journals, as noted above, carry a full range of studies ranging from those conceived on a 'hard science' model (the majority) to any number of alternative research philosophies.

At a more rudimentary level, a theory is any kind of abstraction which can allow some understanding or even prediction. For example, if you have seen rain before, then you can generalize from experience that unless you take an umbrella with you when you go out, you will get wet. Many practice-oriented Marketing texts make their appeal to theory at this level, where 'theory' can be virtually any kind of abstraction or crude generalization which can guide behaviour. Marketing's classic ideas of customer orientation, positioning, targeting and segmentation can be understood as theories of this kind in the sense that they can, in principle, guide and direct managerial behaviour. This 'normative' tradition of theory in Marketing (Baker, 1999; Hackley, 1998) has been highly influential in framing the way popular Marketing texts and courses are conceived and understood. But the dominance of the normative tradition in typical Marketing textbooks and courses leaves the field open to charges of intellectual superficiality.

## Marketing Studies as Resistance

While Marketing studies has generally had a strongly managerial emphasis (Skålen et al., 2008), it has also been a site of passionate intellectual debate and conflict. Even if it is not evident in the typical taught course, elements of critique have characterized Marketing studies since its origin. Indeed, Marketing began as a critical subject in the sense that it originated as a reaction to, and a rejection of, the values and priorities of another subject. As we have seen earlier in the book, the point of departure for Marketing studies was microeconomics (Baker, 1974, 2000b), but you will find little or no economic theory in the great majority of popular Marketing textbooks. Marketing is essentially about manipulating demand within competitive supply conditions, but few Marketing texts include anything on supply and demand, elasticity or market structure. This might be because Marketing emerged from a sense of discontent with economics, a rejection of it, rather than as a development of it.

Marketing is 'informed' by economic theory in the sense that it nailed its objections to the economists' door and went off to form its own group, its own values defined by those it rejected. For example, the economists' assumption of perfect information in competitive markets was replaced, by Marketers, by theories of advertising persuasion that drew on social psychology, literary analysis, cultural anthropology, psychoanalysis and other eclectic branches of social science. Alderson's heterogeneous family buying units were theorized by drawing on, for example, sociological work in the family life cycle, dispensing with the economic notion of the homogeneous consumer. Economic rationality, the idea that consumers maximize their utility by evaluating the price and 'utility' (or usefulness) of goods, was replaced by consumer behaviour theory drawing on Ernest Dichter's motivation research (mentioned above) and Herbert Simon's (1976) research, among many other influences. Consumers were seen to be motivated by emotional and social factors which sometimes cohere with economic rationality, but often do not. The notion of 'utility' explains but a proportion of buying behaviour, perhaps a small proportion. Few would argue that the rise of brand culture today is driven by the increased economic rationality of consumers.

The first college courses in Marketing, then, evolved because of perceived gaps in microeconomic theory. Academics were trying to understand more explicitly the 'invisible hand' of the market. The microeconomics of perfect competition suggested that markets would clear as long as price, demand and supply could find a state of equilibrium. But equilibrium is a notional state, and the ways in which market forces adjust are (still) poorly understood. In any case, economists understand perfect competition as an enlightening fiction that assumes perfect knowledge, no barriers to market entry, numerous providers who all have the same cost base and homogeneous consumers who are all driven by the same motive – to maximize their economic utility. Early Marketing scholars apparently felt that it might be fruitful to see what theory could develop if these simplifying assumptions were abandoned.

## Wroe Alderson

One personality, briefly discussed in Chapter 1, whose influence is still discussed by Marketing scholars was Wroe Alderson (1957, 1965). Alderson was a consultant without a PhD who became a leading light at the Wharton School of Finance and Commerce, University of Pennsylvania, and an influential figure in the development of the subject from a branch of microeconomics to the managerial discipline which it became in the 1950s. Like some earlier authors (Converse, 1930; Fulbrook, 1940; Ryan, 1935), Alderson developed a functionalist theoretical approach to Marketing, adapting sociologist Emile Durkheim's systemic metaphor. The functional perspective referred to the way parts of a whole, organic system acted in interaction with each other. The parts make sense only in terms of their relation to the whole. Marketing institutions and activities were concerned with the efficiency of markets, in interaction with the surrounding environment. In contrast with economists, Alderson assumed that the consuming units in markets – households – were heterogeneous. In other words, buyers acted from a diverse range of motives and preferences using widely differing resources. The efficiency of markets, particularly with regard to demand management, became an increasingly pressing topic during the post-war economic boom in Europe and America, when excess productive capacity had to be satisfied by increased consumption to maintain growth.

Alderson's theories have continued to generate much interest from Marketing scholars, although for many readers, his writing style stubbornly resists even the most erudite attempts to understand it (Brown, 2002). His continuing influence within the Marketing field is confined to a small but dedicated band of scholars (Smalley and Fraedrich, 1995; Wooliscroft, 2003; Wooliscroft et al., 2005). Alderson's writing is said to have contributed mightily to the intellectual development of Marketing, if not to the plain English movement.

## Ways of Thinking About Marketing

It might be useful here to revisit the contested area of Marketing-as-practice in order to try to categorize ways of thinking about the practical field which inform attempts to theorize it. Practical Marketing situations are invariably more complex, unpredictable and uncontrollable than they seem in the textbook models. Attempts to describe managerial Marketing situations invariably suffer from the philosophical problem of under-specificity – they leave out situational context and present a grossly simplified reality. When action is located in that reality, there is a need for large elements of 'tacit' knowledge, details of information necessary for action but which cannot be represented in a text (Hackley, 1999). There is a gap between books and practical skill in Marketing (Gummesson, 2002a), a gap which Marketing shares with other practical fields from surgery to bricklaying. Readers of managerially oriented Marketing texts know that many Marketing experts learned their skills by doing Marketing, and not from books, and many Marketing practitioners seem to make no use at all of the common currency of Marketing tools and concepts (Ardley, 2005).

By the same token, when academic writers try to generalize about the world, they usually acknowledge many exceptions to, and contradictions in, their theoretical scheme. Theoretical approaches give shape to investigation and frame the level of explanation which is possible. In Marketing studies, one might crudely categorize theoretical positions (implicit or explicit) along two continua, in Table 6.1:

**Table 6.1**   Dimensions of Marketing Thought

| Managerial/normative | Sociological/intellectual |
|---|---|
| Scientific | Humanistic |

## Managerial/Normative Marketing Studies

The first dimension in Table 6.1 distinguishes managerial scholarship from sociological scholarship in Marketing. The managerial 'school' of Marketing (Sheth et al., 1988), as we have seen, positions itself as an endeavour which supports the aims and values of organizational Marketing managers. The stated end of such work is to help improve Marketing performance by being either directly or indirectly[13] relevant to practitioners. Research publications in this vein tend to focus on the implications of research findings for managerial action and Marketing efficiency. For example, managerial research and scholarship in Marketing might aim to help managers improve salesforce performance; it might try to increase the validity and accuracy of market research methods; or it could try to discover ways to increase the efficiency and effectiveness of an organization through achieving a higher degree of orientation to Marketing principles. So the Managerial 'school' of Marketing is defined by the main intended audience for its theories and textbooks, namely managers or aspiring managers. It is also characterized by the assumption that this way of thinking about Marketing is legitimate and valid.

## Sociological/Intellectual Values in Marketing Studies

So, the managerial/normative dimension of Marketing thought confines study of the subject within the aims, values and interests of organizational managers. Managerial Marketing texts and research have a normative character in that they seek to offer solutions to managerial problems. The sociological dimension, on the other hand, takes Marketing as a starting point for studies which might well have managerial implications, but which are not conducted with that aim. Rather, they are conducted in a spirit of sociological inquiry. Examples of this kind of research might include studies of consumer culture (including its negative as well as positive aspects); first-hand explorations of the way that Marketing practice is actually conducted in organizations (e.g. Hackley, 2000; Svensson, 2007); or investigations of the ethical or social effects of Marketing activity in particular ethnic, national and cultural contexts.

The distinction between managerial and sociological research and writing in Marketing is, of course, a false one. The two are inseparable. Marketing academics and researchers who would describe themselves as managerial in their orientation use the methods and concepts of social study to achieve their aims. After all, who can doubt that Marketing is fundamentally about people? Marketing, then, could be seen as a branch of sociology, or perhaps psycho-sociology, but seeing Marketing as sociology opens up two difficult issues. One is that its claims to being a discipline rest on its managerial origins. In other words, the academic and scholarly discipline of Marketing loses its legitimacy if it is separated from the management discipline of Marketing. The other is, if Marketing is just social study with an emphasis on organizations, commerce and consumption, then do certain intellectual methods and values distinguish it from other branches of social study? Marketing academics acknowledge that their discipline derives its rationale, its methods and its conceptual vocabulary from other fields of inquiry. Marketing is a hybrid field, but many claim that this multi- and cross-disciplinarity, not to mention its long and distinguished record of theoretical work, make it a unique subject entirely worthy of its own distinct place in the university curriculum.

## Scientific–Humanistic Values in Marketing Studies

The second dimension listed in Table 6.1, scientific–humanistic, maps on to the first. The managerial school of Marketing tends to have two aspects: the normative and the scientific. The latter is the endeavour to produce solid and verifiable facts and causal relationships which can be used to ground the former. So the idea is that normative prescriptions for Marketing management action are derived from positive scientific facts about Marketing (Hackley, 1998). This is a philosophically problematic position called the 'is–ought' problem because normative prescriptions do not follow logically from positive scientific facts. But managerial Marketing academics sometimes argue that Marketing is yet a relatively young science in comparison to, say, medicine or engineering, and it is still trying to develop a body of factual and theoretical knowledge which can ultimately form the basis for a scientific discipline of Marketing practice. The Marketing science endeavour draws on the methods of the biological and physical sciences to seek objective and independent knowledge which will help organizations achieve their aims of profit maximization and long-term competitive success.

The humanistic research tradition, on the other hand, draws on the liberal and aesthetic arts (art history, literary studies) and human sciences (linguistics, history, geography, social science) to place human beings at the centre of research and scholarship. The aim is not necessarily to help commercial organizations achieve profit maximization (or non-profit organizations to achieve their objectives) but to enrich humanity and satisfy curiosity. The values underpinning such research and scholarship might be ethical, intellectual, therapeutic, educational, or even the desire to entertain. One key assumption of humanistic research is that researchers and scholars cannot detach themselves from their research – they cannot be considered as objective in the way that medical or physical scientists are considered to be. Humanistic research starts from the inquiring mind of the person and seeks to connect with the world at a human level. Humanistic research and scholarship in Marketing (Hirschman, 1986) differs radically from scientific research in the field in style, aims and values.

As we have noted, the differences in methods, vocabularies, assumptions and values between the arts and humanities, on the one hand, and the physical and statistical sciences on the other, underlie many key debates in Marketing (Brown, 1996). To some extent, the different perspectives result from the varied educational backgrounds of Marketing academics. Most academic sociologists, historians, philosophers or chemists would be likely to have a first degree in that subject. Not so for Marketing, or indeed management studies in general. People gravitate to academic careers in Marketing from all sorts of backgrounds. Perhaps the diversity of educational background of Marketing scholars explains something of the diversity of thought in Marketing.

## Research in Marketing Studies: Cultural Alternatives

This chapter then has outlined some of the debates over research philosophies and methods in Marketing studies. These debates have been characterized in many, often dichotomous, ways, such as the virtues of positivism versus interpretivism (Holbrook and O'Shaughnessy, 1988), realism or relativism (Anderson, 1986; Hunt, 1989, 1990, 1992; Kavanagh, 1994), modernism and postmodernism (Brown, 1994; Firat et al., 1995), art and science (Anderson, 1983; Brown, 1996, 1997; Charnes et al., 1985; Saren, 1999) and, more generally, in terms of competing quantitative and qualitative research approaches (Hackley, 2001b; Sheth, 1971).

Tadajewski (2006a) argues that the dominant managerial Marketing approach evolved under particular influences, notably the Cold War and McCarthyism in the USA. Brown (1995) has suggested that research in Marketing was especially influenced by the Ford and Carnegie reports into Marketing management education in the USA in the 1950s. The Ford and Carnegie reports (Gordon and Howell, 1959; Pierson, 1959) into the status and relevance of research in Marketing in the USA and the American Marketing Association Task Force (1988) have influenced the emphasis on quantification and model-building as a legitimizing rhetoric in the field. Today, the majority of papers in the major journals, including those devoted mainly to consumer research or advertising, reflect this emphasis on quantification, in spite of calls for 'paradigm pluralism' in Marketing (e.g. Arndt, 1985). Nevertheless, interpretive theoretical perspectives occupy the attention of a significant number of researchers and there are many interpretive theoretical strands (for example, Belk et al., 1988; Ritson and Elliott, 1999; Sherry, 1991; Stern, 1990, 1998; see also an overview in Hackley, 2003b).

We have explored debates concerning not only which research perspectives have internal coherence and intellectual integrity, but also which approaches mirror the practices of Marketing and consumption phenomena in the most appropriate way. One further perspective remains to be reviewed here. There is an argument that the political influences which impose theoretical limitations on the scope and methods of research in Marketing studies mean that it is simply not the best discipline for generating insights into its own subject matter. Perhaps one can learn more about Marketing from movies, art, literature, the press and experience than one can from Marketing textbooks. In fact, Marketing is best explored as a text.

## Cultural Marketing Research

Brown and Jensen-Schau (2008) quote arch Marketing guru Ted Levitt expounding the higher virtue of art over science, while other prominent Marketing academics have spent many years arguing the case for a more eclectic, humanities-driven understanding of the Marketing world. Brown (1995) has gone further in arguing that 'extra-marketing marketing', by which he means sources of Marketing insight emanating from outside the Marketing studies discipline, can offer far more penetrating analyses of Marketing and consumption phenomena than most Marketing textbooks and research tracts.

Reading F. Scott Fitzgerald's *The Great Gatsby* or Tolstoy's *Anna Karenina* won't necessarily help a hotel manager improve his service quality ratings. Conventional Marketing research, no doubt, has its place, but works of art might well connect vividly with Marketing phenomena. What is more, brands can be understood as texts.

Brands can be seen as texts in the sense that they are combinations of signs that tell a story. In social research traditions such as semiotics and discourse analysis, the term 'text' has a broader meaning than just the conventional meaning of 'text' as the printed word. The textuality of brands refers to the combining of 'signifying elements (words, sounds, images, etc.) to produce a meaningful message' (Danesi, 2006, p. 69). The textuality of brands is reflected in the way that 'brand stories' are promoted, for example on the websites of global brands such as Cadbury's which detail the history, positioning, advertising campaigns and other stories about their brands.[14] The Marketing activity behind brands can be seen as a process of adding paragraphs and chapters to the brand story. This way of conceptualizing brands has direct implications for Marketing research. The stories consumers tell of their experience of brands can be elicited through qualitative techniques such as phenomenological interviews and consumer diaries and those stories can be reflected in the Marketing campaigns surrounding the brand.

The Marketing-as-text perspective is continued in Chapter 7.

## CHAPTER SUMMARY

Chapter 6 has outlined the vast range of philosophical and methodological debates surrounding theory and research in Marketing. It has reviewed arguments about the relevance to practice of research in the field and looked at putative political and institutional influences on the way research and science are conceived. It has also explored the often-criticized links between the normative, a-theoretical approach of typical managerial Marketing textbooks and courses and the obscure, statistically sophisticated research which dominates the top journals in the field. The chapter also reviewed the variety of research in the field which has been present from the beginning but which has been subject to political influences shaping the ways in which Marketing is understood, talked about and theorized.

Chapter 7 develops the theme of Marketing-as-text by exploring one obvious but usually ignored aspect of Marketing studies. That is, it is a field which is predominantly constructed through text.

## CHAPTER REVIEW QUESTIONS

1. Does the increase in interest in 'experiential' Marketing, that is, inserting Marketing interventions into the everyday experience of consumers, pose a challenge to the dominant model of qualitative scientific research in academic Marketing studies?
2. Historical accounts of Marketing studies suggest that it has always been a deeply contested area, reflected in the rise and fall of debates about research and theory in the field.

Discuss and evaluate some of the institutional influences on research in Marketing outlined above.
3. Distinguish between market research, research in Marketing, and Marketing research. Are these distinctions important in terms of the categories of critique in Marketing from Chapter 1?

---

## CHAPTER CASE

### Blogging Marketing Strategies

The continuing revolution in communications technology is generating new Marketing media so quickly that many established Marketing agencies are struggling to keep up with developments. These are often driven by unpaid enthusiasts, and do not fit easily within the framework of orthodox Marketing concepts. One exception is MWW, owned by Interpublic, which started a weblog Marketing practice consultancy called Blog 360.[15] They consider that weblogs or blogs have become such an important vehicle for public communication that they can be used by Marketing companies to leverage their brands and achieve positive corporate PR. It can be important, though, not to use blogs as propaganda vehicles carrying one-way corporate sponsored information but also to enable stakeholders to respond and communicate with each other.[16] Weblogs began as personal diaries or journals written on any topic and published to the internet so anyone could read and exchange views. There was normally no charge, no restriction on who could read or respond, and no conscious strategy or purpose behind the blog other than the ethos of free speech and public debate.[17] Blogs can cover any subject from new product reviews,[18] showbiz gossip[19] or practically anything else.[20] A problem for Marketers is that weblogs work both ways: disgruntled customers can publicize their grievances about organizations very quickly and effectively to millions of people. One Dell customer, dissatisfied with the customer service he was getting, complained in a blog that was getting 10,000 visits a day.[21] Eventually, Dell created a blog of their own, and offered to fix the blogger's problem.[22]

### Case Questions

1. In what ways might a blog constitute a *critical* Marketing resource? What categories of research in Marketing might best generate practical insights from the world of blogging?

2.  Does the rising influence of weblogs on Marketing practice fall within the scope of the managerial Marketing paradigm, or is it an example of 'new' Marketing which needs new concepts in order to understand it?
3.  Could the blog initiative be an example of *critical* Marketing practice?

## Notes

1  This table is adapted from one written by the author for the Market Research module of the University of London distance learning BSc in Management, 2007.
2  ESOMAR is the European Society for Opinion and Marketing Research.
3  See www.semioticsolutions.com/
4  See www.happydoggroup.com/
5  See www.bookmarketing.co.uk/
6  See www.bmrb.co.uk/utility.asp?p=7&r=7296.496
7  See www.b2binternational.com/
8  See www.brainjuicer.com/
9  See www.euromonitor.com/default.asp
10  See www.mori.com/qualitative/approach.shtml
11  Source: the *Independent* Media Weekly, 27 June 2005, 'The Man With The $6bn Plan', by Raymond Snoddy.
12  See www.marketingpower.com/
13  A lot of academic marketing research which is positioned as managerial in its aims focuses on the technical and methodological detail of theoretical approaches. So, while in principle the work may be indirectly relevant to management, it is part of an esoteric conversation between scholars rather than an address to management.
14  www.cadbury.co.uk/NR/exeres/0A4DEDE0-2FDC-4940-839E-CB306BB 33C17. htm (accessed on 2 September 2006).
15  See www.clickz.com/news/article.php/3454471 (accessed 20 July 2006).
16  Sites such as buzz.blogger.com/ and uk.blog.com/ explain the basics of blogging.
17  en.wikipedia.org
18  See www.strangenewproducts.com/
19  See trent.blogspot.com/
20  See blogsearch.google.com/
21  Source: 'Bloggers put the boot into business', by Dominic Rushe, *Sunday Times* Business, July 2006, p. 8.
22  If you want to find out more about the scope of blogging topics on the web, technorati.com is a blog search engine.

# CHAPTER 7

# THE 'REAL WORLD' OF MARKETING AS LITERARY CONSTRUCTION

---

## CHAPTER OUTLINE

Chapter 7 looks at managerial Marketing studies as a genre of writing. It explores the ways in which Marketing topics, such as the role of the Marketing manager or the nature of the consumer, are worked up and represented in typical textbooks. This line of critical thinking in Marketing is important because education in the field is dominated by a particular genre of textbook: the shiny-covered, 1000-page Marketing megatext with its distinctively direct and un-academic prose style.

---

## Introduction: Marketing as Literature

Writing is important in social study. In his 1959 book *The Sociological Imagination,* the renowned sociologist C. Wright Mills claimed that any writing that could not be imagined as human speech is bad writing. Good writing, he wrote, has a voice. It may be neurotic or confident, direct or indirect, but it identifies a human source of experience and knowledge which speaks to the reader. He made an exception for a tiny number of prose stylists of genius. The rest of us are instructed to write in our own voice, to be intelligible, and to respect our readership. He also noted that the vast bulk of social scientific writing was dressed to impress, with arcane, polysyllabic words (like arcane and polysyllabic), long-winded abstraction and an impersonal register. He called it 'prose manufactured by a machine' (p. 221). These literary venalities, according to Wright Mills, usually conceal a poverty of ideas, pretentiousness and lack of intellectual confidence.

Wright Mills's advice has not been heeded. What he wrote about social scientific writing is probably truer today than it has ever been. There are certainly examples of a new consciousness of stylistic approaches emerging in the academic Marketing literature. But the mainstream managerial textbooks generally retain a very characteristic, though quite effective, impersonality. Marketing texts may not satisfy literary standards of good writing but they have a style which achieves its purpose.

The scholarly discipline of Marketing is a body of writing. Criticism of the entity, its institutions, practices, traditions and achievements is often conflated with criticism of its literary and rhetorical styles. Managerial Marketing can be described as a genre because, as Brown (1999, 2005) demonstrates, the written word is the medium through which Marketing ideas have become popularized, and its leading proselytisers, especially Philip Kotler and Ted Levitt, have been distinguished literary stylists. Indeed, Marketing is writing, to a considerable extent, with regard not only to its research papers, PhD theses, lecture notes and works of scholarship, but also to its practices which are realized in the form of reports, minutes, speeches, books, brochures and briefings. All writing constructs its sense of reality through literary tropes, styles and rhetorical devices. Writing does not offer direct access to the world of experience beyond reading. It constructs that world. Style and substance in writing are not two opposing things: they are the same thing.

The role and importance of writing has been profoundly neglected in Marketing studies (Brown, 2005; Brownlie, 1997). Much of academic/ practitioner Marketing writing refers unreflexively or without self-awareness to worlds beyond the text, worlds of management practice and of consumption. Marketing texts describe these worlds but one cannot get away from the textual basis of the Marketing discipline.

Marketing writing, in its popular management texts, is often characterized by a progressive, modernist tone cast within platitudinous rhetoric (Brown, 2005; Furusten, 1999; Hackley, 2003a). The need for organizations to become evermore infused with the Marketing concept in order to increase wealth, economic efficiency and consumer well-being gives these texts their sense of moral imperative, dismissing dissent and creating a romantic vision of a Utopian Marketing world (Brown et al., 1998). The recidivism of organizations and managers in lapsing back into their tainted production-orientated ways is a cause for some regret, attributed to the difficulties of implementation (King, 1985). The failings of the Marketing discipline are sometimes alluded to by senior authors in the field (Thomas, 1994, 1996), but very often this critical reflection is turned to a renewed sense of purpose for the discipline to sell its messages harder, louder and with greater scientific rigour (Baker, 2000b; Brown et al., 1998; Deshpande, 1999). Marketing texts have a narrative form often featuring trials and tribulations crowned with a happily triumphant ending.

The relentlessly upward-and-onward yet also platitudinous tone of Marketing management texts has a rhetorical purpose.

> Marketing is more than a business function: it is a philosophy that guides an entire organization ... the goal of marketing is to create customer satisfaction profitably ... Marketing is all around us. We are all customers now ... from the supply and consumption of education and health care to the queue in the post office ... lawyers, accountants and doctors use marketing ... so do hospitals, museums and arts groups ... no politician can get the needed votes and no resort the needed tourists, without marketing. (Kotler et al., 1999, p. xv)[1]

This extract from a mainstream Marketing management textbook illustrates something of the turgid literary style with which the field is closely identified. Marketing writing is often said to lack a quality of reflexivity. Reflexivity in writing refers broadly to a quality of self-awareness, an acknowledgment that what is said is provisional, tentative, closely argued and is offered as one of many possible alternative points of view. Marketing writing, in its popular forms, lacks all of these qualities in a style more closely resembling a Tom Peters consulting harangue[2] than academic argument.

This particular approach in Marketing textbooks, practically invented by Philip Kotler (1967) in his definitive textbook and re-invented since by countless imitators, forms the core syllabus of most introductory Marketing courses that are taught as part of business and management degrees. Professor Kotler didn't invent the ideas of managerial Marketing, at least not all of them, but he did sense the latent popularity of the prescriptive style of management thinking emerging in the *Journal of Marketing* and *Harvard Business Review* in the late 1950s and early 1960s. He wrapped the ideas together with a stylistic flair and proselytizing fervour which cornered the Marketing textbook market for the next 50 years, and there is no sign of any waning in the popularity of this style. The typical textbook approach in Marketing offers a sense of a direct and uncomplicated engagement with Marketing practice which is, in fact, a construction of literary artifice. It is a style which collapses the world into text and dissolves the ontological space between the classroom and the world of Marketing practice.

# Writing Marketing Theory: Constructing Marketing Relevance

Marketing, then, is defined by its language. A focus on the language itself (in terms of rhetoric and/or writing craft) is far from irrelevant to critique in the field. Indeed, the relative lack of language conscious-ness in Marketing writing is a serious impediment to a critical under-standing of the discipline. The appeal to a direct and immediate form of understanding which characterizes so many mass-market Marketing texts is itself a rhetorical device which obscures the way in which forms of representation can mask ideological content (Hackley, 2003a). Marketing texts which claim to offer 'tools and ideas' unmediated by text or by theory are conveying an implicit theory of reading, assuming a 'hegemonic' relationship between the text and the uncritical and unreflective reader (Scott, 1994).

## Writing Research in Marketing

As we indicated previously, the impetus for American academic Marketing to be more scientific came from the Ford and Carnegie reports (Pierson, 1959). Subsequently, the American Marketing Association Task Force (1988) responded to criticisms of the intellectual standards in Marketing scholarship by urging academic researchers to adopt the approach of the physical sciences, or at least to try to mimic that approach. The stated aim is often to discover more general facts about Marketing so that Marketing managers can, in principle, base their deci-sion making on firmer factual grounds[3] (Day and Montgomery, 1999). This orientation places research and scholarship in Marketing firmly within the applied domain, though there have been arguments that a 'pure' research orientation might ultimately yield more telling practical insights. The point here is that, in the matter of literary style, such writing emphasizes the concreteness of Marketing phenomena.

For example, if we assume that the correct model for academic research in Marketing is the model of natural science, then it makes sense to represent Marketing phenomena as relatively solid and sta-ble entities, rather like physical phenomena. One example is shown in Table 7.1 below.

Many forms of codified knowledge tend to build on a taxonomy of key concepts, categories or constructs. Physical science is the obvious example. But is Kotler's taxonomy of foundational Marketing concepts

**Table 7.1**   Kotler et al. (2005) list the key concepts of Marketing as:

- needs
- wants
- demands
- markets
- exchange
- transactions and relationships
- value and satisfaction
- products (services, offers, experiences)

appropriate to a disciplinary field so riven with paradox? Implicit in managerial Marketing texts is the idea that Marketing is a profession with a relatively unified set of values and practices. Consequently, the application of Marketing practice can be learned *in the abstract* through the acquisition of an agreed body of knowledge and skills. On the other hand, as we have seen, Marketing practice may be conducted in a socially constructed world of meaning transfer (McCracken, 2005; Mick and Buhl, 1992). Consequently, it demands kinds of knowledge and skill which are very difficult, if not impossible, to codify and learn in abstractions because of their tacit dimension which is embedded in situational, and interactional, social context (Hackley, 1999). So, we can ask, do typical Marketing texts overgeneralize about the nature of Marketing practice? When we consider the mind-boggling range of activities, skills and knowledge which could be grouped under 'Marketing', it becomes difficult to see how a unified body of knowledge and skill could adequately encompass the huckstering, streetsmart, quicksilver character of Marketing savvy. This does not mean that trying to articulate and understand Marketing practices is not a serious and legitimate endeavour of social study, but it does imply that it is an endeavour which is grounded in specific social situations which are not easy to reduce to simplistic generalizations.

The Marketing science agenda, for all its domination of the top journals in the field, has been criticized, as we have seen in the previous chapter, for assuming that the natural world parallels the social world (Willmott, 1999). This is not only a question of style of course but also of philosophical conviction. Should social study assume that the ontology or essence of the physical world equates to that of the social world? Or is the social world a rather different thing with its own rules and dynamics (Berger and Luckmann, 1966)?

There are paradoxes in this managerial positioning. We have noted one, which is that much academic management research is so technical that practising managers don't read it. Yet typical taught courses seldom deal in the advanced research. The drive to be 'more' scientific has narrowed the management studies syllabus so that in many universities it is intellectually risky for educators to draw on liberal arts perspectives in their teaching, valuable though these may be. So another paradox is that the 'scientism' (Willmott, 1999) of the managerial Marketing genre, pursued in the drive for increased managerial relevance, might actually make Marketing studies less relevant to practice by driving much of its research and theory development into an esoteric silo.

We should acknowledge the risk of overgeneralizing here. If 'typical' Marketing texts sometimes represent a caricature of Marketing practice, perhaps this book is working up a caricature of Marketing texts. Many academic Marketing journal editors are eager to see more original contributions, and they complain about formulaic submissions which offer incremental developments of well-established theories, which perpetrate myths about the field and overstate the generalizability of their insights. As Brown (1995) noted, the traditional Marketing curriculum has 'come under attack' on various grounds (p. 50). So the field does have many dissenters and alternative voices. It is far from a unified vision. Nevertheless, there are themes which frequently recur in criticisms of the way Marketing is written about and represented. In particular, constructions of the Marketing manager and of Marketing work in popular textbooks seem profoundly artificial.

## Theory/Practice in Marketing Writing

A focus on the language and texts of Marketing is a form of intellectual critique which focuses on representation. We are not looking through the texts of Marketing at a world of practice, but rather at the ways in which Marketing texts work up that world through language and rhetoric. Marketing texts, like other texts on organization, produce a representation of work in order to ground, and give credence to, their perspective (Parker, 2006). We can see, for example, that some forms of language are designed for effect. A CEO's speech, say, will adopt different rhetorical strategies to an academic giving a lecture to MBA students or to a mass-market Marketing textbook or a book aimed at practising managers. The use of theory and language in texts can become itself a tool for framing certain aims of reader response. Marketing texts which claim to have directly practical relevance are seeking immunity from critical scrutiny. Practical ideas for organizational application might be subject to functional critique in the sense that they can be judged effective or ineffective in practice. But then again, Marketing prescriptions are not formulae which can be applied and measured for effect. They are, rather, forms of management language the practical effectiveness of which is locked into the context of practice. Theory and language in academic Marketing studies social science are inseparable.

Books aimed at the popular end of the Marketing market often play up their non- or anti-theoretical credentials by claiming to bypass theory. Hackley (2003a) has argued that theory in Marketing occupies a deeply contradictory position and illustrates this with a number of examples. In one, Piercy (2002b)[4] claims that much of Marketing thinking is '... idealistic, ivory-tower … not reality …' (p. 4). Piercy (2002b) in contrast, having 'no patience with academic views … instead offers students and managers … tools and ideas for achieving superior performance in the market place' (p. vii). There is a long tradition of such anti-theoretical prose in Marketing. Some of the discipline's most eminent academic consulting gurus achieve a prose style which distances them from the intellectual introspections of 'academics' and foregrounds the common-sense appeal of their management solutions (Aherne, 2006). Nevertheless, anti-theoretical rhetoric in Marketing places the academic discipline deeply at odds with other intellectual fields.

In many practically oriented texts, Marketing academics use metaphors for theory (such as 'tools' and 'ideas') to deny that theory matters. But, as Brown (2005) has demonstrated, becoming a management guru is as much to do with rhetorical gifts as business acumen and Marketing texts are often positioned, successfully or not, at a managerial as well as an academic audience. Brown (2005) finds that an ability to write in a vivid and direct style lends credibility to gurus' claims to have insights into business practice. This is no mean feat. Many British Marketing academics, for example, have admitted in a survey that they have difficulty connecting with practitioners.[5] Engagement with day-to-day organizational concerns would, on the face of it, seem essential to the thinking of a Marketing academic, but some admit that their research has become disconnected with practice (Piercy, 2002).

Hackley (2005b) has suggested that the tension in Marketing between theory and writing style is mutually productive. Practical Marketing action, and organizational Marketing roles, are produced and reproduced through text and language (Ardley, 2005; Svensson, 2007). Clarity, force and richness of communication are important in all works of life, and no less for Marketing academics – Sawyer et al. (2008) created an admittedly crude scale of 'readability' for Marketing papers in academic journals to suggest that the award-winning ones were better written than others, regardless of their content. Academic Marketing departments in universities rarely ask their PhD candidates to focus at all on writing skill, yet it is the keystone of all accomplishment in academic Marketing studies and a hugely important element, of a different kind, in Marketing practice. Indeed, as Tonks (2002) indicated, an analysis of the metaphors, tropes and rhetorical strategies of academic Marketing writing can be an enlightening research exercise in itself.

## The One-Dimensional Marketing World in Popular Texts

The way in which management is (and managers are) represented in Marketing texts has been described as one-dimensional (Brownlie and Saren, 1997) since it lacks nuance and context. The absence of a realistic management person at the heart of Marketing's managerial project draws the criticism even of other management disciplines, especially organization studies. Taught Marketing courses seldom ponder the obstinate un-manageability of consumers (Gabriel and Lang, 2006) or the serendipity, angst, politics and sheer accident that constitutes organizational management (Mintzberg and Waters, 1985; Watson, 1994, 2001a, b). In a naive Marketing world-view, consumers can be controlled using the scientific techniques which are devised and owned by Marketing managers. Marketing courses seldom question the viability in practice of the Marketing management toolbox of concepts and models. Neither do they tend to question the status, authority or command over resources enjoyed by the Marketing manager, in spite of evidence that Marketing managers often lack the credibility and authority within their organization to make decisions on Marketing policy (Willmott, 1999). Anecdotally, many MBA students who actually were Marketing managers before they stepped up to the academic plate regard the model of the Marketing manager portrayed in typical texts and courses as simply implausible. Organizational complexity is not taken into account in the usual textbook Marketing scheme.

Not only do most courses presume a one-dimensional organizational and consumer world, they also adopt a profoundly naive position toward the language of Marketing and consulting. For example, they seldom allow that the doctrine of customer orientation or other business process discourses might sometimes be a device of control (over employees and over customers) rather than only a neutral tool for ensuring the satisfaction of customers (see, for example, Case, 1999; Gamble, 2007; and Morgan, 1992, on 'business process engineering'). The rhetoric of Marketing texts has seldom been critically deconstructed in mainstream research studies, illustrating the relative lack of reflexivity (or critical self-reflection) for which Marketing studies is widely excoriated (Hackley, 2003a). Indeed, merely asking whether consumers can, really, be managed, or suggesting that managers can sometimes be stressed, neurotic, disempowered and mistaken would be greeted with a deep silence in most Marketing classes. There is little in the canon of Marketing theory which equips students or teachers to address such difficult issues with anything but whimsy (Hackley, 2001b) or scepticism (Brownlie and Saren, 1997).

## Language and Marketing Practice

While the broad categories of Marketing management activity are relatively easy to infer, the way these are enacted in local contexts might vary widely (Hackley, 1999). Studies of what Marketing professionals actually do suffer from several intractable problems. One is the problem of self-reporting – asking people what they do and giving them set choices with which to respond is a very poor way of getting at real behaviour in action, but ethnographic studies directly observing Marketing practitioners in action are relatively rare. Another is the problem of categorization – Marketing practice covers a diverse range of activities and many similar job titles might be very different in their range of activities and scope of responsibility. The question, then, of exactly who is the Marketing manager and what he or she (Maclaran and Catterall, 2000) does in practice is one which is seriously under-investigated in the Marketing literature.

Typical Marketing management texts and courses portray the 'Marketing manager' as someone who is part of a managerial discipline which uses prescribed skills to analyse, plan and control Marketing programmes (Kotler et al., 1999, p. 4). Following Kotler and Levy (1969), this approach is extended across every conceivable kind of business, service, public sector or non-profit enterprise. Yet the scope of Marketing work encompasses a huge range of tasks in widely differing contexts. Think about the tasks that might be involved in, say, running a small supplier of bathroom fittings; setting up a website with a customer interface to market a management consultancy service; commissioning a research study for a large financial services organization which wants to market insurance products to young people; recruiting students for a Master's degree in Marketing; undertaking a brand analysis and strategy plan for a university; and negotiating with potential authors to commission and sell new texts for the Marketing education textbook market. All these activities are concerned with markets and customers. In other words, they are Marketing activities. But do they really involve the same sets of implicit models and personal skills? Moreover, would the knowledge provided in typical Marketing texts be essential or even useful to people doing such tasks?

What is more, Marketing texts might seriously underplay the role of language and rhetoric in Marketing practice. Some theorists argue that a Marketing manager is a class of worker for whom skills and knowledge are less important than language. Language, spoken, written and read, is one of the main elements in the enactment of professional practices in Marketing (Brownlie and Saren, 1997; see also Ardley, 2005). People engaged in Marketing meet, discuss, write reports, conduct presentations, collect and read market and competitive data, persuade, predict, advocate, negotiate, create and decide. Marketing work is a 'social and symbolic practice' (Svensson, 2003, 2007). Marketing models, concepts and rhetoric form part of a symbolic vocabulary with which Marketing people can articulate and perform their expertise.

The focus on language as a key tool of Marketing management could have a vast range of application. Marketing personnel can be involved in negotiating with buyers, customers or suppliers; calculating demand forecasts and profit projections; maintaining client relationships; coordinating or co-creating promotional programmes with agencies and designers; building and maintaining customer databases; generating new business by selling and 'cold calling'; writing Marketing plans; recruiting Marketing personnel; commissioning or designing Marketing and consumer research; training, motivating and setting targets for Marketing staff; conducting internal negotiations for more resources for the Marketing function; taking part in strategic planning meetings; and many more activities (Hackley, 2001a, pp. 90–91). The key issue here is whether this linguistic expertise can be performed adequately though a grasp of Marketing's managerial models and concepts, or whether more sophisticated linguistic training might help. Ardley (2005) asked a selection of professional Marketing managers to articulate their daily work. None used the conventional text-book vocabulary of Marketing concepts. Instead, they used creative metaphors to describe what they did. Hackley (2000) also found, in his interviews with advertising agency professionals, that none resorted to the vocabulary of Marketing concepts in talking about their work.

## Marketing Practice and Social Context

Marketing texts have to maintain that their concepts have relevance to a vast and diverse field of practice, but the context of Marketing roles, as we have already noted, varies enormously. Some Marketing jobs might focus on just one activity, say personal selling for long periods of time. Others might involve most of them by turns, depending on the industry, the individual and the organizational culture, style and priorities. By looking at the very limited sample of tasks above, we can see that there is a rich texture to what people involved with Marketing do in and around organizations. Marketing activity is often represented in typical texts in terms of input–output models, but we can see from these few examples that it is often also defined by language and social interaction. The particulars of practical action, in Marketing as in other fields of activity, are often understood as tacit rather than explicit knowledge (Hackley, 1999). Marketing in specified fields can undoubtedly be learned 'on the job' without the aid of books. It is reasonable, though, to suppose that practical skill in almost any field can be increased by thinking and reading about that field, and by learning about theories and ideas that might be analogous to other situations of potential application. The rationale for management studies in general is just this: such studies are not necessary for competent practice, but they might improve practice both individually, by stimulating better quality reasoning and decision making in the individual, and collectively, by making good practice more widely understood. These vocational benefits are, of course, additional to the intrinsic benefits of study as an intellectual end in itself.

The possible disconnection between Marketing textbooks and practice may go further than the lack of specificity in particular fields of application. Marketing managers, in practice, often lack political authority in their organizations (Willmott, 1993, p. 213, quoted in Brown, 1995, p. 54; see also Willmott, 1999, in Brownlie et al., 1999) and consequently may not have the resources or authority to make autonomous judgements on any of the key Marketing Mix elements. The Marketing manager is not necessarily, or even normally, the locus of authority and autonomy portrayed in the books. Furthermore, Marketing textbooks and curricula typically pay much more attention to large, multinational, fast-moving consumer goods organizations than to small, local enterprises. Large, well-resourced organizations naturally present a very different working environment for Marketers to the small- to medium-sized organizations in which most will work. Marketers, in practice, often have to work with decisions over which they have no authority on such key Marketing issues as price, product and promotion. They have, therefore, scope only to make decisions on sub-sections of the Marketing Mix, perhaps based on little or no Marketing information and sometimes with little or no budget or personnel. In other words, the 'real world' of Marketing management may bear little resemblance to the way it is described in textbooks and courses.

## Managerialism and Marketing Text Work

Managerialism in Marketing, then, is more than simply a set of assumptions about legitimate research methods and topics. It also embraces particular textual representations of the manager as a class of worker with skills, attributes, (gendered) values and power.

So the idea of management crafted in commercial contexts (in, say, a factory of unskilled production operatives) is extended to cover many other types of organization. Managerialism, in part, casts the manager as a key worker in the capitalist enterprise, controlling resources and organizing (and disciplining) lower grades of worker involved in the production process. Managerial Marketing texts effectively take this cult of the manager and place the Marketing manager at its pinnacle as the controller of demand, and therefore as the person who holds the key to the company's destiny. Moreover, this management discipline could be reduced to simple aphorisms, back-of-the-envelope models and normative[6] concepts. The normative strain of managerial Marketing is often linked with the generic idea of the Marketing concept and presented as universal prescriptions applicable to almost any Marketing context, though as Wilkinson and Young (2005) point out, the normative action suitable in a given situation is invariably contingent on the firm's strategic response to its particular operating environment.

The early, and still key, articles on Marketing management placed the manager at the centre of economic success and contributed to the general movement for the professionalization of management. Marketing has been instrumental in this movement, representing the manager as someone whose decisions, informed by his (this has been a highly gendered movement) or her knowledge and skills, was a key determinant of organizational success: 'marketers manage demand and build profitable customer relationships' (Kotler et al., 1999 p. 4). Not only are Marketers constructed as key to the success of commercial organizations, but their skills render them central to the success of any organization, and even to the role of wealth creation in society as a whole.

# Marketing Meaning

More generally, managerialist Marketing texts construct a world of work in which meaning seems relatively uncontested and one-dimensional. In typical texts, the Marketing manager adjusts the Marketing Mix variables for the brands under his or her control, using the firm's Marketing information system as input data for managerial decisions. In other words, the Marketing manager is constructed as a scientist/manager who operates in an objective world of marketed brands. But this realist world-view may be a caricature of the world of Marketing work. Brands and Marketing are social constructions (Hackley, 2001a; Hirschman, 1986). The world of Marketing is a relative one in which the cultural meanings of brands shift. In this sense, according to some authors, the thinking in the typical textbooks lags well behind that of the practitioners. Holt (2004) remarks on this neglect of the cultural perspective in typical treatments of Marketing, as does McCracken (2005):

> The *practice* [original italics] of marketing long ago came to terms with the role of meaning. Every manager is a de facto meaning-manager. Unofficially and implicitly, firms operate with the battle-weary understanding that well-constructed, well-managed meanings add value, create customers, sell products, advance careers, generate profit and raise stock prices even as they have come to see that badly-constructed, badly-managed meanings confuse the customer, diminish brands, damage careers, generate losses, and help pull stock prices down. The real problem often is the academic models. I believe they fail to give us a formal and exhaustive understanding of the role of meaning. (p. 175)

In managerial Marketing texts, the mobility of meaning tends to be underplayed in the interests of a tangible world which responds in predictable ways to Marketing interventions. The realism of the Marketing world is worked up by listing its basic constructs, as in Table 7.1 above, with the world of Marketing practice reduce to the simplicity of a set of 'building blocks'.

## Contradictions of Identity in Marketing Work

Svensson (2003) draws attention to the fluid and negotiated character of Marketers' professional identity. This fluidity results from several contradictions arising in the course of Marketing work. These contradictions arise because Marketers operate to certain idealized norms which do not obtain in practice. For example, on the one hand, the Marketing management approach positions Marketers as owners of a set of 'concepts and tools' through which they can enact their role as controllers of demand. On the other hand, the Marketing concept asserts that Marketers are essentially reactive, i.e. they respond to consumer needs and wants. Of course, in practice, neither obtains. In many accounts of Marketing work, the consumer is ignored: as Schudson (1993, in Svensson, 2003, p. 226) asserts, the idea of Marketing is to make money, not to please people.

In many other accounts, Marketers are blocked from carrying out their ideological role as controllers of demand by internal resource and power constraints and by external competitive factors. Therefore, Marketers face a problem resolving their professional identity because of the lack or scarcity of discursive resources for so doing. Hackley and Kover (2007) make a similar point with regard to advertising agency creative professionals. Managerial workers have to construct their professional persona, their credibility, by using the discursive resources at their disposal (Hackley, 2000). Outcomes might be claimed but the credit for Marketing success, and the blame for failure, are invariably contested in organizations because there are always unknown and unpredictable variables which could account for the outcomes of a given Marketing initiative. So Marketing discourse, the language, conceptual vocabulary and literary tropes and rhetoric (Tonks, 2002) of Marketing can be seen as a resource with which managers can try to construct a sense of professional presence and authority.

Marketing discourse, then, is a way of constructing meaning in organizations. It may be irrelevant to ask if Marketing concepts and techniques *work*. It might be more instructive to ask if they sound plausible. In fact, arguably, the real success of Marketing lies in the plausibility and resonance of its rhetoric. This success is not merely a matter of words but also of the ways in which they tap into wider discourses of power, neoliberalism and consumer sovereignty.

## Cultural Marketing

Another illustration of the role of meaning in Marketing practice comes from the Marketing of culture itself. Not only is Marketing sold as a commodity, but culture itself is often commodified and marketed. For example, Australian tourist venues sell Aboriginal art, while English tourist venues sell experiences of their Royal heritage. Management and Marketing of the arts has become a significant sub-specialism of Marketing, applied to cultural events, opera houses, tourist venues, and more. There is a view that art can be marketed like any other commodity. Artists themselves can be understood as a brand, though the success of someone like Andy Warhol as an artist cannot be understood properly in naive managerial terms (Schroeder, 2005). The analogy between Marketing and arts management is resisted by those who feel that this view is naive or simplistic (Chong, 2002). Arts management approaches, informed by major arts institutions[7] such as the Arts Council of England and the US National Endowment for the Arts, have highlighted the many ways in which arts and culture are managed, funded and promoted.

Of course, if all Marketing is conceived as a cultural enterprise through and through, then the arts can be understood as no more or less a cultural product than a car or a brand of beer. Some dislike the Marketing analogy because they feel that art has a higher moral value than a branded product. But some theorists, such as Bordieu (1977, 1984, 1990) felt that 'art' is neither high nor low but is, simply, what is considered as art. On this reasoning, consumers' search for authenticity may equally be found in a Modigliani painting or a Coors beer, or as Andy Warhol demonstrated, in a can of Heinz Baked Beans.

## The Marketing of Marketing Textbooks

As we have seen, Marketing studies is itself a marketed commodity. Marketing texts have an interest in claiming that their subject area is central to the well-being of all citizens – they are, after all, marketing themselves. Academic textbook sales are big business and Marketing texts enjoy bigger sales and profits than those of most other management subjects. But do they do justice to the heterogeneity of Marketing work? Typical texts and courses maintain that successful Marketing sustains successful organizations. They draw on a range of theoretical traditions for inspiration but they are concerned with Marketing not as a topic of intellectual study but as a kind of work, normally in the service of organizations. Marketing is seen as something people do, usually in a professional capacity at a managerial level. This category of work is positioned as one that serves not only commercial and non-commercial organizations but also society as a whole, because Marketing delivers a lifestyle and helps allocate scarce resources efficiently. This claim seems to group all Marketing activity together as a relatively unified set of professionalized activities which have similar aims and methods. Moreover, these methods can be applied across a limitless range of Marketing applications, from the Marketing of sausages to religion.

Some academics have argued that the idea of Marketing has been taken too far. Marketing, they suggest, should question its paradigm-broadening agenda and 'reconsider the conventional business domain as the conceptual foundation for contemporary Marketing thought' (Shaw and Jones, 2005, p. 273). Then again, periodic reviews and reassertions of Marketing's fundamental domain are part of the mechanism by which the ideological tenets of Marketing management are maintained in their original form (Brown, 1995; Hackley, 2003a). Marketing management texts contain largely the same basic concepts and theories as they did in the 1970s. Review, critique and reiteration is the cycle through which the managerial Marketing genre of writing and research maintains its relatively unchanging character.

Marketing texts, then, do a kind of work (Hackley, 2003a). They 'produce' the discipline of Marketing. Marketing management is a field identified with enthusiasm; it is treated as an ideology[8] (Brown, 1999; Marion, 2005). Marketing principles are a matter of faith, not intellect: they are 'accepted' (Day and Montgomery, 1999) and doubters are 'converted' (Baker, 1999). Perhaps these typical Marketing texts do something that Holt (2004) referred to when he talked about iconic brands. Perhaps they perform an identity myth, resolving the cultural conflicts of interest that arise in all capitalistic economies, and acting as an identity resource for people who aspire to be part of the new cultural technocracy.[9] Managerial Marketing texts embrace everyone into the neo-liberal economic agenda, either as a consumer or as an aspiring manager. Marketing is the biggest attraction in the business school curriculum, though the reasons for this may not be simply that Marketing academics are the cleverest researchers and most compelling teachers.

Marketing, broadly conceived, is an activity in which many of us have an interest as consumers, and often also as economic actors in labour markets dominated by the logic of market economics. Marketing texts and courses, and the professional and academic infrastructure surrounding them, perform a dual task: the ideological one of legitimizing market capitalism and the more prosaic one of providing resources for performing Marketing within this kind of political economy. Ideological strains can be read into all texts, and Marketing texts, including this one, are no exception.

---

## CHAPTER SUMMARY

Chapter 7 has developed some issues around the inescapable contradiction between Marketing's 'practical' basis and the literary mediation upon which it depends for its status as a constellation of educational courses, ideas, theories, books, reports and so on. The chapter outlined criticisms of Marketing studies which focus on the ways in which its popular texts construct a Marketing world which is accessible to the manipulations of a Marketing manager. Some of these criticisms point out that the way these texts work up a concrete world of Marketing entails gross simplification. What is more, the way they work up a sense of a Marketing manager as a controller of techniques and resources and a holder of authority within the organization is equally simplistic. Marketing texts' rhetoric is overreliant on metaphors which reify Marketing and Marketers as solid, one-dimensional things in order to play up the control offered by Marketing techniques and concepts. In so doing, they ignore the complex social texture of organizations and of the worlds of Marketing. Seen in these ways, the use of words in Marketing texts is seen as a fertile site for critical intellectual analysis of Marketing studies, while the actual language and symbolic communication of Marketing practice is seen as an equally important site of future research into Marketing.

Chapter 8 will summarize some key issues of critique raised in the book and review some of the major directions in which a critical Marketing studies might be taken.

---

# CHAPTER REVIEW QUESTIONS

**?**

1. Does it make sense to argue that attention ought to be paid to the writing of Marketing? Or should such attention be confined to literary studies?
2. Perform a literary deconstruction of a passage from any Marketing textbook. Compare the interpretations of several friends. What, if anything, have you learned about Marketing and Marketing studies from this exercise?
3. Brown (2005) has maintained that the leading gurus of Marketing owe much of their success not to the efficacy of their business solutions but to the force of their rhetoric. Take three 'seminal' Marketing research articles and analyse the literary style of each. Can you discern any 'success factors' of Marketing writing?

---

## CHAPTER CASE

### Marketing in Publishing

Publishing an academic book is a Marketing activity through and through, although many academics would not like to have their intellectual endeavours associated with 'Marketing'. The process of publishing a book such as this one is fairly typical. Firstly, the aspiring author writes a proposal and sends it to a publisher. The proposal should contain some detail about the concept, content and style of the book. It will also contain some thoughts on market positioning and competition. The proposal has to show that the book will fill some kind of gap not adequately served by current books. If the publisher's subject area editor likes the proposal, it will be sent out for appraisal by other people working in the same field. The author might have to make changes before the proposal goes before the publisher's editorial committee. If the idea is approved, a contract is issued and the author gets writing. The publisher's people design an attractive cover, write some copy for the sleeve, design flyers for distribution at conferences, add the book to their catalogues, lobby libraries and book clubs to order it, put it on the publisher's website, and perhaps add sample pages and favourable reviews of the book to its page on amazon.com. They send out free copies to other academics and to journals who might publish a review of it, and they display it on their stall at relevant conferences and book fairs. Some big-budget Marketing books have their own dedicated website and perhaps even a public book launch event.

Surprisingly few academic Marketing books have discussed the Marketing of Marketing books. Chandler (2006) points out that all writing is Marketing. No one writes not to be read, and to be read, your writing has to persuade readers to read and buyers to buy. And, as Brown (2005) avers, Marketing (academic Marketing, at least) is writing. Academics live by writing, research papers, books and courses. Marketing practitioners also spend a lot of time writing reports, Marketing plans, promotional copy, new business pitches, presentations and so on. Marketing and publishing are sometimes thought to be incompatible, especially by purist book lovers, but Chandler (2006) shows that Marketing, seen broadly as persuasion, looms large even for academic books. Moreover, even though the book business has been revolutionized in recent years by digital technology, C. Brown (2006c, p. 10) points out that slick Marketing in the book trade is far from new: 'The book business, in truth, has always been Marketing orientated. Its Marketing orientation pre-dates the emergence of the modern Marketing concept'. C. Brown (2006c) notes many more book Marketing practices, especially those related to PR and the complex promotional efforts behind the modern book trade.

Hackley (2006) refers to the way some book sellers (like Waterstones) are responding to authors' entrepreneurial spirit by offering the service of printing and binding a book and placing it on the shelf of one of their shops, for a relatively modest price. This is possible because the cost of printing a book has come down. The internet is also changing the economics of the book business. Waterstones can carry about 100,000 titles in a high street store, while Amazon.com can carry 3.7 million[10]. This means that the majority of books which are not blockbusters are now profitable to keep in print.

## Case Questions

1.  Look up some book retailing and publisher's websites and see if you can list more Marketing activities in book Marketing in addition to those mentioned above.
2.  From your selection of publisher's websites, can you discern differences in the Marketing approach with regard to particular publishing brands? In what ways are these publishing brands differentiated?
3.  What Marketing activities can you discern in the second-hand book trade?
4.  In what ways do you think the book business conforms to the conventional Marketing management paradigm view of marketing orientation?

5.  How did you make the choice to buy this book? Reflect on the Marketing influences that may (or may not) have surrounded your decision. In your view, were they effective? Would you be able to improve on Sage's Marketing activity for this book?

## Notes

1  I cite this passage in a spirit of quite undeserved mockery in Hackley (2003a, p. 1327).
2  Tom Peters, of Peters and Waterman fame, conducts expensive management consulting seminars (recordings of which are available to purchase) to large audiences of managers in hotels. He walks around the dinner tables shouting platitudes at the post-prandial assembled.  The audience, wisely anaesthetized with food and alcohol, greet this ritual humiliation with rounds of ecstatic applause. As Peters himself might say, go figure.
3  As noted in the previous chapter, Professor Morris Holbrook of Columbia Business School is perhaps the most eminent proponent of  'pure' as opposed to 'applied' research in Marketing but, in general, practical managerial application has been and continues to be the dominant rhetoric justifying research in the field.
4  Nigel Piercy is one of the foremost Marketing thinkers on either side of the Atlantic, and Professor of Marketing at the University of Warwick.
5  Reported in *THES* (Times Higher Education Supplement), 10 May 2008.
6  The 'normative' here refers to what ought to be done in a given situation. 'Normative' marketing theory (see Baker, J. (ed.) (1995) *Marketing: Theory and Practice*, 3rd edn., Basingstoke, McMillan) refers to norms of practice that can be communicated in the form of simple rules of thumb.
7  See www.nea.gov and www.artscouncil.org.uk
8  Whittington and Whipp (1992) have argued that Marketing has failed to establish a sufficiently strong professional ideology and this accounts for the relative weakness of its implementation.
9  Technocrat? Moi?
10 Source: 'Net delivers consumer nirvana', *Talking Point* feature by Simon Crerar in the *Sunday Times*, 23 July 2006.

# CHAPTER 8

# CONSUMER RATIONALITY, CRITICAL THEORY AND ETHICS: THREE ISSUES FOR A CRITICAL MARKETING STUDIES

---

## CHAPTER OUTLINE

Chapter 8 develops three of the topics which represent critical points of debate in Marketing studies. The aim of the book has been to acknowledge, open up and explore critical debates in the field, not to set out an agenda for a critical Marketing studies. However, there are important issues in the typical Marketing studies curriculum which might serve as particularly fertile points of departure for critical debate. Consumer rationality, the role of Critical Theory and ethical issues represent three of the many possible critical areas in the field. The chapter discusses these and makes use of case examples to try to illustrate their pertinence to a critical Marketing studies.

---

# Introduction: Critical Standpoints in Marketing Studies Revisited

This book has reviewed some uncompromising criticisms of Marketing studies, touching on the functional or practical, intellectual, ethical, and political or axiological assumptions of its research, its textbooks and its practice. In the preceding chapters, there have also been many examples cited of scholarship in the field which acknowledge criticisms of the discipline and offers ways of engaging with them. A secondary theme running through the book has concerned the ways in which many criticisms of Marketing studies reverberate around the political and institutional infrastructure of the discipline, and specifically point to the agenda of managerial ideology in Marketing studies which is set by the top US Marketing departments and journals. Many criticisms of Marketing studies are aimed at the managerial ideology in the discipline which, it is argued, promote instrumentalism, intellectual shallowness and a narrow idea of the aims and constituency of Marketing studies. This managerially focused works tends to ignore the wider constellation of Marketing scholarship and practice.

This is not to suggest that judgements about values, methods or vested interests in Marketing studies and practice can be closed or final. One of the main aims of this book has been to make more visible the impassioned and detailed debates which continue in the whole field, but which are seldom acknowledged in typical managerially focused courses. In spite of appearances to the contrary, Marketing studies is not an area of benign consensus and happy agreement but of persistent intellectual tension. What appears in a Marketing book or course is the shiny tip of a very craggy iceberg. This book is one attempt to engage criticisms of the field by opening up critical debates and exposing more of the variety of scholarship in the field in a way which might connect with typical courses and textbook topics. As such, it seems appropriate to refer to some particular sites of critical engagement for Marketing studies in this final chapter. The chapter selects three broad issues which are interpenetrated by the categories of critique framework. These seem particularly important sites for critique, though there are others which equally deserve attention.

The first focuses on debates about the model of consumer driving the Marketing management enterprise. This issue also touches on the broader issues of meaning and culture in Marketing. The second issue returns to Critical Theory and its role, if any, in a critical Marketing studies. The third focuses on ethics in Marketing, outlining some Western notions of ethical analysis and applying them to an area of ethical debate.

# Rationalist and Interpretive Visions of the Consumer

## From Levy to Holbrook and Hirschman

An aim of this book has been to show that Marketing studies is far from the seamless and consensual vehicle of managerial ideology it is often supposed to be by critics from other disciplines. This point is made to show that the field is as provisional and contested as any other academic area and to underline that it is a mistake to take the most popular forms of Marketing studies to be representative of the whole, pervasive as the managerial genre of Marketing may be.

Another of the fundamental debates which thrive beneath the shiny surface of Marketing studies concerns the model of the consumer which underpins the Marketing concept. Wroe Alderson (discussed previously) had challenged the conventional, economic model of the consumer which obtained in Marketing scholarship during the 1940s and 1950s. Sidney Levy also challenged conventional assumptions about the nature of consumers and consumer decision making but from a different perspective (Heath, 2007). Using ideas from anthropology, Levy investigated the symbolic and cultural role of products and services. He suggested that products, services and brands have a symbolic role, following anthropologists who had written of the role of possessions in social status, group membership and identity. Levy (1959) introduced the idea of symbolic brand image and argued against the prevailing assumption of economic rationality. In doing so, he challenged the philosophical basis of conventional Marketing thought at the time. Today, 'brand image' is part of the lexicon of business, though the full implications of thinking about Marketing as a cultural process (Holt, 2004), rather than a mechanical technique of management, are still underplayed today. In typical texts, brand image is treated as a taken-for-granted idea without any discussion, in typical texts, of the anthropological heritage of the idea nor of the implications of brand symbolism for Marketing management.

But this being Marketing, the debate didn't end there. The tendency to place a rational, instrumental model of the consumer at the centre of Marketing studies was attacked 40 years later by Morris Holbrook and Elizabeth Hirschman. The Marketing concept places an understanding of consumers' needs, motivations and drives at the centre of organizational activity. Yet, by the 1980s, Holbrook and Hirschman argued that many Marketing courses and research studies were still making the same assumptions about consumer rationality and product utility that Levy had criticized 40 years before. In a series of influential papers (especially Hirschman and Holbrook, 1982; Holbrook and Hirschman, 1982), they argued that consumers are often motivated by a desire for fantasy, fun and symbolic value through consumption. Consumers, they argued, are not motivated only by a rational evaluation of product utility but also by experiential, psychodynamic and emotional drives which are not necessarily connected with utility. Consumption is clearly something which is indulged in not only as a means to a problem-solving end but as an end in itself. This end might be irrational, on the face of it, in the sense that it is an expression of deeply personal inner drives (Gould, 1991) or existential desire (Elliott, 1997). On the one hand, the suggestion that consumer rationality is often deeply subjective, that is, they (we) are often irrational, might make them (and us) easier to manipulate and 'manage', or perhaps to exploit. On the other hand, irrational consumer behaviour is difficult to measure and to reduce to cause–effect models, and therefore poses a challenge to a simplistic managerial model of Marketing.

Tadajewski (2006b) has written of similar issues in consumer research, suggesting that the work of Ernest Dichter (1947, 1949, 1955, 1979) established the field of interpretive consumer research but has been largely forgotten by the mainstream. Some ten years after their ground-breaking papers, Holbrook and Hirschman (1982) set out a range of philosophical traditions which, they argued, could be used by Marketing academics to explore consumers' symbolic, emotional and social motivations in new and fruitful ways. These methods, based mainly on the theoretical interpretation of qualitative data sets, remain rather outside the scope of the typical Marketing course, reflecting the way that the managerial mainstream has generally resisted the theoretical implications of Levy's (1959) argument.

Levy (1996, in Tadajewski, 2008a) has written of his apparent frustration in advancing the same argument for an anthropological mentality in Marketing for 50 years. Other Marketing academics, such as McCracken (2005) and Belk et al. (1988), have advanced arguments in favour of an interpretive research approach which uses theoretical analyses of qualitative research data to generate insights into the quality of consumer experience, reflecting the symbolic role of branded goods and services and the meaning-making character of Marketing management. But, in spite of some 50 years of argument and research, the typical Marketing studies textbook or university curriculum, and the typical research study published in the top academic Marketing journals, rest on an implicit or explicit model of a rational consumer motivated by utility. It should be conceded that the tendency to model consumers as if they are machines is not confined to Marketing academics: advertising professionals, for example, adopt similar machine metaphors when talking about consumers (Hackley, 2003c), though the input–output model of the consumer is contested in the industry. Academic Marketing studies continues the debate at a deeply theoretical level, but, in its popular forms, Marketing education carries little of these debates and instead relies largely on conventional assumptions about consumer behaviour which have remained the same for over 50 years.

In history, the social sciences and humanities, the very nature of the human being supposed by researchers is fiercely debated and discussed. In typical Marketing studies texts and courses, a naive and simplistic model of a one-dimensional consumer tends to be assumed. Given that, as we have seen, the rejection of the microeconomic assumption of consumer rationality was the basis for the foundation of the Marketing studies discipline, it is odd that debates about the nature of the consumer have been largely marginalized from mainstream textbooks, academic journals and courses to the sub-field of consumer research. Marketing's intuitive appeal is based partly on the idea that it is the discipline which is close to the consumer, and it deals in turning insights into consumers to managerial advantage, yet the typical approach in the field emphasizes the managerial dimension and neglects the consumer dimension. There have been calls to reinstate the experiential voice of the consumer to the heart of the discipline (e.g. Wensley, 1990) but, generally speaking, the discussion on the nature of the consumer takes place in consumer research, separated from the Marketing management positioning in academic departments and academic research.

## Biometrics and Consumer Co-creation of Marketing

Models of the consumer play an important part in defining the scope, methods and aims of Marketing studies. A case example might illustrate the problematic nature of the model of the consumer in Marketing studies. VIP customers of a nightclub called The Baja Beach Club in Barcelona, Spain were reported to be having microchips implanted in their bodies to avoid queues and make paying easier.[1] On entrance to the club, and each time they order drinks from the bar, they simply wave their arm over a microchip scanner. Customers pay 125 Euros to have the chips implanted. They are programmed with a ten-digit number which can be linked to the customer's bank account. Clearly, these consumers are not worried about the lack of privacy entailed in this practice. Whatever they buy can be traced, and of course their presence in the club is on record. Is biometric consumption the future of Marketing? Might all consumers be implanted with chips recording and paying for their purchases and, potentially, betraying their whereabouts, like a micro-chipped house pet? If so, what does this imply for consumer choice and Marketing management? Location technology is already present in mobile phones, but in principle this is voluntary. What are the implications for individual freedom of biometric Marketing?

Biometric Marketing might take Marketing practice to the extremes of segmentation and control. What implications might this have for individual identity, privacy and freedom? Neuro-Marketing, similarly, is beginning to earn attention as some major global consumer goods manufacturers purchase their own Magnetic Resonance Imaging (MRI) scanners to conduct experiments in consumer control. This might not lead to the sinister Marketing world Vance Packard (1957) wrote about (Hackley, 2007c), but it does require Marketing studies to develop a critical vocabulary to take seriously the implications of developments in Marketing practice for identity and freedom.

Another element of the new engagement with consumer experience in Marketing practice is seen in the example of BootB,[2] a web-based company which takes actual advertising briefs and invites ordinary people to pitch for the brief. This is taking the idea of user-generated content, already important in social networking websites such as YouTube and Facebook, to a point where the notion of the Marketing (or advertising) professional seems undermined. Of course, it remains to be seen how successful the initiative is but it is one of many which are engaging with consumers in a new and deeper way. In such a model of Marketing practice, consumers are not passive dupes being 'acted upon' by the powerful techniques of Marketing managers. They are offering their own solutions on their own terms. Arguably, the classic Marketing concepts cannot adequately theorize such developments.

This refers to the co-creation of brand meaning by consumers, mobilized by the internet and other technological advances in communication. According to scholarship categorized as Consumer Culture Theory by Arnould and Thompson (2005), brands can be understood as units of meaning while Marketing has the task of managing or influencing that meaning (McCracken, 2005). The scholarship in Marketing which deals with this perspective, and the challenge cultural Marketing poses to the managerial paradigm (Holt, 2004) is, as discussed extensively in the book, predominantly excluded from the typical Marketing course and textbook.

# Critical Theory Perspectives in Marketing and Management Studies

So, a critical Marketing studies which is engaged with the interpretive character of social life and the symbolic aspects of consumption would place a study of meaning, identity and symbolic consumption in wider societies at the centre of a social scientific discipline of Marketing studies. But, while calls for broadening the theoretical range of scholarship in managerial Marketing studies have been made for a number of years (Arndt, 1985), an intellectually more engaged discipline would not satisfy the critical inclinations of other scholars who argue that critique in Marketing studies requires a contribution from the traditions of Critical Theory (Bradshaw and Firat, 2007).

For many academics, what is needed in Marketing studies is a fundamental critique which problematizes and explodes the deep and ideologically driven assumptions around which the discipline turns. One group of intellectual traditions which have become associated with critique in cultural and social studies, including management and Marketing studies, is labelled Critical Theory.

Chapter 1 touched on the meanings of being critical. For academics, the word 'critical' usually implies one of two things. On the one hand, 'critical' is used as a generic label by teachers for thinking and reasoning which is considered deeper and more sophisticated than superficial learning. This involves asking penetrating questions about the assumptions which underlie a way of talking about or theorizing something.

On the other hand, the word 'critical' is also used by many academics in connection with specific intellectual traditions. In particular, Critical Theory is a branch of political and literary studies which draws on post-Marxian theory. Academics sometimes use the word 'critical' in connection with scholarship to mean this particular intellectual tradition, as well as to refer in a general way to higher intellectual standards.

The question of what, exactly, critical scholarship in management should or can mean is not one asked exclusively in Marketing studies. The idea of 'critical management' studies (Alvesson and Willmott, 1992) has almost become an academic brand, even though there is considerable variation of thought within it which cuts across well-established sub-disciplines like 'critical accounting' and 'critical HRM'. Other disciplines have their own elements, for example Critical Psychology (Fox and Prilleltensky, 1997).

The key tradition of critical scholarship is based on the ideas of thinkers who critiqued the very foundations of capitalist society. This intellectual perspective (or, more accurately, these intellectual perspectives), applied to Marketing, management or other subject areas, tend to be labelled Critical Theory (with capitals). Writers like Horkheimer and Adorno (1944) and later Marketing, management and consumer research scholars such as Alvesson (1993), Alvesson and Willmott (1992), Brownlie et al., 1999, Hetrick and Lozada (1994), Murray and Ozanne (1991), and Parker (2006) have contributed to a thriving genre of critical Marketing and management scholarship which positions Marketing activity as a major cultural influence on the way we live, even forming our subjective values and framing our relationships in terms of commodities and transactions. From this perspective, the ideology of the market, presented in its own discipline, can be understood on one level as an expression of the neo-liberal capitalist consensus (Witkowski, 2005). The values of the market, often expressed in the language of Marketing, are set above other values and, in the view of some authors, reach out beyond the inward-looking worlds of textbooks and educational syllabi into the wider worlds of politics, government and citizenship (Willmott, 1999). The Critical Theory perspective is very significant in the idea of Critical Marketing scholarship though, like any intellectual tradition, it is itself the subject of heated debates about its relevance for Marketing studies (see Burton, 2001, 2005; Tadajewski and Brownlie, 2008; Saren et al., 2007; see also Alvesson and Deetz, 2000).

## CT and Ideology in Marketing

In Chapter 3 we touched upon some ideas of Critical Theory in the context of the political category of Marketing critique. One key element of Critical

Theory (or CT) approaches concerns ideology (with a small 'i'). Ideology in Marketing refers, broadly speaking, to conventional and relatively unquestioned ways of representing (writing, talking about) Marketing. 'Ideology' is not a concept found frequently in Marketing texts (Marion, 2006) but it does nevertheless occur (e.g. in Deshpande, 1999; Hackley, 2001b), though we should acknowledge that, in Marketing writing, the uses of the term seldom do justice to its 200-year history (O'Reilly, 2006). One usage identifies the term pejoratively with neo-Marxism. In this view, critical Marketing is against Marketing. Another view uses the term ideology to refer to the Marketing concept as a foundational, normative idea around which Marketing knowledge is built (Whittington and Whipp, 1992). The third refers to ideology as a kind of silence, whereby particular, conventional and accepted ways of expressing knowledge in Marketing silence other, alternative modes of expression, values or interests (see the discussions in Alvesson and Deetz, 2000 and Alvesson and Willmott, 1992; see also Hackley, 2003a).

One difficulty of CT approaches to Marketing critique is that they often carry an implied ethical stance. Of course, this is not necessarily problematic – integrity in knowledge demands that truth is the ultimate standard, and perpetuating untruth is, one might suppose, unethical by any standard. It is suggested here that the primary value of CT perspectives in Marketing are that they open up areas of investigation and lines of argument which are closed down by managerial ideology. The aim, realistically, is not political emancipation but intellectual rigour in the pursuit of truth.

The reason why neo-Marxist critical theory is seen as relevant to critique in Marketing studies is that Marketing discourse can be seen broadly to construct subjectivities in social relationships in ways which are taken for granted. Marketing discourse – the managerial genre of talking and writing about markets and Marketing – is seen to have a role in constructing consumers' (Elliott and Wattanasuwan, 1998) and workers' (Brownlie and Saren, 1997; Willmott, 1999) sense of identity and also in reproducing relations of power and authority that (arguably) serve the vested interests of consultants, governments, organizations and other institutions. In other words, Marketing can be seen as a tool of domination. Marketing discourse informs ways of thinking about our own values and identity which, some theorists argue, limit our personal freedoms in ways which are moral or intellectual, and perhaps material. Critical Theory in Marketing, drawing on the work of Horkheimer and Adorno (1944) and the Frankfurt School of neo-Marxian scholars, is thought to be useful in casting light on the interests served by particular ways of representing knowledge, and especially by representing knowledge as neutral, benign and in the universal interest (Hetrick and Lozada, 1994; Murray and Ozanne, 1991; Murray et al., 1994). There is a connection with ethical criticisms of Marketing in that the way in which typical Marketing studies texts and courses tend to represent Marketing, as a neutral problem-solving discipline which managers exercise in the interests of all citizens, obscures ethical problems in the discipline and deflects ethical criticisms. If Marketing is in the interests of all, how can it be bad?

Critical Theory is not easy for students of Marketing to apply, not least because it presents them with an ideological dilemma – how does one apply a theoretical approach in Marketing studies which appears to undermine the claims of the entire field? For PhD students in particular, this can create political issues within Marketing departments. What is more, Marketing knowledge has itself evolved into a commodity (Holbrook, 1995) which is packaged and sold. So one could in principle take the same CT approaches to critique any other field of knowledge. Perhaps it serves to say that power, the primary focus of CT approaches, is completely ignored in mainstream Marketing textbooks and educational courses when, arguably, it should be a foundational concept in any social study for the light it casts on the implications of knowledge for the less powerful in society. And a serious consideration of power in cultural or social studies must take account of class and capital.

Marketing has, perhaps, become an ideological imperative in the neoliberal era – to criticize it is almost to criticize freedom and capitalism, or at least a pinkish hue is sometimes cast on those who draw attention to Marketing's excesses. Yet it can also be argued that Marketing excesses restrict freedoms by limiting choices and even restrict competition through abuse of market power. A more general criticism is that Marketing marketizes many areas of life, including the media, by commodifying relationships, information and politics (Reuter and Zitzewitz, 2006). Hence, a CT perspective is required to reveal and generate insight into the ways in which Marketing activities, discourses, practices and theories construct their subjects, workers, managers, citizens and consumers, and marketize social institutions, relationships and experiences.

## Marketing Studies and Ethical Critique

Many examples of practice in this book have carried implied ethical dimensions. In the final section of the book, ethical analysis in Marketing is outlined briefly in the context of one example of ethically problematic Marketing practice. For many people, the ethical critique of Marketing practice, and the role of Marketing studies in framing that practice, are the key imperatives in a critical appraisal of the discipline. But where does one begin to evaluate the ethical status of Marketing initiatives?

Ethics in Marketing is, in itself, a problematic area. For those with money, Marketing is a byword for fun. It's about frivolity and venality with a touch of mendacity. It is about making money and buying stuff. For most of the world's population, making money is a daily imperative because they don't have nearly enough. To those who see poverty every day, anything in the name of Marketing is virtuous because the alternative is horrible to behold:

hunger, homelessness, destitution and preventable disease. Wealth creation is seen as good, because poverty is the greater evil. Economically advanced Western nations preach to developing nations about carbon emissions, workers' rights, the welfare of children, and health and safety issues at work. But, in general, Western populations are not hungry. Inequality does not invalidate ethical considerations in Marketing, but it does place them in a wider context. Marketing is seen as part of a route to more wealth creation, less hunger, and greater social mobility in the developing countries in Asia and Africa, and also Eastern Europe and South America. Developing nations do not have the institutional, legal and regulatory infrastructure within which Marketing activity operates, as developed nations do. The point to remember must be that ethical issues are culturally and economically relative. This, of course, makes them all the harder to agree on.

In spite of the imperative for economic growth in the developed and developing worlds, much that is labelled 'Marketing' attracts concern, criticism, even vituperation. Ethical criticism of Marketing practices is widespread (see, especially, Klein, 2000), in spite of the social Marketing movement (Hastings and Haywood, 1994), which uses Marketing techniques to promote socially beneficial ends such as safer driving, responsible consumption and environmental awareness. Marketing practices are not the only aspect criticized – as we have seen, the ways that academics and consultants conceive of, write about, research in and offer advice on Marketing are also criticized, often by their peers, and often because they seem to legitimize the practices.

Ethical criticisms of Marketing are very tangible when they focus on waste or overuse of natural resources, unsustainable levels of consumption, social and environmental pollution, exploitation of the vulnerable and so forth. Ethical criticisms also overlap with political levels of critique when they focus on the ethicality of freedom and truth. Lowe et al. (2005) argue that Marketing studies is profoundly implicated in supporting and legitimizing what is widely perceived as an 'amoral scientism' at the heart of Marketing practice, which has led to nothing less than 'the material enslavement of modern societies' (p. 198). Marketing practice, driven by Marketing studies, here stands accused of promoting an unsustainable and morally defective materialism as a lifestyle. As a result of this perception, Lowe et al. (2005) argue that there is a need for 'formal education programmes for managers and administrators to be re-focused – away from a heavy, positivist, technical orientation and more toward a value reflexive and processual dialectic orientation' (p. 199).

Lowe et al. (2005) clearly see Marketing studies as a matter of management education which has an important role in maintaining intellectual and, closely linked, ethical standards in management practice, with implications for the wider world in terms of the effects of organizational Marketing activity on economies, societies and citizens. The 'amoral scientism' to which they refer results in people being treated as a means to Marketing ends with other consequences of Marketing activity (such as environmental degradation or reduction in the social welfare of non-consumers) being marginalized or disregarded. Examples of this conflict might include, say, the Marketing of products which have negative social effects in some circumstances, like alcohol or cigarettes, or the location of a new office block or retail store in a conservation area.

## Marketing's Lack of Proportion

For Witkowski (2005), many criticisms of Marketing studies reflect a loss of proportion in the discipline, and a tendency toward immoderation in all things. Marketing is closely associated with an upbeat, positive tone of relentless wealth creation driven by endless growth in consumption. Witkowski (2005) argues that this immoderation can be traced to three main sources. These are:

> the grounding of marketing in a neo-liberal and distinctly American world-view: the ascendancy of a managerial paradigm focused on customer satisfaction, competitive strategy and tactics, and continuous sales growth; and the application of marketing principles to an ever-broader range of international and non-commercial institutions and exchanges. (p. 222)

The social welfare and historical perspectives which once lay at the heart of the discipline have, he argues, been abandoned in favour of an uncritical, and instrumental, managerialism. As a result, 'the trajectory of the field poses greater and greater social, environmental and cultural risks. Marketing educators should lead a movement toward a more balanced discipline' (p. 228). Witkowski (2005) suggests that this means changing the emphasis away from teaching the simplistic managerial techniques with which the discipline is so closely identified and towards a renewed emphasis on intellectual rigour (especially through a historical perspective) and issues of social welfare and public policy and Marketing.

## The Academic Marketing Field as Social and Cultural Studies

While Witkowski (2005) and Lowe et al. (2005) envision a critical Marketing which is firmly rooted in management education, Tadajewski and Brownlie (2008a) look at Marketing as a field of social and cultural studies as well as a set of social practices. They argue that subjecting Marketing studies to a far wider range of intellectual influences might go some way to addressing the discipline's managerialist solipsism, and might help it to engage meaningfully with environmental, cultural and political issues. For example, they suggest (citing Firat and Dholakia, 1982, among others) that in its typical forms, thinking and teaching in Marketing and consumer research uncritically supports a 'techno-managerial' perspective and reduces the consumer to a one-dimensional parody of a human being – one which exists only through consumption (p. 15). Once again, this implies that Marketing practice can have a rather one-way, means–ends relationship with the social world in which it operates. Bradshaw and Firat (2007), on the other hand, warn of the dangers of retaining a focus on managerial practice. Instead, following trends in critical management studies, they offer an agenda for critical Marketing studies which draws on the neo-Marxist intellectual tradition of the Frankfurt School and Critical Theory as a 'unifying pillar' (p. 41). Bradshaw and Firat (2007) offer a warning that unless a critical Marketing studies uses powerful concepts of social critique advocated by theorists such as Horkheimer and Adorno (1944), there is a risk that critique in and of Marketing and Marketing studies might simply lack the intellectual force to make a difference.

## Ethical Analysis in Marketing Studies

Marketing theory, textbooks, practice and education, then, can be open to critique on many differing ethical grounds. Western ethical concepts of moral philosophy have been used in categorizing ethical analyses in response to criticisms (Laczniak and Murphy, 2006; Murphy et al., 2005; Smith, 1995). There are the usual macro-level criticisms including mis- or over-use of raw material resources, a poor record on conservation of the environment, exploitation of minorities, misleading claims, a tendency to foster greed and materialism, and so on (Hackley et al., 2008a). There are also more micro-level criticisms including inaccurate food labelling, the promotion of products or practices damaging to health, the promotion of stereotypes of race, gender and body type through its advertising, the exploitation of the vulnerable, especially children (Nicholls and Cullen, 2004; Nwachukwu et al., 1997), and the exploitation of those with less educational or monetary resources. But how might one judge the ethical status of a particular Marketing topic or practice in a world of competing values and interest? Ethicality is generally concerned with what is considered good or right by some standard or other. Formal ethical analysis in the field has often been based around three Western traditions of moral philosophy (Robin and Reidenbach, 1987), which are briefly outlined here and placed in the context of one topical example.

## Deontology

The deontological approach to ethical analysis holds that acts can be good or not, in and of themselves, regardless of their consequences. So the ethical status of Marketing activities would be judged on *a priori* moral principles, such as those prescribed in religious traditions. This might seem quite sensible, since Marketing acts often seem unfair, exploitative, vulgar or offensive, misleading and so on. The problem comes with the relativity of moral principles – your sense of what constitutes offence, for example, is not the same as mine. Different cultural, religious and ethnic backgrounds tend to carry quite different values. Infamous cases of Marketing giving offence include advertising campaigns for French Connection UK, Benetton and Calvin Klein (discussed in Hackley, 2005a). The interesting thing about these campaigns is that they generated offence from particular groups for particular ads, and while they received a lot of press attention, the actual number of complaints received by the UK Advertising Standards Authority was quite small, usually in the dozens. So even campaigns as notorious as these were not found to be offensive by everyone. Indeed, they were all commercially successful campaigns in their time. Consequently, arguments about their ethical status on deontological grounds would be divided along religious and cultural grounds.

Deontology is concerned with an individual's duty to act morally. So if an advertisement is accused of being ethically dubious, who is responsible? The advertising agency creative team? The brand manufacturer? Or the owner of the broadcast medium? And do they not owe their primary duty to the shareholders and other stakeholders in their company? Marketers seldom attract criticism for campaigns which failed, but it is difficult to be successful in Marketing. Perhaps success is bound to be offensive to someone.

The relativity of deontological judgements is particularly problematic for Marketing regulators. In societies with one pre-eminent religious tradition, deontological judgements are not so difficult to make, being judgements of theological authority. Standards of moral duty can be widely agreed upon, but in religiously plural societies, there are competing moral standards which cannot easily be satisfied by one deontologically informed ruling on, say, an offensive advertisement or a morally illegitimate product. The Marketing and advertising of birth control pills and condoms, alcohol, cigarettes, food, dating services, pornography and movies are obvious examples which cannot conform equally to different religious standards. Less obviously, but equally significant, are issues of whether the advertising of toys to children, or the promotion of loans to people who might already be in debt, is intrinsically wrong.

## Virtue Ethics

Dating from Aristotle's *Nicomachean Ethics* (Aristotle, trans., 1985), virtue ethics holds that moderation is a virtue – people should strive to strike a balance between excess on the one hand and insufficiency on the other. Aristotle's famous 'Golden Mean' expressed this principle in terms of personal conduct. So virtue ethics emphasizes virtuous behaviour by individuals rather than the ethical status of acts in themselves. Once again, its problem as well as its strength is its very subjectivity. What is considered virtuous to one person may not be to another. Marketing executives, for example, may wish to behave virtuously in their professional work by, say, not exaggerating or over-selling the benefits of their product. But, on the other hand, they may be coerced into doing just that by senior managers who feel that maximizing sales is the most important task of their company, since by doing so, they serve the interests of shareholders. The manager must balance his or her duty to the company with a duty to their family and to themselves to work hard, please their superiors and earn money. So virtue rests on a highly subjective judgement.

## Virtue and Trust

Virtue ethics also rests on an implicit assumption that individuals are morally developed in the sense that they have had a moral education. Some theorists have assumed that conscience, the inner sense of right and wrong, is innate to human beings, but this need not be so. If someone grows up in a highly competitive and relatively unregulated environment, then they might feel that their primary duty is to their family and themselves. Others must look out for themselves. This might seem a cynical or selfish outlook, but in a world of scarce resources and competitive markets, people should not be judged too harshly for doing the best they can for themselves in their commercial life.

That there are many people with this attitude leads to another ethical problem. If people operating within capitalistic systems tend to act in their own interests, then it is a duty of governments to create legal and regulatory systems which force them to act fairly, for the greater good. So it cannot be a matter only for individual judgement to decide whether or not to sell products which are defective or dangerous, for example. It is a matter of legal compulsion. So governments around the world do try to create regulatory frameworks which give consumers some degree of confidence in the quality of products and services they buy.

Even with effective regulatory systems, business activity requires an element of trust. If a person pays for a service, they trust the provider to deliver on that promise. Or if a seller gives a service or product to the consumer, they are trusting the consumer to eventually pay for that. Governments have to create policy frameworks which provide both consumers and producers and suppliers with some recourse to the law if that trust is exploited.

## Utilitarianism

Utilitarianism is the third main ethical principle used in Marketing analysis. It considers the ethical status of the consequences of Marketing acts rather than the ethical status of the acts themselves. So, for example, a public service advertisement designed to reduce car crashes through drink driving may be offensive to some for its graphic depiction of personal injuries sustained in a violent car crash. Similarly, a public service campaign promoting 'safe' sex might be considered offensive by people who feel that sexual behaviour outside marriage is immoral. But in both cases the ads would be considered on ethical or utilitarian grounds if they resulted in less sexually transmitted disease or fewer traffic accidents. Some people may find the ads intrinsically offensive because of their content and, therefore, immoral on deontological grounds. But this would not influence the utilitarian position, which is based on outcomes not content.

The problem here, of course, lies with the judgement of which good should be served. There are invariably competing interests in any society. Ultimately, there will be different ideas about what is the greater good, for example between censorship of TV advertising and social problems. Who has the right to say that one ethical issue is more important than another?

Another issue concerns the right of anyone to censor public communication. There comes a point where state-imposed restrictions on public communication limit individual freedom and free speech (see the discussion in Hackley and Kitchen, 1999). Then again, in many countries, the neo-liberal ideas of individual freedom and free speech are considered secondary in importance to the greater good of society in general. In any state, there has to be some trade-off between control and regulation of the activities of the population, including control of Marketing activity, and freedom to act independently and creatively. The point where individual freedom, uncontrolled, begins to harm society, is as key a debate in Marketing ethics as it is in political science in general.

---

## CHAPTER SUMMARY

Chapter 8 concluded the book by referring to three chosen topics which seem particularly accessible to critical analysis: the nature of the consumer in Marketing studies, the role of Critical Theory and, thirdly, how ethical issues are treated. These are just three of many possible points of connection between the typical, managerial Marketing topics and a critical Marketing studies. They are issues which interpenetrate the four categories of critique in Marketing which have been the basis of the book – functional/practical, intellectual, ethical and political critique. The chapter reviewed various issues touched upon previously to try to generate viable points of departure for critical reappraisal of the discipline. It concludes with a case example focusing on ethical issues in alcohol promotion in the UK.

---

# CHAPTER REVIEW QUESTIONS ?

1. Discuss the contrasts in the model of the consumer assumed by Levy (1959) and others who emphasize consumer fantasy, fun and symbolism, and the 'black box' cause–effect model (e.g. Howard and Sheth, 1968) of buyer behaviour which tends to be more popular in typical textbooks. What are the key points of connection and divergence between the two?
2. Does it matter to Marketing managers whether consumers are supposed to be motivated by rationality or symbolism?
3. In what ways is the use of Critical Theory relevant and useful, or irrelevant and useless, in Marketing studies?
4. What, in your opinion, are the key ethical issues in Marketing? Is an ethical stance important for a Marketing manager? If so, why?

## CHAPTER CASE

### Alcohol Advertising in the UK

The UK has experienced rising rates of alcohol-related illness in recent years across all age groups, but most alarmingly among younger drinkers (Szmigin et al., 2008). The alcohol Marketing industry has attracted complaints for its role in this trend (Hackley et al., 2008b). Alcohol advertising has received particular criticism, so much so that the UK advertising regulator, the Advertising Standards Authority (ASA), imposed a new code of practice for alcohol advertising on TV on 1 January 2005. These changes were imposed:

> as a result of widespread concern about drinking behaviour among young people, including excessive or binge drinking and anti-social behaviour. These changes were intended to prevent alcohol ads having a strong appeal to those under 18 years of age and being associated with youth culture.[3]

The ASA operates a system of advertising regulation which acts on public complaints. Anyone can contact the ASA to complain about any advertisement if they feel it is offensive or ethically unacceptable in any way. Even if there is just one complaint, the ASA will then examine the offending advertisement to see if it contravenes any of the ASA codes of practice.

In September 2006, the ASA banned television advertisements for two alcohol brands, WKD[4] and Smirnoff Ice,[5] under the revised code of practice. For some time, the codes of practice have forbidden advertisers to make ads that appeal to youth culture, but many observers have felt that the advertisers have flouted this rule by using talking animals, surreal animations and adolescent hi-jinks in their alcohol advertising. The manufacturers, Diageo Great Britain and Beverage Brands UK Ltd, objected to the adjudication. Both ads had been passed by the pre-vetting committee for broadcast ads. However, they received a complaint which the ASA was duty bound to investigate. Its committee ruled that each ad contravened the new regulations by appealing to youth culture. Clearly, there is some scope for interpretation in such a judgement. Smirnoff has been described as the world's most 'powerful' alcohol brand because of its global distribution and its appeal to 'consumers of all ages',[6] while WKD advertising has used the theme 'do you have a wicked side?' through its promotions on TV and the internet featuring adolescent jokes and pranks.

## Ethical Issues

From a deontological point of view, any alcohol advertisements would be deemed unethical by people who regard alcohol itself as unethical, for example Muslim countries do not permit the consumption or sale of alcohol. But the UK is a country where the sale, promotion and consumption of alcohol are legal. There are limits on its legality, for example driving while under the influence of alcohol is not permitted, and persons under 18 years of age are not legally entitled to drink alcohol. But deontological judgements also extend to duty to others. Do the alcohol manufacturers not owe a duty of care to people to advertise responsibly so that people, and especially younger people, are not encouraged to drink to excess? Then again, the alcohol industry and advertising industry executives are promoting a legal product and they were trying to operate within the existing ASA guidelines. As a result of the ban, a lot of shareholders' money was wasted making the ads.

## Case Questions

1.  Is it ethically acceptable to advertise alcohol (in countries where it is legal to do so) in ways which are attractive to young people? Discuss this question with reference to the three main Western concepts of ethical analysis, deontology, virtue ethics and utilitarianism.
2.  Does it make sense to say that alcohol consumption and promotion are legal (with age restrictions), but certain forms of advertising alcohol are ethically unacceptable?
3.  It is widely agreed in the UK that alcohol over-use is a social problem with wide ramifications for public and personal health, crime and the economy. Many doctors want alcohol advertising banned altogether, just

as cigarette advertising was banned in the UK on public health grounds. Discuss the ethical arguments for and against an alcohol ban in the UK.

4. Is 'Marketing ethics' a contradiction in terms? Evaluate this statement with regard to the alcohol issue in the UK.

## Notes

1  Source: 'Now we can start paying by chip in skin', by Graham Keeley, London *Evening Standard*, 11 October 2006, p. 22.

2  See www.bootb.com/en/ (accessed 11 January 2008).

3  See www.asa.org.uk/asa/adjudications/Public/TF_ADJ_41791.htm

4  Adjudication at www.asa.org.uk/asa/adjudications/Public/TF_ADJ_41792.htm

5  Adjudication at www.asa.org.uk/asa/adjudications/Public/TF ADJ 41791.htm

6  See  www.just-drinks.com/article.aspx?id=86380&lk=nd02  (accessed 20 October 2006).

# GLOSSARY

**Axiology**   Values (including ethical and economic) and aims underlying research, scholarship and thinking around a particular topic area.

**Critical Theory**   An influential intellectual tradition of cultural critique based on the ideas of Horkheimer and Adorno and the 'Frankfurt School' of neo-Marxist theorists.

**Critique**   A systematic, reflective examination of the values of a thing, or more loosely, any examination of the qualities of a thing (such as a system of thinking or writing). Kant opposed critical judgement to dogmatism. In this book, it is implied that typical Marketing textbooks tend toward dogmatism (about the efficacy of the Marketing concept, for example) and lack an element of critique.

**Consumer culture**   The ways in which humans use consumption to impose meaning onto their lives.

**Culture**   Broadly, the numerous ways in which human beings impose meaning onto their lives through ritual, belief systems, symbolism and symbolic interaction.

**Discourse**   Discourse refers to a given set of conventions for talking and thinking about and describing a given phenomenon or activity. Thus, for example, one might have the discourse of film criticism or the discourse of medical diagnosis.

**Economic utility**   The assumption of microeconomics that consumers make rational judgements on purchase decisions based on utility, a subjective judgement of practical usefulness or benefit.

**Epistemology**   The study of the philosophy of knowledge.

**Functional(ism)**   Used in three ways in Marketing studies, to refer to (a) the organizational function of Marketing and its sub-functions of product development, promotion, distribution, service, pricing etc., and differentiated from the other organizational functions of human resource management, accounting, operations or strategy; (b) the effectiveness (functionality) of Marketing techniques; and (c) functionalist research philosophy, derived from the sociologist Durkheim and taking a systemic approach to the interdependence of social institutions.

**Homogeneous and Heterogeneous**   Same and different. Homogeneous consumers all have the same drives, preferences and motivations. Heterogeneous consumers are all different individuals with different preferences etc.

**Ideology**   Ideology with a small 'i' refers to beliefs which are widely regarded as taken-for-granted and unquestionable, but which might well reflect the interests of one group more than those of others. These beliefs might constitute a way of looking at the world which is implicit in forms of communication.

**Instrumental**   Treating humans as a means to an end: this is goal-oriented problem-solving without regard for human values. The discipline of managerial Marketing studies is accused of instrumentalism in that it is conceived as an ethically neutral problem-solving discipline

**Interpretive**   An approach to social research and scholarship which assumes that the social world is co-constructed through interaction. Is often associated with theoretically informed analyses of qualitative research data sets.

**Managerialism**   Managerialism is the idea that management can be reduced to generic skills applicable in any context. The term is also used to refer pejoratively to the idea that managerial skills, values and priorities are given too much credence and have a greater presence than they ought to have in organizational, social and economic life. Managerialist Marketing texts and courses assume that the (supposed) interests, values and priorities of organizational managers should be the guiding values of Marketing studies.

**Managerial ideology**   The discipline of Marketing studies is said to be a vehicle of managerial ideology in that its popular texts and courses implicitly assume that managers are a powerful class of skilled individuals in whom is vested the responsibility for general economic and social welfare. A further element of this term is the argument that managerial ideology carries many assumptions of neo-liberalism including the ideas of individualism, political freedom, capitalism, consumption as a lifestyle and the belief in the value of technological progress as a cure for mankind's problems.

**Neo-liberal**   See 'managerialism'.

**Normative**   The normative in Marketing studies refers to situational norms of action, what one ought to do for best results in a given situation. Managerial Marketing studies is a normative discipline in that it purports to show how-to-do-Marketing.

**Objectivity**   The idea that human understanding stands apart from experience. Interpretive research assumes that the researcher is a part of the phenomenon being studied and should reflect on that in the research process. Positivistic research assumes that the researcher is independent of the world which is being researched.

**Ontology**   Ontological assumptions are to do with the basic assumptions made about the nature or essence of social life for research purposes. For example, positivist research would usually suppose that the social world is analagous to the physical world, with patterns of cause and effect which are accessible to quantitative research techniques.

**Paradigm**   A term often used in social science to refer to a given set of conventional assumptions or norms about the way research in a particular area should proceed.

**Positivistic**   A short-hand term often used to refer to academic research which is based on the hypothetico-deductive method and statistical measurement. More broadly, it refers to research which assumes ontological parity between the social and the physical worlds. In its common usage, it is unconnected with A. J. Ayer's philosophy of logical positivism.

**'Pure' and 'applied' research**   In science, some research has a more 'blue skies' and speculative character (pure research), while other research projects are more directly linked to immediate practical problems (applied). Research in Marketing is often justified on grounds of relevance to management, but some academics have argued that there is a case for pure research in the field which does not have to justify itself with claims of managerial relevance.

**Rationality**   A term referring to the ways in which we consciously justify our actions and beliefs. Rational consumer behaviour, for example, can be contrasted with consumer behaviour which is driven by emotion, spontaneity, peer pressure, symbolic desires, whimsy, etc. Rationalization refers to fitting our behaviour and beliefs after the fact to a preconceived idea of rational behaviour.

**Realist**   The philosophical assumption underlying academic research which holds that social entities, such as attitude, belief, personality or emotion, can be treated as if they are physical entities for the purpose of research. Is usually linked with the 'positivist' research approach.

**Reification**   Treating metaphors as if they have a physical reality: treating social relations as if they are things.

**Reflexivity**   Being aware of being aware: reflexivity in writing is a quality of self-consciousness and self-critique often said to be lacking in typical Marketing studies texts and courses.

**Representation**   Referring to ways in which the world of sense experience is portrayed in text, words, pictures or other forms of representation.

**Rhetoric**   The arts of persuasion in communication.

**Social construction**   An ontological position which holds that the social world is not analogous to the physical world because social reality has a quality of self-generation which the physical world lacks. Berger and Luckman's (1966) classic example refers to a book, read and interpreted by one person, and discussed with another and another. Eventually, a lot of people have an idea of that book which is real enough to them, even though they haven't necessarily read it. In branding, the idea of a Mercedes Benz as a symbol of affluence and success is real enough to millions who will never own or ride in one.

**Text**   In social research, a text is said to be anything which can be described.

# REFERENCES

Aherne, A. (2006) 'Exploit the Levitt Write Cycle', *Journal of Strategic Marketing*, 14 (1): 77–87 (with S. Brown).

Ajzen, I. (1991) 'The theory of planned behavior', *Organizational Behavior and Human Decision Processes*, 50: 179–211.

Ajzen, I. (2002) 'Perceived behavioral control, self-efficacy, locus of control, and the theory of planned behavior', *Journal of Applied Social Psychology*, 32: 665–683.

Alderson, W. (1957) *Marketing Behavior and Executive Action: A Functionalist Approach to Marketing*. Homewood, IL: Richard D. Irwin.

Alderson, W. (1965) *Dynamic Marketing Behaviour: A Functionalist Theory of Marketing*. Homewood, IL: Richard D. Irwin.

Alvesson, M. (1994) 'Critical theory and consumer marketing', *Scandinavian Journal of Marketing*, 9: 291–313.

Alvesson, M. and Willmott, H. (1992) *Critical Management Studies*. London: Sage.

Alvesson, M. and Deetz, S. (2000) *Doing Critical Management Research*. London: Sage.

AMA (2008) www.marketingpower.com/AboutAMA/Pages/DefinitionofMarketing.aspx (Accessed 24 September 2008)

American Marketing Association (AMA) Task Force on the Development of Marketing Thought (1988) 'Developing, disseminating and utilising marketing knowledge', *Journal of Marketing*, 52 (Oct.): 1–25.

Anderson, P. F. (1983) 'Marketing, scientific progress and scientific method', *Journal of Marketing*, 4: 18–31.

Anderson, P. F. (1986) 'On method in consumer research: a critical relativist perspective', *Journal of Consumer Research*, 13 (Sept.): 108–114.

Ansoff, H. I. (1965) *Business Strategy*. London: Penguin.

Ardley, B. (2005) 'Marketing managers and their life world: explorations in strategic planning using the phenomenological interview', *The Marketing Review*, 21 (7/8), June.

Aristotle (trans., 1985) *Nicomachean Ethics*. Trans. T. Irwin. Indianapolis, IN: Hackett Publishing.

Arndt, J. (1985) 'The tyranny of paradigms: the case for paradigmatic pluralism in marketing', in N. Dholakia and J. Arndt (eds), *Changing the Course of Marketing: Alternative Paradigms for Widening Marketing Theory*. Research in Marketing, Supplement 2. Greenwich, CT: JAI Press.

Arnould, E. and Thompson, C. J. (2005) 'Consumer culture theory: 20 years of research', *Journal of Consumer Research*, 31 (March): 868–882.

Bagozzi, R. P. (1975) 'Marketing as exchange', *Journal of Marketing*, 39/4 (Oct): 32–39.

Baker, M. J. (1974) *Marketing: An Introductory Text*. London: Macmillan.

Baker, M. J. (1976) 'Evolution of the marketing concept', in M. J. Baker (ed.), *Marketing Theory and Practice*. London: Macmillan.

Baker, M. J. (ed.) (1995) *Marketing: Theory and Practice*, 3rd edn. Basingstoke: Macmillan.

Baker, M. J. (ed.) (1999) *The Marketing Book*, 4th edn. Oxford: Butterworth Heinemann, Chartered Institute of Marketing.

Baker, M. J. (2000a) 'Marketing: philosophy or function?', in M. J. Baker (ed.), *Marketing Theory: A Student Text*. London: Thomson Learning Business Press, pp. 1–20.

Baker, M. J. (2000b) *Marketing Strategy and Management*, 3rd edn. London: Macmillan Business.

Baker, M. J. (2000c) (ed.) *Marketing Theory: A Student Text*. London: Thomson Learning Business Press.

Bartels, R. (1951) 'Influences on the development of marketing thought: 1900–1923', *Journal of Marketing*, 16 (1): 1–17.

Bartels, R. (1988) *The History of Marketing Thought*. Columbus, OH: Publishing Horizons Inc.

Baumgartner, H. and Pieters, R. (2003) 'The structural influence of marketing journals: a citation analysis of the discipline and its subareas over time', *Journal of Marketing*, 67 (April): 123–139.

Belk, R. (1986) 'Art Versus Science as Ways of Generating Knowledge About Materialism', in D. Brinberg and R. J. Lutz (eds), *Perspectives on Methodology in Consumer Research*. New York: Springer-Verlag, pp. 3–36.

Belk, R. W., Sherry, J. F. and Wallendorf, M. (1988) 'A naturalistic enquiry into buyer and seller behaviour at a swap meet', *Journal of Consumer Research*, 14 (4): 449–470.

Berger, P. and Luckmann, T. (1966) *The Social Construction of Reality: A Treatise in the Sociology of Knowledge*. London: Penguin.

Berry, L. (1983) 'Relationship marketing', in L. Berry (ed.), *Emerging Perspectives on Services Marketing*. Chicago: American Marketing Association, pp. 25–28.

Biggadike, R. E. (1981) 'The contributions of marketing to strategic management', *Academy of Management Review*, 6 (4): 621–632.

Bolton, R. (2005) 'Marketing renaissance: opportunities and imperatives for improving marketing thought, practice and infrastructure', *Journal of Marketing*, 69 (October): 1–25.

Booms, B. H. and Bitner, M. J. (1981) 'Marketing strategies and organization structures for service firms', in J. H. Donnelly and W. R. George (eds), *Marketing of Services*. Chicago: American Marketing Association.

Bordern, N. (1964) 'The concept of the marketing mix', *Journal of Advertising Research*. Reprinted in B. Enis, K. Cox and M. Mokwa, (eds) (1995) *Marketing Classics: A Selection of Influential Articles*, 8th edn. Englewood Cliffs, NJ: Prentice-Hall.

Bordieu, P. (1977) *Outline of a Theory of Practice*. Cambridge: Cambridge University Press.

Bourdieu, P. (1984) *Distinction: A Critique of the Judgement of Taste*. London: Routledge.

Bourdieu, P. (1990) *The Logic of Practice*. Cambridge: Polity Press.

Borsch, F. J. (1958) 'The Marketing Philosophy as a Way of Life', in E. J. Kelley and W. Lazer (eds), *Managerial Marketing: Perspectives and Viewpoints: A Source Book*. Homewood: IL. Richard D. Irwin, pp.18–24.

Bradshaw, A. and Firat, A. F. (2007) 'Rethinking critical marketing', in M. Saren, P. Maclaran, C. Goulding, R. Elliott, A. Shankar and M. Catterall (eds), *Critical Marketing: Defining the Field*. Oxford: Butterworth-Heinemann, pp. 30–43.

Bradshaw, A. and Holbrook, M. B. (2007) 'Remembering Chet: theorizing the mythology of the self-destructive bohemian artist as self-producer and self-consumer in the market for romanticism', *Marketing Theory*, 7: 115–136.

Bradshaw, A., McDonagh, P. and Marshall, D. (2006) 'No space – new blood and the production of brand culture colonies', *Journal of Marketing Management*, 22 (5): 579–599.

Brassington, F. and Pettitt, S. (2006) *Principles of Marketing*, 4th edn. London: Financial Times Prentice Hall.

Brenkert, G. G. (2002) 'Ethical challenges of social marketing', *Journal of Public Policy and Marketing*, 21 (Spring): 14–25.

Brown, C. (ed.) (2006) *Consuming Books: The Marketing and Consumption of Literature*. London: Routledge, pp. 167–174.

Brown, N. (2007) 'The relevance of judgment and decision making research for marketing: introduction to the special issue', *Marketing Theory,* 7 (1): 5–11.

Brown, S. W. (2005) 'When executives speak, we should listen and act differently', in R. Bolton (ed.), 'Marketing renaissance' Opportunities and imperatives for improving marketing thought, practice and infrastructure, *Journal of Marketing,* 69 (October): 1–25.

Brown, S. (1994) 'Marketing as multiplex: screening postmodernism', *European Journal of Marketing,* 28 (8–9): 27–51.

Brown, S. (1995a) *Postmodern Marketing.* London: ITBP.

Brown, S. (1995b) 'Life begins at 40? Further thoughts on marketing's mid-life crisis', *Marketing Intelligence and Planning,* 13 (1): 4–17.

Brown, S. (1996) 'Art of Science? Fifty years of marketing debate', *Journal of Marketing Management,* 12 (4): 243–267.

Brown, S. (1997) 'Marketing science in a postmodern world: introduction to the special issue', *European Journal of Marketing,* 31 (3–4): 167–182.

Brown, S. (1999) 'Marketing and Literature – the anxiety of academic influence', *Journal of Marketing,* 63(1): 1–15.

Brown, S. (2001a) 'Torment your customers: they'll love it!', *Harvard Business Review,* Vol. 79, September, pp. 82–88.

Brown, S. (2001b) *Marketing: The Retro Revolution.* London: Sage.

Brown, S. (2002) 'Reading Wroe: on the biopoetics of Alderson's functionalism', *Marketing Theory,* 2 (3): 243–271.

Brown, S. (2003) *Free Gift Inside!* London: Capstone.

Brown, S. (2005a) *Writing Marketing: Literary Lessons from Academic Authorities.* London: Sage.

Brown, S. (2005b) *Wizard! Harry Potter's Brand Magic.* London: Cyan Press.

Brown, S. (2006a) 'Ambi-Brand Culture: on a wing and a swear with Ryanair', in J. E. Schroeder and M. Salzer-Morling (eds), *Brand Culture.* London: Routledge, pp. 50–67.

Brown, S. (ed.) (2006b) 'Rattles from the swill bucket', in *Consuming Books: The Marketing and Consumption of Literature.* London: Routledge, pp. 1–17.

Brown, S. (2007) 'Are we nearly there yet? On the retro-dominant logic of marketing', *Marketing Theory,* 7: 291–300.

Brown, S. and Jensen-Schau, H. (2008) 'Writing Russell Belk: excess all areas', *Marketing Theory,* 8 (2): 143–165.

Brown, S. and Sherry, J. F. (2002) (eds) *Time, Space and the Market: Retroscapes Rising.* New York: M. E. Sharpe.

Brown, S., Doherty, A.-M. and Clarke, W. (1998) 'Stoning the romance: on marketing's mind-forg'd manacles', in S. Brown, A.-M. Doherty and W. Clarke (eds), *Romancing the Market.* London: Routledge, pp. 1–22.

Brown, S. and Patterson, A. (eds) (2000) *Imagning Marketing: Art, Aesthetics and the Avant-Grade.* London: Routledge.

Brown, S., Hirschman, E. and Maclaran, P. (2001) 'Always historicize!: researching marketing history in a post-historical epoch', *Marketing Theory,* 1 (1): 49–89.

Brown, S., Kozinets, R. and Sherry, J. F. (2003) 'Teaching old brands new tricks: retro branding and the revival of brand meaning', *Journal of Marketing,* 67 (3): 19–33.

Brownlie, D. (1997) 'Beyond ethnography: towards more writerly accounts of organizing in marketing', *European Journal of Marketing,* 31 (3): 27–44.

Brownlie, D. (2006) 'Emancipation, epiphany and resistance, on the underimagined and overdetermined in critical marketing', *Journal of Marketing Management,* 22: 505–508.

Brownlie, D. and Saren, M. (1992) 'The four Ps of the marketing concept: prescriptive, polemical, permanent and problematical', *European Journal of Marketing,* 26 (4): 34–47.

Brownlie, D., Saren, M., Wensley, R. and Whittington, R. (eds) (1999) *Re-Thinking Marketing: Towards Critical Marketing Accountings*. London: Sage.

Brownlie, D. and Saren, M. (1997) 'Beyond the one-dimensional marketing manager: the discourse of theory, practice and relevance', *International Journal of Research in Marketing*, 14 (2): 146–161.

Brownlie, D. and Saren, M. (1995) 'On the commodification of marketing: opening themes', *Journal of the Market Research Society*, Vol. 36 (2): 97–104.

Burrell, G. and Morgan, G. (1979) *Sociological Paradigms and Organizational Research*. London: Heinemann.

Burton, D. (2001) 'Critical marketing theory: the blueprint?', *European Journal of Marketing*, 35 (5–6): 722–743.

Burton, D. (2005) 'Marketing theory matters', *British Journal of Management*, 16 (1): 5–18.

Buttle, F. (1995) 'Marketing communications theory: what do the texts teach our students?', *International Journal of Advertising*, 14: 297–313.

Carson, D. (1993) 'A philosophy for marketing education in small firms', *Journal of Marketing Management*, 9 (2): 189–204.

Carson, D., Cromie, S., McGowan, P. and Hill, J. (1995) *Marketing and Entrepreneurship in SMEs: An Innovative Approach*. Hertfordshire: Prentice Hall.

Case, P. (1999) 'Remember re-engineering? The rhetorical appeal of a managerial salvation device', *Journal of Management Studies*, 36 (4): 419–442.

Catterall, M., Maclaran, P. and Stephens, L. (eds) (2000) *Marketing and Feminism: Current Issues and Research*. London: Routledge.

Catterall, M., Maclaran, P. and Stevens, L. (2005) 'Postmodern paralysis: the critical impasse in feminist perspectives on consumers', *Journal of Marketing Management*, 21 (5–6): 489–504.

Chadha, R. and Husband, P. (2006) *The Cult of the Luxury Brand: Inside Asia's Love Affair with Luxury*. London: Nicholas Brealy.

Chajet, (1991) *Image by Design*. Reading, MA: Addison-Wesley in Schroeder, J. E. (2002) *Visual Consumption*. London: Routledge (p. 4)

Chalmers, L. V. (2001) *Marketing Masculinities: Gender and Management Politics in Marketing Work*. Greenwood: Westport.

Chandler, C. (2006) 'No experience necessary, or how I learned to stop worrying and love marketing', in C. Brown, (ed.) (2006c) *Consuming Books: The Marketing and Consumption of Lliterature*. London: Routledge, pp. 167–174.

Charnes, T., Cooper, R., Lerner, P. and Phillips, R. (1985) 'Management science and marketing management', *Journal of Marketing*, Spring: 93–105.

Chong, D. (2002) *Arts Management: Critical Perspectives on a New Sub-discipline*. London: Routledge.

Contardo, R. and Wensley, J. R. C. (2004) 'The Harvard Business School story: avoiding knowledge by being relevant', *Organization*, 11: 211–231.

Converse, P. (1930) *The Elements of Marketing*. New York: Prentice Hall.

Converse, P. (1945) 'The development of the science of marketing', *Journal of Marketing*, 10 (July): 14–23.

Cousins, L. (1990) 'Marketing planning in the public and non-profit sectors', *European Journal of Marketing*, 24 (7): 25–30.

Cova, B. (2005) 'Thinking of marketing in meridian terms', *Marketing Theory*, 5: 205–214.

Cova, B. and Svanfeldt, C. (1992) 'Marketing beyond marketing in a postmodern Europe: the creation of societal innovations', in K. G. Grunert and D. Fuglede (eds), *Marketing for Europe – Marketing for the Future*, EMAC, Aarhus, May, pp. 155–71.

Cox, W. (1967) 'Product Life Cycles as marketing models', *Journal of Business*, November.

Crane, A. (2000) *Marketing, Morality and the Natural Environment*. London: Routledge.

Cranfield School of Management (2000) *Marketing Management: A Relationship Marketing Perspective*. London: MacMillan.

Danesi, M. (2006) *Brands*. London and New York: Taylor and Francis and Routledge.

Davies, A. and Elliott, R. (2006) 'The evolution of the empowered consumer', *European Journal of Marketing*, 40 (9/10): 1106–1121.

Day, G. (1981) 'The product life cycle: analysis and applications issues', *Journal of Marketing*, 45, Autumn, pp. 60–67.

Day, G. S. and Wensley, R. (1983) 'Marketing theory with a strategic orientation', *Journal of Marketing*, 47 (autumn): 43–55.

Day, G. S. and Montgomery, D. B. (1999) 'Charting new directions for marketing', *Journal of Marketing*, Special Issue, 63: 3–13.

Derrida, J. (1979) 'Lining on: border lines', in H. Bloom (ed.), *Deconstruction and Criticism*, trans. J. Hulbert. New York: Seabury, pp. 75–175.

Deshpande, R. (1999) 'Forseeing marketing', *Journal of Marketing*, Special Issue, 63: 164–167.

Dibb, S. (2005) *Marketing Concepts Strategies*. London: Houghton Mifflin (Academic); Euro Ed. Edition.

Dichter, E. (1947) 'Psychology in market research', *Harvard Business Review*, 25 (4): 432–443.

Dichter, E. (1949) 'A psychological view of advertising effectiveness', *Journal of Marketing*, 14 (1): 61–67.

Dichter, E. (1955) 'Scientifically predicting and understanding consumer behavior', in R. H. Cole (ed.), *Consumer Behavior and Motivation*. Urbana: University of Illinois, pp. 26–37.

Dichter, E. (1979) *Getting Motivated by Ernest Dichter: The Secret Behind Individual Motivation by the Man Who Was Not Afraid to Ask 'Why?'*. New York: Pergamon Press.

Dixon, D. (1979) 'Prejudice v. marketing? An examination of some historical sources', originally published in the *Akron Business and Economic Review*, autumn: 37–42. Reprinted in M. Tadajewski and D. Brownlie (eds), *Critical Marketing: Issues in Contemporary Marketing*. London: Wiley, pp. 33–44.

Dholakia, N., Firat, A. F. and Bagozzi, R. P. (1980) 'The de-Americanization of marketing thought: in search of a universal basis', in C. W. Lamb and P. M. Dunne (eds), *Theoretical Developments in Marketing*. Chicago: American Marketing Association, pp. 25–29.

Doyle, P. (1989) 'Building successful brands: the strategic options', *Journal of Marketing Management*, 5 (1): 77–95.

Doyle, P. (2001) *Marketing Management and Strategy*. London: Financial Times Prentice Hall.

Drucker, P. (1954) *The Practice of Management*. Oxford: Butterworth Heinemann (reprinted 1993).

Dumont, L. (1977) *From Mandeville to Marx*. Chicago, IL: University of Chicago Press.

Eagleton, T. (1991) *Ideology*. London: Verso.

Elliott, R. (1997) 'Existential consumption and irrational desire', *European Journal of Marketing*, 34 (4): 285–296.

Elliott, R. and Wattanasuwan, K. (1998) 'Brands as symbolic resources for the construction of identity', *International Journal of Advertising*, 17 (2): 131–144.

Enteman, W. F. (1993) *Managerialism: The Emergence of a New Ideology*. Wisconsin, Madison: University of Wisconsin Press.

Firat, A. F. (1985) 'Ideology versus science in marketing', in *Changing the Course of Marketing: Alternative Paradigms for Widening Marketing Theory – Research in Marketing*, Supplement 2, pp. 135–146.

Firat, A. F. and Dholakia, N. (1982) 'Consumption choices at the macro level', *Journal of Macromarketing*, 2 (Autumn): 6–15.

Firat, A. F. and Dholakia, N. (2006) 'Theoretical and philosophical implications of postmodern debates: some challenges to modern marketing', *Marketing Theory*, 6 (2): 123–162.

Firat, A. F., Dholakia, N. and Venkatesh, A. (1995) 'Marketing in a Postmodern World', *European Journal of Marketing*, 29, 40–56, in J. E. Schroeder (2002) *Visual Consumption*. London: Routledge, p.4.

Firat, A. F. and Venkatesh, A. (1995) 'Liberatory postmodernism and the reenchantment of consumption', *Journal of Consumer Research*, 22 (3): 239–267.

Fischer, E. and Britor, J. (1994) 'A feminist poststructuralist analysis of the rhetoric of marketing "relationships"', *International Journal of Research in Marketing*, 11 (4): 317–331.

Fisk, G. (1971) 'The role of marketing theory', in G. Fisk (ed.), *New Essays in Marketing Theory*. Boston: Allyn and Bacon, pp. 1–6.

Foucault, M. (1977) *Discipline and Punish: The Birth of the Prison*. London: Penguin.

Foucault, M. (2000) 'The subject and power', in J. D. Faubion (ed.), *Power: The Essential Works of Foucault*, Vol. 3. New York: The Free Press, pp. 326–348.

Fox, D. and Prilleltensky, I. (1997) *Critical Psychology: An Introduction*. London: Sage.

Fox, K. F., Skorobogatykh, I. I. and Saginova, O. V. (2005) 'The Soviet evolution of marketing thought 1961–1991: from Marx to marketing', *Marketing Theory*, 5 (3): 283–307.

Foxall, G. (2000) 'The psychological basis of marketing', in M. J. Baker (ed.), *Marketing Theory: A Student Text*. London: Thomson Learning Business Press.

Fullbrook, E. (1940) 'The functional concept in marketing', *Journal of Marketing*, 4: 229–237.

Fullerton, R. A. (2007) 'Psychoanalyzing kleptomania', *Marketing Theory*, 7: 335–352.

Fullerton, R. (1987) 'The poverty of ahistorical analysis: present weakness and future cure on US marketing thought', in F. Firat, N. Dholakia and R. Bagozzi (eds), *Philosophical and Radical Thought in Marketing*. Lexington, MA: Lexington Books.

Fullerton, R. (1988) 'How modern is modern marketing thought? Marketing's evolution and the myth of the production era', *Journal of Marketing*, 52, (Jan.): 108–125.

Furusten, S. (1999) *Popular Management Books: How They Are Made and What They Mean for Organisations*. London: Routledge.

Gabriel, Y. and Lang, T. (2006) *The Unmanageable Consumer*. London: Sage.

Gamble, J. (2007) 'The rhetoric of the consumer and customer control in China', *Work, Employment and Society*, 21 (1): 7–25.

Gardner, B. and Levy, S. (1955) 'The product and the brand', *Harvard Business Review*, March–April: 33–39.

Gordon, R. and Howell, J. E. (1959) *Higher Education for Business*. New York: Columbia University Press.

Gordon, R., Hastings, G., McDermott, L. and Siqier, P. (2007) 'The critical role of social marketing', in M. Saren, P. Maclaran, C. Goulding, R. Elliott, A. Shankar and M. Catterall (eds), *Critical Marketing: Defining the Field*. London: Elsevier and Burtterworth-Heinemann, pp. 159–177.

Gould, S. J. (1991) 'The self-manipulation of my pervasive, perceived vital energy through product use: an introspective-praxis perspective', *Journal of Consumer Research*, 18 (2): 194–207.

Gramsci, A. (1971) *Selections from the Prison Notebooks*. New York: International.

Gronhaug, K. (2000) 'The sociological basis of marketing', in M. J. Baker (ed.), *Marketing Theory: A Student Text*. London: Thomson Learning Business Press, pp. 102–118.

Gronroos, C. (1994) 'From marketing mix to relationship marketing: towards a paradigm shift in marketing', *Asia–Australia Marketing Journal*, 2 (1): 9–29.

Gronroos, C. (2006) 'On defining marketing: finding a new roadmap for marketing', *Marketing Theory*, 6 (Dec.): 395–417.

Gummesson, E. (2002a) 'Practical value of adequate marketing management theory', *European Journal of Marketing*, 36 (3): 325–349.

Gummesson, E. (2002b) *Total Relationship Marketing*. Oxford: Butterworth Heinemann/Elsevier (revised 2nd edition).

Hackley, C. (1998a) 'Management learning and normative marketing theory: learning from the life-world', *Management Learning*, 29 (1): 91–104.

Hackley, C. (1998b) 'Mission statements as corporate communications: the consequences of social constructionism', *Corporate Communications: An International Journal*, 3 (3): 92–98.

Hackley, C. (1999) 'Tacit knowledge and the epistemology of expertise in strategic marketing management', *European Journal of Marketing*, Special Edition: Marketing Pedagogy, 33 (7–8): 720–735.

Hackley, C. (2000) 'Silent running: tacit, discursive and psychological aspects of management in a top UK advertising agency', *British Journal of Management*, 11 (3): 239–254.

Hackley, C. (2001a) *Marketing and Social Construction*. London: Routledge.

Hackley, C. (2001b) 'Towards a post-structuralist marketing pedagogy: from irony to despair (a two by two matrix approach)', *European Journal of Marketing*, 35 (11–12): 1184–1196.

Hackley, C. (2001c) 'Looking at me, looking at you: qualitative research and the politics of knowledge representations in advertising and academia', *Qualitative Market Research: An International Journal*, 4 (1): 42–51.

Hackley, C. (2003a) '"We are all customers now": rhetorical strategy and ideological control in marketing management texts', *Journal of Management Studies*, 40 (5): 1325–1352.

Hackley, C. (2003b) *Doing Research Projects in Marketing, Management and Consumer Research*. London: Routledge.

Hackley, C. (2003c) 'How divergent beliefs cause account team conflict', *International Journal of Advertising*, 22 (3): 313–332.

Hackley, C. (2003d) 'IMC and Hollywood – What Brand Managers Need to Know', *Admap*, pp. 44–47 November.

Hackley, C. (2005a) *Advertising and Promotion: Communicating Brands*. London: Sage.

Hackley (2005b) 'High anxiety: a decidedly partial review of Stephen Brown's *Writing Marketing: Literary Lessons from Academic Authorities*, interpolated with some no-doubt ephebic ruminations on the meanings of the Brown ouvre' published as a 'Commentary' in *Journal of Marketing Management,* 22: 883–890.

Hackley, C. (2007a) 'Auto-ethnographic consumer research and creative non-fiction: exploring connections and contrasts from a literary perspective', *Qualitative Market Research: An International Journal,* 10 (1): 1352–2752.

Hackley, C. (2007b) 'A Celtic crossing: a personal, biographical exploration of the subjective meaning of the Celtic brand and its role in social identity formation', *Journal of Strategic Marketing*, Special Issue on Celtic Marketing Concepts, 14 (1–2): 69–76.

Hackley, C. (2007c) 'Marketing psychology and the hidden persuaders', *The Psychologist*, 20 (8): 488–490.

Hackley, C. and Kitchen, P. J. (1997) 'Creative problem solving as a technology of expert behaviour within marketing management', *Creativity and Innovation Management*, 6 (1): 45–59.

Hackley, C. (2006) 'I write marketing textbooks but I'm really a swill guy', in C. Brown (ed.) (2006c) *Consuming Books: the marketing and consumption of literature*. London: Routledge, pp. 167–174.

Hackley, C. and Tiwsakul, R. (2006) 'Entertainment marketing and experiential consumption', *Journal of Marketing Communications*, 12 (1): 63–75.

Hackley, C. and Kitchen, P. J. (1999) 'Ethical perspectives on the postmodern communications Leviathan', *Journal of Business Ethics,* 20 (1): 15–26.

Hackley, C. and Kover, A. J. (2007) 'The trouble with creatives: Negotiating creative identity in advertising agencies', *International Journal of Advertising*, 26 (1): 63–78.

Hackley, C., Griffin, C., Szmigin, I., Mistral, W. and Bengry-Howell, A. (2008a) 'The discursive constitution of the UK alcohol problem', in *Safe, Sensible, Social: A Discussion of Policy Implications – Drugs: Education, Prevention and Policy* (in press).

Hackley, C., Tiwsakul, R. and Preuss, L. (2008b) 'An ethical evaluation of product placement – A deceptive practice?', *Business Ethics – A European Review*, 17(2) (April): 109–120.

Hastings, G. B. and Haywood, A. J. (1994) 'Social marketing: a critical response', *Health Promotion International*, 6 (2): 135–145.

Halbert, M. (1965) *The Meaning and Sources of Marketing Theory*. New York: McGraw-Hill.

Hamal, G. and Prahalad, C. K. (1994) *Competing for the Future*, Harvard Business School Press.

Heath, G. E. (2007) 'Sidney Levy: challenging the philosophical assumptions of marketing', *Journal of Macromarketing*, 27 (1): 7–14.

Heath, R. G. and Feldwick, P. (2008) '50 years using the wrong model of advertising', *International Journal of Market Research,* 50 (1): 29–59.

Heilbrunn, B. (1996) 'In search of the hidden g(o)od', in S. Brown, J. Bell and D. Carson (eds), *Marketing Apocalypse: Eschatology, Escapology and the Illusion of the End*. London: Routledge.

Hetrick, W. P. and Lozada, H. R. (1994) 'Construing the critical imagination: comments and necessary diversions', *Journal of Consumer Research*, 21 (Dec.): 548–558.

Hills, G. E. (1994) *Marketing and Entrepreneurship: Research Ideas and Opportunities*. Westport, CT: Quorum Books (Greenwood Publishing Group Inc.).

Hirschman, E. C. (1983) 'Aesthetics, ideologies and the limits of the marketing concept', *Journal of Marketing*, 47 (summer): 45–55.

Hirschman, E. C. (1986) 'Humanistic inquiry in consumer research: philosophy, method and criteria', *Journal of Marketing Research*, 23: 237–249.

Hirschman, E. C. (1993) 'Ideology in consumer research, 1980 and 1990: a Marxist and feminist critique', *Journal of Consumer Research*, 19 (March): 537–555.

Hirschman, E. C. and Holbrook, M. B. (1982) 'Hedonic consumption: emerging concepts, methods and propositions', *Journal of Marketing*, 46 (summer): 92–101.

Hirschman, E. C. and Holbrook, M. B. (1992) *Postmodern Consumer Research: The Study of Consumption as Text*. California: Sage and the Association for Consumer Research.

Holbrook, M. B. (1995) 'The four faces of commodification in the development of marketing knowledge', *Journal of Marketing Management*, 11: 641–654.

Holbrook, M. B. (1999) 'Introduction to consumer value', in M. B. Holbrook (ed.), *Consumer Value: A Framework for Analysis and Research*. London: Routledge.

Holbrook, M. and Hirschman, E. (1982) 'The experiential aspects of consumption: consumer feelings, fantasies and fun', *Journal of Consumer Research*, 9 (Sept.): 132–140.

Holbrook, M. and O'Shaughnessy, J. (1988) 'On the scientific status of consumer research and the need for an interpretive approach to studying consumer behaviour', *Journal of Consumer Research*, 15: 398–403.

Hollander, S. C. (1986) 'The marketing concept: a déjà vu', in G. Fisk (ed.), *Marketing Management as a Technology as a Social Process*. New York: Praeger, pp. 2–29.

Hollander, S. C., Rassuli, K. M., Jones, D. G. and Farlow Dix, L. (2005) 'Periodization in marketing history', *Journal of Macromarketing*, 25 (1): 32–41.

Hooley, G. J. (1994) 'The product life-cycle revisited: aid or albatross?', *Journal of Strategic Marketing*, 3 (1): 23–40.

Hooley, G. J. (2000) 'Positioning', in M. J. Baker (ed.), *Marketing Theory*. London: Business Press, pp. 206–215.

Hooley, G., Saunders, J. and Piercy, N. (2003) *Marketing Strategy and Competitive Positioning*, 3rd edn. London: FT Prentice Hall.

Hooley, G. J., Piercy, N. F. and Nicoulaud, B. (2008) *Marketing Strategy and Competitive Positioning*, 4th edn. London: Pearson/Prentice Hall.

Holt, D. (2004) *How Brands Become Icons: The Principles of Cultural Branding*. Harvard, MA: Harvard Business School Press.

Horkheimer, M. and Adorno, T. W. (1944) *Dialectic of Enlightenment*. New York: Continuum.

Houston, F. S. and Gassenheimer, J. B. (1987) 'Marketing and exchange', *Journal of Marketing*, 51: 3–18.

Howard, J. and Sheth, J. N. (1968) *Theory of Buyer Behavior*. New York: J. Wiley & Sons.

Hulthén, K. and Gadde, L. E. (2007) 'Understanding the "new" distribution reality through "old" concepts: a renaissance … for transvection and sorting', *Marketing Theory,* 7: 184–207.

Hunt, S. D. (1989) 'Reification and realism in marketing: in defence of reason', *Journal of Macromarketing*, 9 (autumn): 4–10.

Hunt, S. D. (1990) 'Truth in marketing theory and research', *Journal of Marketing*, 54 (July): 1–15.

Hunt, S. D. (1991) *Modern Marketing Theory: Critical Issues in the Philosophy of Marketing Science.* Cincinnati: Southwestern Publishing Co.

Hunt, S. D. (1992) 'For reason and realism in marketing', *Journal of Marketing*, 56 (April): 89–102.

Hunt, S. D. (1994) 'On rethinking marketing: our discipline, our practice, our methods', *European Journal of Marketing*, 28 (3): 13–21.

Hunt, S. D. (2002) *Foundations of Marketing Theory: Toward a General Theory of Marketing.* Armonik, NY: Sharpe.

Jack, G. (2008) 'Postcolonialism and marketing', in M. Tadajewski and D. Brownlie (eds), *Critical Marketing: Issues in Contemporary Marketing*. Chichester: Wiley, pp. 363–383.

Jobber, D. (2003) *Principles and Practice of Marketing*, 4th revised edition. London: McGraw-Hill.

Jones, D. G. B. and Monieson, D. D. (1990) 'Early development of the philosophy of marketing thought', *Journal of Marketing*, 54 (Jan.): 102–113.

Katsikeas, C. S., Robson, M. J. and Hulbert, J. M. (2004) 'In search of relevance and rigour for research in marketing', *Marketing Intelligence and Planning,* 22 (5): 568–578.

Kavanagh, D. (1994) 'Hunt vs Anderson: round 16', *European Journal of Marketing*, 28 (3): 26–41.

Keith, R. J. (1960) 'The marketing revolution', *Journal of Marketing*, 24 (Jan.): 35–38.

King, S. (1985) 'Has marketing failed or has it never really tried?', *Journal of Marketing Management*, 1 (1): 1–19.

Klein, N. (2000) *No Logo: Taking Aim at the Brand Bullies*. London: Flamingo.

Kniffin, F. W. (1966) 'Is marketing education drifting?', *Journal of Marketing*, 30 (1): 4–6.

Knights, D. and Morgan, G. (1991) 'Strategic discourse and subjectivity: towards a critical analysis of corporate strategy in organizations', *Organization Studies*, 12 (2): 251–274.

Köse, Y. (2007) 'Nestlé: a brief history of the marketing strategies of the first multinational company in the Ottoman Empire', *Journal of Macromarketing*, Special Issue on Marketing History, 27 (1): 74–85.

Kotler, P. (1967) *Marketing Management: Analysis, Planning, Implementation and Control*. Englewood Cliffs, NJ: Prentice Hall.

Kotler, P. (1972) 'A generic concept of marketing', *Journal of Marketing*, 36 (April): 46–54.

Kolter, P. (1988) *Marketing Management Analysis, Planning, Implementation and Control*, 6th edn. New York: Prentice Hall.

Kotler, P. (2003) 'Brands', in *Marketing Insights from A to Z*. New York: John Wiley, pp. 8–14.

Kotler, P. and Levy, S. (1969) 'Broadening the concept of marketing', *Journal of Marketing*, 33 (Jan.): 10–15.

Kotler, P. and Zaltman, G. (1971) 'Social marketing: an approach to planned social change', *Journal of Marketing*, 35 (July): 3–12.

Kotler, P. and Roberto, E. L. (1989) *Social Marketing: Strategies for Changing Public Behaviour*. New York: The Free Press.

Kolter, P., Armstrong, G., Saunders, J. and Wong, V. (1999) *Principles of Marketing*, 2nd European edn. New Jersey: Prentice Hall.

Kotitt, P., Wong, V., Saunders, J. and Armstrong, G. (2005) *Marketing Principles*, 4th European edn. London: Pearson Prentice/Hall.

Kotler, P., Wong, V., Armstrong, G. and Saunders, J. (2007) *Principles of Marketing: Enhanced Media European Edition* 4th edn. London: Financial Times/Prentice Hall.

Laczniak, G. R. and Murphy, E. (2006) 'Normative perspectives for ethical and socially responsible marketing', *Journal of Macromarketing*, 26 (2): 154–177.

Laing, A. (2003) 'Marketing in the public sector: towards a typology of public services', *Marketing Theory*, 3 (4): 427–445.

Latour, B. (1987) *Science in Action: How to Follow Scientists and Engineers Through Society*. Cambridge, MA: Harvard University Press.

Lee, N. and Lings, I. (2008) *Doing Business Research: A Guide to Theory and Practice*. London: Sage.

Letiche, H. (2002) 'Viagra(ization) or technoromanticism', *Consumption, Markets and Culture*, 5 (3): 247–260.

Levitt, T. (1960) 'Marketing myopia', *Harvard Business Review*, July–August: 45–56.

Levitt, T. (1965) 'Exploit the product life cycle', *Harvard Business Review*, 43: 81–94, November–December.

Levy, S. (1959) 'Symbols for sale', *Harvard Business Review*, 37 (July): 117–124.

Levy, S. (1996) 'Stalking the amphisbaena', *Journal of Consumer Research*, 23 (3): 163–176.

Levy, S. (2003) 'Roots of marketing and consumer research at the University of Chicago', *Consumption, Markets and Culture*, 6 (2): 99–110.

Lowe, S., Carr, A. N., Thomas, M. and Watkins-Mathys, L. (2005) 'The fourth hemeneutic in marketing theory', *Marketing Theory*, 5 (2): 185–203.

Lusch, R. E. (1999) 'From the editor', *Journal of Marketing*, 63/4 (October): 1.

Macdonald, M. (1999) 'Strategic Marketing Planning: Theory and Practice', in M. J. Baker (ed.) (1999) *The Marketing Book*, 4th edn. Oxford: Butterworth Heinemann, Chartered Institute of Marketing, pp. 50–77.

Maclaran, P. and Brown, S. (2005), 'The center cannot hold: consuming the utopian marketplace', *Journal of Consumer Research*, 32 (September): pp. 311–323.

Maclaran, P. and Catterall, M. (2000) 'Bridging the knowledge divide: issues on the feminisation of marketing practice', *Journal of Marketing Management*, 16 (6): pp. 635–646.

Maldonado, R., Tansuhaj, P. and Muehling, D. (2003) 'Impact of gender on ad processing: a social identity perspective', *Academy of Marketing Science Review,* 3: 1–15.

Malhotra, N. and Birks, D. (2006) *Marketing Research: An Applied Perspective*. London: Financial Times Prentice Hall.

Marchand, R. (1998) *Creating the Corporate Soul: The Rise of Public Relations and Corporate Imagery in American Big Business*. Los Angeles: University of California Press.

Marion, G. (1993) 'The marketing management discourse: what's new since the 1960s', in M. J. Baker (ed.), *Perspectives on Marketing Management*. Vol. 3. Chichester: Wiley, pp. 143–168.

Marion, G. (2005) 'Marketing ideology: legitimacy and legitimization', Paper presented at the 4th International Critical Management Studies Conference, University of Cambridge.

Marion, G. (2006) 'Marketing ideology and criticism', *Marketing Theory*, 6 (2): 245–262.

Maynard, H. H. (1941) 'Marketing courses prior to 1910', *Journal of Marketing*, 5 (April): 382–384.

McCarthy, E. J. (1960) *Basic Marketing: A Managerial Approach*. Homewood, IL: Irwin.

McCracken, G. (2005) *Culture and Consumption 11: Markets, Meaning and Brand Management*. Bloomington, IN: Indiana University Press.

McFall, L. (2004) *Advertising: A Cultural Economy*. London: Sage.

Michaelson, G. A. and Michaelson, S. G. (2003) *Sun Tzu Strategies for Marketing: 12 Essential Principles for Winning the War for Customers*. New York: McGraw-Hill Professional.

Mick, D. G. and Buhl, C. (1992) 'A meaning-based model of advertising experiences', *Journal of Consumer Research*, 19: 317–338.

Mintzberg, H. (1994) *The Rise and Fall of Strategic Planning*. New York and London: Prentice-Hall.

Mintzberg, H. and Waters, J. (1985) 'Of strategies, deliberate and emergent', *Strategic Management Journal*, 6: 257–272.

Mittlestaedt, R. A. (1989) 'Economics and the development of the sub-discipline of consumer behavior in marketing', in T. Nevett, K. R. Whitney and S. C. Hollander (eds), *Marketing History: The Emerging Discipline*, pp. 3–21. Michigan: Michigan State University.

Mittlestaedt, R. A. (1990) 'Economics, psychology and the literature of the sub-discipline of consumer behavior', *Journal of the Academy of Marketing Science*, 18 (4): 303–311.

Moisio, R. and Arnould, E. (2005) 'Extending the dramaturgical framework in marketing: drama structure, drama interaction and drama content in shopping experiences', *Journal of Consumer Behaviour*, 4 (4): 246–256.

Morgan, G. (1992) 'Marketing discourse and practice: towards a critical analysis', in M. Alvesson and H. Willmott (eds), *Critical Management Studies*. London: Sage.

Morgan, G. (2003) 'Marketing and critique: prospects and problems', in M. Alvesson and H. Willmott (eds), *Studying Management Critically*, pp. 111–131. London: Sage.

Morley, D. and Robins, K. (1992) 'Techno-orientalism: futures, foreigners and phobias', *New Foundations*, 16: 136–156.

Mumby-Croft, R. and Hackley, C. (1997) 'The social construction of market entrepreneurship: a case analysis in the UK fishing industry', *Marketing Education Review*, Special Edition on the Marketing/Entrepreneurship Interface, 7 (3): 87–94.

Murphy, E., Laczniak, G. R., Bowie, N. E. and Klein, T. A. (2005) *Ethical Marketing*. Upper Saddle River, NJ: Prentice Hall.

Murray, J. B. and Ozanne, J. L. (1991) 'The critical imagination: emancipatory interests in consumer research', *Journal of Consumer Research*, 18 (2): 129–144.

Murray, J. B., Ozanne, J. L. and Shapiro, J. M. (1994) 'Revitalising the critical imagination: unleashing the crouched tiger', *Journal of Consumer Research*, 21: 559–565.

Narver, J. C. and Slater, S. E. (1990) 'The effect of a market orientation on business profitability', *Journal of Marketing*, 54: 20–35.

Newman, J. W. (1958) *Motivation Research and Marketing Management*. Boston: Harvard Business School, Division of Research.

Nicholls, A. J. and Cullen, P. (2004) 'The child–parent purchase relationship: "pester power", human rights and retail ethics', *Journal of Retailing and Consumer Services*, 11 (2): 75–86.

Notani, A. S. (1998) 'Moderators of perceived behavioral control's predictiveness in the theory of planned behavior: a meta-analysis', *Journal of Consumer Psychology*, 7: 247–271.

Nwachukwu, S. L. S., Vitell, S. J., Gilbert, F. W. and Barnes, J. H. (1997) 'Ethics and social responsibility in marketing: an examination of the ethical evaluation of advertising strategies', *Journal of Business Research*, 39 (2): 107–118.

O'Reilly, D. (2006) 'Commentary: branding ideology', *Marketing Theory*, 6 (2): 263–271.

O'Malley, L. and Patterson, M. (1998) 'Vanishing Point: the mix management paradigm re-viewed', *Journal of Marketing Management*, 14 (8): 829–851.

O'Malley, L., Patterson, M. and Kelly-Holmes, H. (2008) 'Death of a metaphor: reviewing the "marketing as relationships" frame', *Marketing Theory*, 8 (2): 167–187.

O'Shaughnessy, N. (1996) 'Social propaganda and social marketing: a critical difference?', *European Journal of Marketing*, 35 (9/10): 1047–1067.

O'Shaughnessy, J. (1997) 'Temerarious directions for marketing', *European Journal of Marketing*, 31 (9/10): 677–705.

O'Shaughnessy, J. and O'Shaughnessy, N. J. (2004) *Persuasion in Advertising*. London: Routledge.

Packard, V. (1957) *The Hidden Persuaders*. New York: Longmans.

Parker, M. (2006) 'The counter culture of organization: towards a cultural studies of representations of work', *Consumption, Markets and Culture*, 9 (1): 1–15.

Patterson, A. and Brown, S. (2007) 'Inventing the pubs of Ireland: the importance of being postcolonial', *Journal of Strategic Marketing*, 15: 41–51.

Patterson, M. and Elliott, R. (2002) 'Negotiating masculinities: advertising and the inversion of the male gaze', *Consumption, Markets and Culture*, 5 (3): 231–249.

Peñaloza, L. (2000) 'The commodification of the American West: marketer's production of cultural meanings at the trade show', *Journal of Marketing*, 64 (4): 82–109.

Peng, N. and Hackley, C. (2005) 'A qualitative case exploration of the use of image political advertising in the Taiwanese presidential election of 2000', Royal Holloway University of London School of Management Working Papers.

Peter, J. P. and Olsen, J. C. (1983) 'Is science marketing?', *Journal of Marketing*, 47 (3): 111–125.

Peters, T. and Waterman, (1982) *In Search of Excellence: Lessons from Amercia's Best-run Companies*. New York: Harper & Row.

Piercy, N. (1998) *Market-led Strategic Change*. Oxford: Butterworth-Heinemann (first edition 1992).

Piercy, N. (2002a) 'Research in marketing: teasing with trivia or risking relevance?', *European Journal of Marketing*, 36 (3): 350–363.

Piercy, N. (2002b) *Market-Led Strategic Change – A Guide to Transforming the Process of Going to Market*, 3rd edn. London: Butterworth-Heinemann.

Pierson, F. C. (1959) *The Education of American Businessmen*. New York: McGraw-Hill.

Pomerantz, A. and Fehr, B. J. (1997) 'Conversation analysis: an approach to the study of social action as sense making practises', in T. A. van Dijk (ed.), *Discourse as Social Interaction*. London: Sage, pp. 64–91.

Quickenden, K. and Kover, A. J. (2007) 'Did Boulton sell silver plate to the middle class? A quantitative study of luxury marketing in late eighteenth-century Britain', *Journal of Macromarketing*, 27: 51–64.

Reuter, J. and Zitzewitz, E. (2006) 'Do ads influence editors? Advertising and bias in the financial media', *Quarterly Journal of Economics*, 121 (1): 197–227.

Ries, J. and Trout, J. (1985) *Positioning: The Battle for Your Mind*. London: McGraw Hill.

Ritson, M. and Elliott, R. (1999) 'The social uses of advertising: an ethnographic study of adolescent advertising audiences', *Journal of Consumer Research*, 26 (3): 260–277.

Robin, D. and Reidenbach, R. E. (1987) 'Social responsibility, ethics, and marketing strategy: closing the gap between concept and application', *Journal of Marketing*, 51 (1): 44–58.

Rogers, E. (2003) *Diffusion of Innovations*, 5th edn. New York: Free Press.

Ryan, F. (1935) 'Functional elements of marketing distribution', *Harvard Business Review*, 13 (Jan): 205–224.

Saren, M. (1999) 'Marketing theory', in M. J. Baker (ed.), *Marketing Theory: A Student Text*. London: Thomson Learning Business Press, pp. 21–42.

Saren, M. (2000) 'Marketing theory', in M. J. Baker (ed.), *IEBM Encyclopaedia of Marketing*. London: International Thomson, pp. 794–809.

Saren, M. and Hastings, G. (2002) *'The Critical Contribution of Social Marketing', Marketing Theory*, 3 (3): 305–322.

Saren, M., Maclaran, P., Goulding, C., Elliott, R., Shankar, A. and Catterall, M. (eds) (2007) *Critical Marketing: Defining the Field*. Oxford: Butterworth-Heinemann.

Saunders, J. (1993) 'Marketing Education Group Conference 1993', in M. Davies (ed.), *Emerging Issues in Marketing*. Loughborough: University of Loughborough Press, pp. ii–iv.

Saunders, J. (1995) 'Invited comment on the market segmentation content of' 'A Critical Review of Research in Marketing', *British Journal of Management*, 6 (1): S89–S91.

Sawyer, A. G., Lara, J. and Xu, J. (2008) 'The readability of marketing journals: are award-winning articles better written?', *Journal of Marketing*, 72 (Jan.): 108–117.

Schroeder, J. E. (2002) *Visual Consumption*. London: Routledge.

Schroeder, J. E. (2005) 'The artist and the brand', *European Journal of Marketing*, 39 (11/12): 1291–1305.

Schroeder, J. E. and Salzer-Mörling, M. (2006) *Brand Culture*. London: Routledge.

Schudson, M. (1993) 'Advertising, Health Messages and Public Policy', in R. L. Rabin and S. D. Sugarman (eds), *Smoking Policy: Law, Politics and Culture*. Oxford University Press, pp. 208–225.

Schultz, D. E., Tannenbaum, S. I. and Lauterborn R. F. (1994) *Integrated Marketing Communications*. Lincolnwood, IL: NTC Business Books.

Scott, L. (1994) 'The bridge from text to mind: adapting reader-response theory to consumer research', *Journal of Consumer Research*, 21: 252–273.

Scott, L. (2007) 'Critical research in marketing: an armchair report', in M. Saren, P. Maclaran, C. Goulding, R. Elliott, A. Shankar and M. Catterall (eds), *Critical Marketing: Defining the Field*. Oxford: Butterworth Heinemann.

Shankar, A., Cherrier, H. and Canniford, R. (2006) 'Consumer empowerment: a Foucauldian interpretation', *European Journal of Marketing*, 40 (9/10): 1013–1130.

Shaw, E. H. and Brian Jones D. G. (2005) 'A history of schools of marketing thought', *Marketing Theory*, 5 (3): 239–281.

Sherry, J. E. (1991) 'Postmodern alternatives: the interpretive turn in consumer research', in T. S. Roberston and H. H. Kasserjan (eds), *Handbook of Consumer Behaviour*. Englewood Cliffs, NJ: Prentice-Hall, pp. 548–591.

Sheth, J. N. and Sisodia, R. S. (2005) 'Does marketing need reform?', *Journal of Marketing*, 69 (Oct.): 10–12.

Sheth, J. N., Gardner, D. M. and Garrett, D. E. (1988) *Marketing Theory: Evolution and Evaluation*. New York: John Wiley.

Sheth, J. N., Sisodia, R. J. and Sharma, A. (2000) 'The antecedents and consequences of customer-centric marketing', *Journal of the Academy of Marketing Science*, 28 (1): 55–66.

Simon, H. (1976) *Administrative Behavior,* 3rd edn. New York: The Free Press.

Sividas, E. and Johnson, M. S. (2005) 'Knowledge flows in marketing: an analysis of journal article references and citations', *Marketing Theory*, 5 (4): 339–361.

Skålén, P., Fougére, M. and Fellesson, M. (2008) *Marketing Discourse – A Critical Perspective*. London: Routledge.

Skålén, P., Fellesson, M. and Fougere, M. (2006) 'The governmentality of marketing discourse', *Scandinavian Journal of Management*, 22: 275–291.

Smalley, R. and Fraedrich, J. (1995) 'Aldersonian Functionalism: an enduring theory of marketing', *Journal of Marketing Theory and Practice*, 3 (Autumn): 2.

Smith, N. C. (1995) 'Marketing strategies for the ethics era', *Sloan Management Review*, 26 (4): 85–97.

Southgate, N. (2003) 'Coolhunting, account planning and the ancient cool of Aristotle', *Marketing Intelligence and Planning*, 21 (7): 453–461.

Steiner, R. (1976) 'The prejudice against marketing', *Journal of Marketing*, 40 (July): 2–9.

Stern, B. (1990) 'Literary criticism and the history of marketing thought: a new perspective on "reading" marketing theory', *Journal of the Academy of Marketing Science*, 18: 329–336.

Stern, B. B. (ed.) (1998) *Representing Consumers: Voices, Views and Visions*. London: Routledge.

Stewart, D. W. (1999) 'Beginning again: change and renewal in intellectual communities', *Journal of Marketing*, 64 (4): 2–4.

Strong, E. K. (1925) *The Psychology of Selling and Advertising*. New York: McGraw-Hill.

Svensson, P. (2003) *Setting the Marketing Scene: Reality Production in Everyday Marketing Work*. Lund, Sweden: Lund Business Press.

Svensson, S. (2007) 'Producing marketing: towards a social-phenomenology of marketing work', *Marketing Theory*, 7: 271–290.

Szmigin, I., Griffin, C., Mistral, W., Bengry-Howell, A., Weale, L. and Hackley, C. (2008) 'Re-framing "binge drinking" as calculated hedonism: empirical evidence from the UK', *International Journal of Drug Policy* (in press).

Tadajewski, M. (2006a) 'The ordering of marketing theory: the influence of McCarthyism and the Cold War', *Marketing Theory*, 6 (2): 163–199.

Tadajewski, M. (2006b) 'Remembering motivation research: resituating the emergence of interpretive research', *Marketing Theory*, 6 (2): 163–199.

Tadajewski, M. and Brownlie, D. (2008a) 'Critical marketing: a limit attitude', in M. Tadajewski and D. Brownlie (eds), *Critical Marketing: Issues in Contemporary Marketing*. London: Wiley, pp. 1–28.

Tadajewski, M. and Brownlie, D. (2008b) 'Rethinking the development of marketing', in M. Tadajewski and D. Brownlie (eds), *Critical Marketing: Issues in Contemporary Marketing*. London: Wiley, pp. 29–31.

Thomas, M. J. (1994) 'Marketing: in chaos or transition?', *European Journal of Marketing*, 28 (3): 55–62.

Thomas, M. J. (1996) 'Marketing adidimus', in S. Brown, J. Bell and D. Carson (eds), *Marketing Apocalypse*. London: Routledge, pp. 189–205.

Thompson, C. J., Locander, W. B. and Pollio, H. R. (1989) 'Putting consumer experience back into consumer research: the philosophy and method of existential phenomenology', *Journal of Consumer Research*, 17: 133–147.

Tiwsakul, R., Hackley, C. and Szmigin, I. (2005) 'Explicit, non-integrated product placement in British television programmes', *International Journal of Advertising*, 24 (1): 95–111.

Tonks, D. (2002) 'Marketing as cooking: return of the sophists', *Journal of Marketing Management*, 18 (7–8): 803–822.

van Waterschoot, W. (2000) 'The marketing mix', in M. J. Baker (ed.), *Marketing Theory*. London: Thomson Learning Business Press, pp. 216–230.

Vargo, S. L. and Lusch, R. F. (2004) 'Evolving to a new dominant logic for marketing', *Journal of Marketing*, 68 (1): 1–17.

Veblen, T. (1899) *The Theory of the Leisure Class: An Economic Study in the Evolution of Institutions*. New York, London: Macmillan.

Watson, T. J. (1994) *In Search of Management: Culture, Chaos and Control in Managerial Work*. London: Routledge.

Watson, T. J. (2001a) 'Management: an activity in search of itself', in E. Antonocopoulou, M. Bresnen, G. Burrell, Collinson, T. Corbett, S. Dale, S. Legge, G. Morgan and J. Swan (eds), *Organisational Studies: Critical Perspectives on Business and Management. Volume 1: Modes of Management*. London: Routledge.

Watson, T. J. (2001b) 'Negotiated orders, in organisations', in N. Smelser and P. Baltes (eds), *International Encyclopaedia of the Social and Behaviour Sciences*, pp. 10965–10967. Amsterdam: Elsevier.

Wensley, J. (1996) *Another Oxymoron in Marketing: Marketing Strategy*, in S. Shaw and N. Hood (eds), *Marketing in Evolution*. London: Macmillan, pp. 36–54.

Wensley, J. (2007) 'Relevance of critique: can and should critical marketing influence practice and policy', in *Critical Marketing: Defining the Field*. Butterworth-Heinemann, pp. 233–243.

Wensley, R. (1988) 'Falling in love with a marketing myth; the story of segmentation and the issue of relevance', in S. Brown, A-M Doherty and W. Clarke (eds), *Romancing the Market*. London: Routledge, pp. 74–85.

Wensley, R. (1990) 'The voice of the consumer? Speculations on the limits to the marketing analogy', *European Journal of Marketing*, 24 (7): 49–60.

Wensley, R. (1995) 'A Critical review of research in marketing', *British Journal of Management*, 6: S63–S82.

Wensley, R. (1999) 'The basics of marketing strategy', in M. J. Baker (ed.), *The Marketing Book*. Oxford: Butterworth Heinemann, pp. 16–49.

Whittington, R. and Whipp, R. (1992) 'Marketing ideology and implementation', *Journal of Marketing*, 26 (1): pp. 52–63.

Wilkie, W. S. and Moore, E. S. (2003) 'Scholarly research in marketing: exploring the four eras of thought development', *Journal of Public Policy and Marketing*, 22 (autumn): 116–46.

Wilkie, W. S. and Moore, E. S. (2006) 'Macromarketing as a pillar of marketing thought', *Journal of Macromarketing*, 26 (2): 224–232.

Wilkinson, I. F. and Young, L. C. (2005) 'Toward a normative theory of normative marketing theory', *Marketing Theory*, 5 (4): 363–396.

Willis, P. (1991) 'The Ethnographic Imagination', in J.E. Schroeder (2002) *Visual Consumption*. Cambridge: Polity. p.4

Willmott, H. (1993) 'Paradoxes of marketing: some critical reflections', in D. Brownlie, M. Saren, R. Wensley and R. Whittington (eds), *Rethinking Marketing*. Coventry: Warwick Business School Research Bureau, pp. 207–221.

Willmott, H. (1999) 'On the idolization of markets and the denigration of marketers: some critical reflections on a professional paradox', in D. Brownlie, M. Saren, R. Wensley, and R. Whittington (eds), *Rethinking Marketing*. London: Sage.

Wind, J. and Robertson, T. (1983) 'Marketing strategy: new directions of theory and research', *Journal of Marketing*, Spring, 12–25.

Witkowski, T. H. (2005) 'Sources of immoderation and proportion in marketing thought: commentary', *Marketing Theory*, 5 (2): 221–231.

Woodruff, R. B. and Gardial, S. F. (1996) *Know Your Customer: New Approaches to Understanding Customer Value and Satisfaction*. Cambridge, MA: Blackwell.

Wooliscroft, B. (2003) 'Wroe Alderson's contribution to marketing theory through his textbooks', *Journal of the Academy of Marketing Science*, 31 (4): 481–485.

Wooliscroft, B., Tamilia, R. and Shapiro, S. (eds) (2005) *A Twenty-first Century Guide to Aldersonian Marketing Thought*. Berlin, Heidelberg and New York: Springer.

Wright Mills, C. (1959) *The Sociological Imagination*. Oxford University Press.

# INDEX

Please note that titles of publications beginning with 'The' will be filed under the first significant word.